T0303960

Managing for Service Effectiveness in Social Welfare Organizations

ABOUT THE EDITORS

Rino J. Patti, DSW, is Professor of management and organization at the University of Washington, School of Social Work. He is the author of the recent book, *Social Welfare Administration: Managing Social Programs in a Developmental Context* and has published extensively on the subject of social welfare management. He is the Associate Editor of the journal, *Administration in Social Work*.

John Poertner, DSW, is Associate Professor at the University of Kansas School of Social Welfare. His work includes designing social programs, development and use of management information systems and measuring clients service benefits.

Charles A. Rapp, PhD, is Associate Professor and Associate Dean at the University of Kansas School of Social Welfare. His teaching and scholarship interests have been focused on the development of a client-centered model of performance management and its application in child welfare and community care of chronically mentally ill individuals.

Managing for Service Effectiveness in Social Welfare Organizations

Rino J. Patti
John Poertner
Charles A. Rapp
Editors

Routledge
Taylor & Francis Group

NEW YORK AND LONDON

First Published by

The Haworth Press, Inc., 12 West 32 Street, New York, NY 10001
EUROSPAN/Haworth, 3 Henrietta Street, London WC2E 8LU England

Transferred to Digital Printing 2010 by Routledge
270 Madison Ave, New York NY 10016
2 Park Square, Milton Park, Abingdon, Oxon, OX14 4RN

Managing for Service Effectiveness in Social Welfare Organizations has also been published as
Administration in Social Work, Volume 11, Numbers 3/4, Fall/Winter 1987.

Library of Congress Cataloging-in-Publication Data

Managing for service effectiveness in social welfare organizations /
  Rino J. Patti, John Poertner, Charles A. Rapp, editors.
    p. cm.
  "Has also been published as Administration in social work, volume 11, numbers 3/4, Fall/
Winter 1987" — T.p. verso.
  Includes bibliographies.
  ISBN 0-86656-687-2
  ISBN 0-86656-823-9 (pbk.)
  1. Social work administration — United States. I. Patti, Rino J. II. Poertner, John. III. Rapp,
Charles A.
HV95.M265 1987   87-22930
361.3'068 — dc19   CIP

Publisher's Note
The publisher has gone to great lengths to ensure the quality of this reprint
but points out that some imperfections in the original may be apparent.

Managing for Service Effectiveness in Social Welfare Organizations

CONTENTS

Managing for Service Effectiveness in Social Welfare Organizations

SECTION ONE: OVERVIEW AND RATIONALE

Introduction to the Special Issue: Managing for Service Effectiveness in Social Welfare Organizations

> The future is not a place we are going.
> The future is a place we are creating.
>
> *— St. Joan D'Arc*

The field of social work administration is at a conceptual and practice crossroad. Some perceive social welfare organizations going down a road of continued budget cuts and program elimination, loss of purpose, and management for survival. Others envision a renewal of social welfare organizations through revitalizing social work's fundamental purpose (producing outcomes for clients) in managerial practice. This second road, that of managing SWOs with service effectiveness at its core, is the central theme of this volume. Collectively, these papers contribute to articulating a model of SWO administration founded on concepts and strategies for connecting managerial action with service effectiveness.

Why this concern with managing for service effectiveness? At a time when budgets are being cut, programs eliminated, and agencies reorganized to deal with threats to their existence, it might seem more appropriate to concern ourselves with managing for survival. Indeed, a good deal of the literature in social welfare administration in recent years has been devoted to this issue (Perlmutter, 1984). By focusing on the matter of service effectiveness we do not mean to divert attention from the very real crisis that confronts the social welfare enterprise, nor to suggest that by simply demonstrating efficacy can SWOs ward off the forces that seek to reduce their scope and significance. On the other hand, a basic source of legitimacy for SWOs is the ability to deliver benefits to consumers and other constituencies. The capacity to demonstrate these effects places the SWO in a stronger position to deal with external threats to its domain and to exploit opportunities and resources in its environment. Seen in this way, managing for service effectiveness becomes a strategy for survival rather than a competing preoccupation.

There are at least two major reasons for focusing on service effectiveness as a principal criterion for social welfare administration. First, service effectiveness is a key objective of social work, and it seems appropriate, therefore, that social work administrators concern themselves with how to maximize this objective. Improving the efficacy of social work practice has been a major professional issue in recent years, but for the most part these efforts have not addressed the organizational conditions and management practices conducive to achieving this end. Orienting the practice of administration to service effectiveness may help to effect a convergence of interest and energy between clinical and management practitioners around a common and fundamental professional purpose.

Second, in recent years there has been an erosion of social work leadership in social welfare. The succession of administrators from other fields and disciplines has been most pronounced in public social services, but it has occurred in other sectors too. In part, the loss of influence in social welfare is attributable to a perception among high-level officials that social workers have no marginal knowledge/skill advantage over their competitors. Social workers, on the other hand, claim greater expertise in the programmatic and interpersonal aspects of management and have sought to make the case that clients are better served when social work managers are at the helm. Unfortunately, the link between these skills and qualities and better services has yet to be documented systematically. The ability of social workers to demonstrate a distinctive expertise that makes a difference in how clients are served should strengthen their claim to leadership. More important, to the extent this can be done, it may help them to mobilize the resources of social agencies around the purpose of client benefit, rather than other indicators of performance such as output and efficiency which, though important, are not the raison d'être of social welfare management.

This volume is the outgrowth of two conferences jointly planned and coordinated by the editors. For several years, Patti at the University of Washington, and Poertner and Rapp at the University of Kansas, had been independently engaged in research and curriculum building efforts aimed at linking administrative theory and practice to the delivery of effective social services. In 1984, the APM of the Council on Social Work Education, the editors became aware of their mutual interest and began the collaboration, one in Lawrence, Kansas, the other in Ossining, New York. In consultation with Dr. Simon Slavin, Editor of *Administration in Social Work*, it was agreed that the subject was sufficiently important to command a special issue of the journal.

The articles in this volume were commissioned by the special issue editors from persons whose previous work indicated an interest and expertise in managing for service effectiveness. The papers were shaped by instructions from the editors prior to each conference and by extended discussion and critique at the conferences. Because of this, the collection, though reflecting diverse views, manages to achieve a degree of coherence not found in most anthologies.

Following the three introductory papers in Section One, the issue is divided into six sections corresponding to the core functions and tasks in an effectiveness driven approach to management. These include measuring performance, program and organizational design, managing people, managing information, managing environmental relations, and the ethics of managing for effectiveness.

The lead papers, by Patti and Rapp and Poertner, set forth the rationale for this approach to management, define terms, and discuss some of the problems and issues that need to be addressed as managing for service effectiveness develops in the coming years.

Patti, offering a definition of service effectiveness and a rationale for why social welfare administration should be primarily directed at promoting this organizational outcome, discusses several issues that are critical to the development of this approach to management. The issues are: particularizing management models to the service outcomes sought in different subsectors of social welfare; managing tradeoffs between effectiveness and other performance outcomes such as output and efficiency; the structural and managerial requisites to promoting effectiveness; and mobilizing external publics around service effectiveness criteria.

Rapp and Poertner argue that social administration is distinct from other disciplines and is consistent with social work when client outcomes are the central focus of attention. Four common myths preventing managers from moving clients center stage are explored and refuted. A typology for classifying and measuring client outcomes is presented. Scholars and practitioners are encouraged to explore, expand, and refine the typology.

We then begin consideration of the substantive dimensions of effectiveness oriented management with several papers on the definition and measurement of service outcomes. The articles by Reid and Hudson, two leaders in the movement to develop an empirically based practice in social work, provide a state-of-the-art review of conceptual and technical developments in assessing the effects of services. Together, these papers reflect the significant progress that has been made in this area and the capabilities that currently exist for detecting whether services have made a difference for clients. Carter, writing from the perspective of a public agency administrator, provides an overview of what is currently being done in agencies to assess the impact of services. Drawing on his own experience and that of other social service managers, Carter suggests administrative strategies for developing outcome oriented social programs. In the last paper in this section, Grasso and Epstein argue that agency efforts to improve service effectiveness through monitoring and evaluation are flawed because the information is used for management control purposes. Pointing to the different functions and interests of frontline and management levels, the authors describe an agency project which illustrates the thesis that the way to improve worker performance is to integrate the assessment of services with staff training and skill improvement.

Program design, the focus of the next section, has to do with the structural and technical arrangements that provide the context for service delivery. The lead paper by Thomas, drawing upon his extensive work in the design and development of practice interventions (D&D, sometimes referred to as R&D) sets forth a model that agencies might use to design organizational conditions and administrative practices for improving the quality and effectiveness of services. Taber's contribution is a specific model of program design. Taber's five program design elements provide managers with a framework for specifying the components of a program, identifying client benefits, and keeping the program operating as intended. In the final paper in this section, Savage reports the findings of a study of women's drug treatment programs which was concerned with determining whether certain organizational and program characteristics were related to client outcome.

The results indicate that a broad and uniformly applied repertoire of services is associated with positive client outcomes, especially when clients' problems are not well understood and technologies are indeterminate.

The morale, job satisfaction, and involvement of direct services workers is generally thought to be a necessary, if not a sufficient condition for service effectiveness. In the section on managing people, Weiner presents a formulation that integrates much of the recent work concerned with integrating personal and organizational goals and applies it to social welfare. Gowdy distills the findings of the quality of work life literature which identifies those elements of organizational process and climate that appear consequential for worker motivation and performance. Taken together, these papers provide an excellent review and synthesis of what managers should do to elicit the best efforts of frontline personnel.

Information about performance is crucial to the implementation of an effectiveness oriented model of management. Although much has been learned about the measurement of service outcomes, the strategic use of this information to support and enhance the delivery of services continues to be more the exception than the rule. The article by Poertner and Rapp sets forth a management information system design which focuses on the achievement of service objectives and shows how this system was implemented in child welfare to improve the quality of the services provided. Taylor draws upon recent research by herself and others to examine how managers can use feedback to motivate subordinate performance. Evidence is presented which confirms the view that when performance standards are understood, the consistent and purposeful use of feedback can have powerful effects on subordinates' work behavior. While the first two articles deal with information generated by workers, Weissman addresses the problems and potentials associated with soliciting feedback from clients. Weissman's analysis suggests that agencies give too little thought to how best to obtain useful information from clients and to how such feedback can be productively employed for agency decision making. He suggests several ways in which agencies can benefit from clients' assessments of their experience in the agency.

If managing for service effectiveness was solely an internal agency matter, the developmental task outlined in this volume would be much simpler. But alas, social agencies are generally not in a position to decide unilaterally their service goals. As a result, SWO managers invariably find it necessary to build external support and acquire resources for the service goals they consider desirable. The problem, as

Martin points out in the first paper in this section, is that powerful external constituents are often less concerned with service effectiveness than with whether the agency is pursuing service goals that are congruent with their ideological and political preferences. The strategy suggested by Martin includes a broad array of administrative tactics aimed at simultaneously securing legitimacy and maximizing autonomy for social agencies in the context of these constraints. The second paper, by Simons, discusses persuasion skills and strategies that can be employed by managers to mobilize support for their programs. In light of the analyses offered by both Martin and Gummer, these skills become central to the repertoire of the effectiveness oriented manager. Simons' perceptive discussion of persuasive tactics suggests that SWO managers can shape the perceptions and priorities of influentials.

The final section in the volume is somewhat of a counterpoint to the preceding ones in that it deals with constraints and obstacles to the development of a service effectiveness driven model of social welfare administration. Neither Gummer nor Lewis argues against the desirability of client benefit as a measure of agency performance, but each is skeptical that agency administrators will be able to focus primarily on this performance outcome. Gummer points to the institutional forces in our society that push social agencies toward efficiency and control. Lewis questions whether the multiple ethical responsibilities of managers allow them to pursue client outcomes to the exclusion of other important values. Together, these articles raise a number of questions that will need to be contended with as we seek to develop and refine a service oriented model of social welfare administration.

The editors wish to acknowledge the generous support provided in this project by Dean Harold Lewis, Hunter College School of Social Work of the City University of New York, and Dean Patricia Ewalt, School of Social Welfare, University of Kansas. The lead editor would also like to express gratitude to the Edwin and Lucy Moses Fund for the support provided to him and for underwriting the costs of the New York conference. We also appreciate the excellent staff support provided by Liz Gowdy and Nadine Patti, whose efforts were instrumental in making the conferences in Kansas and New York successful.

REFERENCE

Perlmutter, F. D. *Human services at risk*. Lexington, MA: D.C. Heath and Co., 1984.

Managing for Service Effectiveness in Social Welfare: Toward a Performance Model

Rino J. Patti, DSW

This volume explores the relationship between what managers in social agencies do, or cause to happen, and the outcomes of services to clients. There are, of course, a number of variables that mediate the effects of management behavior and a number, outside the control of managers, that independently influence service outcomes. Still, it appears that managerial practices are consequential for how services are provided and with what effects. Our purpose in this issue is to identify what is known about how administrators facilitate and support service effectiveness and to formulate an agenda for the development of practice knowledge in this field.

This approach to management practice is to be distinguished from traditional ways of thinking about managerial effectiveness in the human services. For the most part, both practice and scholarship have been concerned with the traits, philosophical orientations, and skills managers should have in order to manage well. Doing well, in this case, usually means being able to handle diverse analytic, interpersonal, fiscal, and political tasks in ways that important constituencies consider desirable. The criterion against which the manager is assessed is likely to be a normative concept of process, i.e., how these tasks should be carried out. The relationship between managerial behavior (especially at middle and upper management levels) and agency service outcomes, when it is considered at all, tends to be seen as indirect and attenuated. While the manager is nominally accountable for the effectiveness of programs, the manner in which an agency is managed is likely to be considered more important than the results it

Dr. Patti is Professor, School of Social Work, University of Washington, Seattle, WA 98195. Dr. Patti is Associate Editor of *Administration in Social Work*.

achieves. This can and frequently does lead to the anomalous situation in which the agency is "well" managed, but has little demonstrable impact on the clientele it serves.

The approach to management with which we shall be concerned in this volume seeks to build practice around the central criterion of service effectiveness. But what is service effectiveness and how does it differ from other kinds of organizational outcomes with which administrators are concerned? Some of the papers to follow will address this question at length, but as a point of departure, we will suggest that service effectiveness is reflected in three kinds of outcomes which may be, but are not necessarily related (Poertner & Rapp, 1983). The first is the extent to which the agency is successful in bringing about desired changes in or for the client systems it serves. In the case of individual clients this may be changes in behaviors, cognitions, skill levels, attitudes, alterations in social status, or modifications in undesirable environmental conditions.

The second aspect of effectiveness is service quality, or the extent to which the organization is competently implementing methods and techniques that are thought necessary to achieving service objectives. Service quality can be measured against standards prescribed by the agency based on prior experience, models used in other organizations or advanced in the professional literature, or those promulgated by regulatory bodies. Accessibility, timeliness, consistency, humaneness, and technical proficiency of services, are examples of service quality.

Client satisfaction, a third dimension of effectiveness, is concerned with how consumers assess the quality and/or impact of the services received. In addition to direct feedback from clients, client satisfaction can sometimes be inferred from attendance rates, premature terminations, reapplications for services, and related types of data.

This definition raises a number of issues such as the extent to which it reflects the construct "effectiveness," e.g., whether the costs associated with outcomes should be an integral element of this definition; whether service quality should be included with service effectiveness outcomes, since it is an indicator of how well services are delivered and not the results achieved; whether client satisfaction can reasonably be used as a measure of effectiveness if it is not supported by other, more "objective" measures of change. In addition, since we know that social agencies will never live by effectiveness alone, a management model built around this criterion must address the interaction between this and other dimensions of performance such as output, efficiency, resource acquisition, and worker satisfaction. These and a host of related issues concerning the definition of effectiveness will be grist for scholars and practitioners. Some of them are addressed in the papers in the next section of this issue.

In what follows, I will propose a rationale for this emerging practice paradigm and then attempt to outline some of the issues which face us if we are to move toward a service effectiveness driven approach to management.

A RATIONALE FOR SERVICE EFFECTIVENESS

The main (and perhaps too obvious to mention) reason why service effectiveness should be the principal concern of management is simply that this is the primary business of the social welfare organization. Changing people and/or the social conditions in which they live is the raison d'être of the human service agency, not the acquisition of resources, the efficient utilization of resources, or the satisfaction and development of staff. All these may be important in their own right, and even instrumental to providing effective services, but they are, or at least should be, subservient to this objective. It is the failure of administrative theory and practice to maintain this primary focus which, in part, explains why management has never been fully understood or accepted in social work and the other human service professions. I have argued elsewhere that "service effectiveness can serve as a philosophical linchpin in a time when external conditions act as a strong centrifugal force pulling administration and direct practice into quite different orbits" (Patti, 1985). To the extent that there is a greater convergence of interest and energy around this central issue, there would seem to be a much better chance of making progress.

For example, it is interesting to note that among the major obstacles to practitioner level evaluation in social agencies is the perceived lack of administrative interest, supportive arrangements, and inducements (Blythe, 1983; Welch, 1983; Mutschler, 1984). Strategies for practice knowledge development, now widely emphasized in the education of direct service workers, would seem likely to thrive only if agency managers are able to utilize such efforts in service of their practice goals. Currently, it appears that case level evaluation efforts are not widely supported or utilized by managers because they are thought to have little relevance to the issues with which they are primarily concerned. When managers come to see their principal task as promoting service effectiveness, albeit from a different vantage point, a convergence of interests can begin to occur.

A somewhat more parochial, self-interested reason for attending to service effectiveness has to do with securing a distinctive competency domain for social workers in management. By and large, social workers in public social welfare, and to a lesser extent in the voluntary field, have sought to gain or retain leadership positions by acquiring the skills and tools of general management – in effect, becoming more like those with whom they are competing. Competing with the products of schools of business or public affairs, who increasingly look upon social welfare as a field of opportunity, makes little sense for social workers in the long term. Schools of social work have neither the curriculum space nor the faculty capability to provide in-depth training in all those skill areas that are now thought to constitute the core of management, e.g., marketing, finance, accounting, etc. (Morris, 1982).

Rather, a more productive strategy would be to concentrate on competencies directed at the design, delivery, and evaluation of social services, with particular attention to how the internal and external environments of agencies can be managed to optimize service effectiveness. This is a formidable agenda, but it is this kind of capability, which generally cannot be acquired in schools of business or public administration, that promises a competitive edge for social workers in management.

DEVELOPING A SERVICE EFFECTIVENESS DRIVEN APPROACH TO MANAGEMENT

There are a number of intellectual and practical problems that confront us in this undertaking, many of which are addressed at length elsewhere in this volume. I will focus on four that seem critical to developing a management model concerned with service effectiveness: the variable definition of service effectiveness in different sectors of social welfare; the matter of trade-offs between effectiveness and efficiency; the identification of organizational and managerial variables that account for variations in service effectiveness; and, the problem of mobilizing external support for effectiveness oriented performance criteria.

Varying Definitions of Effectiveness

The search for service effectiveness in social welfare is complicated by the fact that the field consists of a very heterogeneous cluster of organizations which vary dramatically by purpose, auspice, technology, clientele, and so forth. Unlike the for-profit field where certain measures of organizational performance (e.g., profitability, market share, debt-equity ratio, etc.) are widely accepted as indicators of corporate effectiveness, and can be used to compare diverse enterprises, the picture in social welfare is more complex. This is not only because different groups involved with social agencies tend to use divergent criteria to judge organizational performance (Whetten, 1978), but also because the intrinsic nature of service effectiveness varies from sector to sector. Service effectiveness looks very different in different types of social agencies. If this is the case and we wish to tie management practice to service effectiveness, we may ultimately be looking for several models of management particularized to the several sectors of social welfare.

For the sake of discussion let us propose a taxonomy of social welfare organizations based on the concept of social purpose or function. This formulation draws upon, but is different from, those proposed by Vinter (1974), Austin (1983), and Kahn (1973). The scheme proposes five types of organizations. (1) Social control agencies, whose primary purpose is to protect society against deviant and disorderly persons. This category includes, for example, prisons, probation and parole programs, and services for the sexual offender. (2) Social care and maintenance agencies, whose purpose is to care for persons unable to care for themselves by virtue of mental and/or physical incapacity or life circumstances, e.g., nursing homes, institutions for the profoundly retarded, income assistance programs, etc. (3) Socialization and prevention agencies, which are concerned mainly with promoting the normal emotional and social development of their clients and transmitting desirable social skills and values. This class includes substitute care arrangements for children, leisure time and recreational programs for the elderly, character building, and youth serving agencies. (4) Rehabilitative and restorative agencies, whose principal purpose is to effect changes in the cognitive, emotional, or interpersonal deficits which clients themselves or others consider undesirable. Community mental health centers, vocational rehabilitation programs, and residential treatment institutions are examples. (5) Advocacy and social change organizations, which seek to promote or protect the political or economic interests of people who have been neglected, stigmatized, or otherwise denied opportunity in our society. Clients' rights organizations, and service agencies set up to deal with the needs of certain minorities (e.g., homosexuals, the homeless, etc.), are included in this category.

An examination of the criteria used to judge service effectiveness in these types of social welfare organizations suggests differences both in the emphasis placed on the three dimensions of effectiveness mentioned earlier (i.e., change, quality, and client satisfaction) and in the nature of the criteria themselves. For example, in socialization and social change organizations, client/member satisfaction with services is more likely to be considered an appropriate indicator of effectiveness than in social control or social care programs. Conversely, outcomes that reflect reduced incidence of problematic behaviors, or changes in behavioral patterns tend to be more salient criteria of effectiveness in social control and rehabilitative agencies than in social care, socialization, or advocacy programs. Finally, it appears that quality of care is more likely to be taken as a proxy of effectiveness in socialization programs where the outcomes of service are often not visible until long after the service has been delivered (e.g., adoption and foster care).

Moreover, for any particular dimension of effectiveness, substantive criteria will tend to vary across types of organizations. On the dimension of changing clients or social conditions for example, there appear to be a number of differences. These are illustrated in Figure 1. In social control agencies, changes in behavior or the reduction of offending behavior, are likely to be the test of effectiveness, even though agencies tend not to fare well against this standard. In social care organizations, effectiveness is often determined by how well client statuses are maintained or improved (e.g., clients kept out of more restrictive settings). In socialization and prevention settings, the acquisition of skills and attitudes, or evidence that clients are mastering normal developmental tasks, tend to be considered desirable outcomes. In rehabilitation programs, the return to normal or near normal modes of functioning is taken as a desirable indicator of change. Finally, in advocacy and social change services, improvements in the social circumstances (e.g., improved access to resources, increased power, and recognition) are often the litmus test of effectiveness.

This speculative exercise is intended to illustrate that effectiveness has many faces in social welfare. To the extent that there are differences in service effectiveness criteria employed in the diverse sectors in social welfare, we may start thinking about the various design and management configurations that are necessary for promoting service effectiveness. At this point it appears that we may be looking at not one but several models.

Figure 1

Selected Criteria of Effectiveness Employed In
Types of Social Welfare Organizations

Type of Organization	Client/Status Condition	Quality of Service	Client Satisfaction
Social Control	Reductions in offending behaviors	Due process for perpetrators, humane treatment, provision for rehabilitation	As expressed in non-compliance, resistance to regulations
Social Care & Maintenance	Maintaining clients in most favorable status	Individ. care, humane treatmt, provision for rehabilitation	As expressed in cooperation with staff and regulations
Socialization & Prevention	Acquisition of new skills, normal development	Attitudes, skills of caretakers	As expressed in demand, attendance, perceptions of service
Restoration & Rehabilitation	Return to role functioning	Credentials of staff, intensity of treatment	As expressed in participation, discontinuance rates & perceptions of service
Advocacy & Social Change	Improved access to resources, power, status	Responsiveness to client needs, client/member involvement in decision making	As expressed in member support, e.g. contributions of time and money

Managing Tradeoffs Between Performance Areas

An approach to management that seeks to maximize service effectiveness must deal with how this performance criterion interacts with other kinds of organizational outcomes such as output and efficiency. There is some agreement among organizational scholars that it is not possible to simultaneously optimize performance in all areas (Steers,

1975; Quinn & Rohrbaugh, 1981). Indeed, it would seem to follow
that as the manager diverts resources to improve service effectiveness,
at some point this will begin to negatively effect output and/or efficiency. One can imagine service technologies that are not only more
effective, but more efficient as well, but the limited available evidence
suggests that these variables are negatively related.

For example, several studies have found an inverse relationship between worker/client ratios, which can be treated as a measure of efficiency and various indices of service effectiveness (Holland, 1973;
Linn, 1970; Moos, 1974; Martin & Segal, 1977). Moos found that
clients in community residential facilities assessed the treatment environments more positively in those settings with more favorable
worker-client ratios. A similar finding is reported by Martin and Segal
in their study of halfway houses for alcoholics. Using staff expectations for client behavior (i.e.. independent and self-responsible versus
dependent, subservient, and conformist) as a measure of service effectiveness, these investigators determined that staff members in facilities
with better staff-client ratios were more likely to expect independent
behaviors from clients than those in halfway houses with higher case-
loads.

Most of the work on the relationship between efficiency as reflected
in staff-client ratios and service outcomes appears to have been done
in inpatient facilities. However, there is some evidence to suggest that
similar trade-offs may occur in outpatient settings. For example, there
is research which indicates a positive relationship between caseload
size and error in the determination of eligibility for public assistance,
though this was true only when worker experience and type of caseload were taken into account (Baker & Vosburgh, 1977). In another
study of several state welfare departments, Newman and Ryder (1978)
found that agencies with lower error rates in AFDC had higher administrative costs, though these higher cost were offset by lower error
costs. They also concluded that some aspects of service quality, such
as providing assistance to clients in the completion of applications,
were negatively associated with output. Further evidence is provided
by Whetten (1978) who found staff members' perceptions of the effectiveness of the service provided in manpower training agencies were
inversely associated with agency output.

None of this is to suggest that agencies must necessarily be inefficient in order to be effective. It is to suggest that service effectiveness
should been seen in the context of other performance goals. Administrators must be in a position to determine how much service effective-

ness can be achieved without posing unacceptable risks to other performance goals.

Management Practices and Organizational Arrangements

The core of a service effectiveness driven model of management is the relationship between managerial practices and organizational arrangements on the one hand, and service effectiveness on the other. Several of the papers to follow (Grasso, Epstein & Savage) will address this subject; but I would like to touch on three aspects of this question which deserve particular attention as we move to flesh out a model of effectiveness oriented management.

The first has to do with a better understanding of how structural arrangements interact with interpersonal and group processes to create the working environment of the worker. This would seem important because many of the structural arrangements that one sees used as independent variables in studies are not very tractable in the short term. Size, dispersion, age, professional complexity, division of labor, and even centralization and formalization are often difficult to change. Each is important to understanding performance levels but such knowledge tends to be unused because it is seen as nonactionable. Concentrating on behavioral and interpersonal variables in the context of structure would yield findings that are more readily translated for practice (Friesen, 1983; Hunt, Osborn & Schuler, 1978).

A second issue is achieving a better understanding of the particular contributions to service effectiveness made by managers at several levels in social agencies what — each does, or causes to happen, that impacts workers' performance. In agencies of any size there are likely to be three levels of management: supervisory, or first line management; program, or middle management: executive, or institutional level administration. As organizations grow larger, it appears that these levels become more functionally differentiated. We have a fairly good idea about the activity configurations at each of these levels (Patti, 1983), but more attention should be directed at sorting out those managerial actions at each level that are most consequential for service effectiveness and the identifying relative contributions each makes to desired client outcomes. Figure 2 is an initial attempt at specifying the behaviors that appear consequential in this regard.

A third, and related issue, has to do with how management behavior at higher levels influences the actions of managers at lower levels. It might be speculated that when the performance priorities at several hierarchical levels are congruent and the behaviors of managers are complementary with respect to these priorities, there is a greater likelihood of obtaining performance targets, other things being equal. Thus, we would expect that when managers and their superiors engage in complementary behavior around service effectiveness, worker performance will improve. An interesting study by Hunt, Osborn, and Larson (1975) provides some support for this contention. In this research, the treatment orientations of upper level managers in a mental

Figure 2

Illustrative Managerial Activities
Associated With Service Effectiveness At
Several Administrative Levels

Administrative Level   Selected Activities/Behaviors

Executive level   - Articulate (within & without)
                             client benefit as a prime cri-
                             terion of agency performance
                           - Mobilize support of external con-
                             stituents that favor service
                             effectiveness as a criterion
                             measure
                           - Build organizational structure
                             which allows for decentralized
                             program decisions
                           - Allocate resources for research
                             and development
                           - Require service effectiveness data
                             as justification for plan and
                             budget submissions

Program level   All of above within program domain

                           - Selecting technologies (with sub-
                             ordinate advice) that work or
                             appear to, based on documented
                             evidence in comparable settings
                           - Provide opportunity for staff par-
                             ticipation in design & implemen-
                             tation of service intervention
                           - Develop performance standards
                             related to service effectiveness
                           - Define indicators of performance
                             & a system for capturing informa-
                             tion about them
                           - Provide feedback to subunits about
                             performance or standards
                           - Identify staff competencies neces-
                             sary to deliver the service tech-
                             nology & recruit personnel
                           - Develop personnel system to
                             attract & reward competent staff

Figure 2 continued

Administrative Level   Selected Activities/Behaviors

Supervisory level   - Set performance targets with
                             workers, determine resources,
                             time, etc., needed to achieve
                             targets
                           - Clarify roles & expectations for
                             each staff person
                           - Provide specific advice about goal
                             related methods & procedures
                           - Give feedback regarding worker
                             performance
                           - Identify skills needed to achieve
                             performance targets & provide re-
                             sources to acquire training, etc.
                           - Mediate, divert or insulate staff
                             from demands or conditions which
                             may undermine service effective-
                             ness efforts
                           - Provide opportunities for staff
                             autonomy & discretion within
                             agreed upon parameters

hospital (i.e., their orientation to either custody or rehabilitation) were found to interact with supervisory behavior to influence the performance and satisfaction of workers at the front line. Also relevant here is some work by Graen and his colleagues (1977) who found that certain dimensions of manager/superior relationships were positively related to manager/subordinate behavior in the same areas. Friesen (1983) reported a similar finding in her study of supervisors in community mental health agencies. Supervisors who assessed their superiors as supportive were much more likely to be perceived as supportive by their subordinates. More work needs to be done. It appears that in order to understand what contributes to worker performance we need to understand not only the behavior of individual administrators, but how managerial behavior at several levels intersects to form an organizational environment supportive of service effectiveness at the front line.

Building External Support for Service Effectiveness

Since social agencies are largely dependent on external decision makers for resources, it would seem to follow that the pursuit of service effectiveness as a prime performance criterion must be supported, or at least tolerated, by these resource providers. Put differently, how likely is it that an agency will invest heavily in effecting changes in clients or their social conditions if achieving these outcomes is not valued by powerful constituents?

This is problematic, because it appears that some kinds of external resource providers in some sectors of social welfare are more interested in other kinds of performance criteria. There are several perspectives on what inspires the priorities of these groups. The first of these, exemplified in the work of Lipsky (1980) and Weatherly (1984), speaks to the discrepancy between the latent and manifest intent of policy makers. The argument, perhaps too simply put, is that many social service systems are really not intended to solve client problems. Their purpose, rather, is to offer the semblance of a service response, but not the substantive resources. The reluctance to commit the resources grows out of ideological ambivalence toward troubled and disadvantaged people, the lack of political power among consumers, and related causes. Several separate studies have shown how front line workers in human service agencies often resort to tactics like rationing and diluting services, creaming clients, and buck passing, in order to manage the chronic mismatch between demand and resources. The objective, under these circumstances, is to maintain a modicum of order in a system that would otherwise become inoperative if operated strictly in accordance with official intent. In this view, the failure of agencies to define performance in service effectiveness terms is quite understandable, because to do so would be to invite utter failure.

Although this line of analysis raises some important questions, it assumes, I think, more rationality and consistency among policy makers and resource controllers than observation would lead one to acknowledge. In addition, it leaves the practitioner with little alternative but to make do in a system which will inevitably undermine efforts to provide effective services.

Another perspective contends that policy makers and funders, for a variety of reasons, employ different criteria when judging agency performance than do agency personnel. Kouzes and Mico (1979) for example, argue that in the policy domain, judgments of effectiveness are likely to revolve around criteria such as equity, distributive justice, responsiveness to community problems, and the like. In a somewhat different vein, Martin (1980) and Whetten (1978) have suggested that resource controllers tend to embrace a normative view which places a high value on such organizational outcomes as expansion and growth, productivity, and the rational management of resources. Finally, Carter (1983) argues that the legislative process mitigator against specifying and holding agencies accountable for service outcomes because of the desire to avoid alienating constituents whose interests are served by maintaining the programs in question.

One is struck with the possibility that all of these views may be right at times, for some resource providers, with respect to some kinds of programs. In other words, it seems plausible to assume that the performance priorities favored by resource controllers will be a product of the social and economic characteristics of the decision makers, the political context within which they operate, and the social purpose of the program, i.e., the sector of social welfare in which the agency operates.

One must also contend with the possibility that the reluctance of resource providers to stress client outcomes as a measure of agency performance is due to a perception that human service agencies do not possess the technology necessary to deliver on change objectives. It is at least conceivable that law makers, high level executives, and others have come to settle for other performance criteria which they take as surrogates of service effectiveness because so little seems to have worked in the past. In any case, it would seem that efforts to mobilize powerful external groups around service effectiveness must rest on a more sophisticated understanding of their preferences and values than is now available.

At the same time, the cause of service effectiveness oriented management would benefit by increased attention to the tactics and strategies of external influence. A field that is so utterly dependent on external decision making has a very impoverished knowledge base regarding means for impacting the perceptions and decision priorities of those who determine our fate. A similar lack of knowledge regarding marketing and advertising in order to shape and stimulate consumer demand would render for-profit organizations vulnerable to a chaotic and unpredictable environment. We would do well to study those instances in which social agencies have been able to shape the performance priorities of resource providers to understand how this has been done. Carter (1983) provides some examples of instances in which this has been done. There is evidence to suggest that agencies are not only influenced, but also influence, and that they are not only dependent, but are also depended upon (Pfeiffer & Salancik, 1978; Austin, 1983; Jansson & Simmons, 1984). We need to know more about how powerful constituents can be mobilized to support service effectiveness and how such support can be reconciled with the other agendas to which they must also be responsive. The articles by Martin and Simons in this volume present some interesting ideas about strategies for achieving this end.

CONCLUSION

Even this partial listing of the issues that need attention in developing a service effectiveness driven approach to management represents a formidable challenge for the practice and scholarly communities. The limited resources available to pursue this task compels closer relationships between agency and university, and between those concerned with direct services and administration. The promotion of service effectiveness serves the interests of all these groups and the more their resources are collaboratively brought to bear on this common ground, the more we in social welfare and those we serve will benefit.

REFERENCES

Austin, D. Administrative practice in human services. *Journal of Applied Behavioral Sciences*, 1983, *19*, 141-152.
Austin, D. The political economy of social benefit organizations. In H. Stein (Ed.). *Organization and the human services*. Philadelphia: Temple University Press, 1981.
Baker, T. & Vosburgh, W. W. Workers, cases, and errors. *Administration in Social Work*, 1977, *1*, 161-170.
Blythe, B. An examination of practice evaluation among social workers. Doctoral dissertation, University of Washington, 1983.
Carter, R. *The accountable agency*. Beverly Hills, CA: Sage Publications, 1983.
Friesen, B. Organization and leader behavior correlates of line worker satisfaction and role clarity. Doctoral dissertation, University of Washington, 1983.
Graen, G. Effects of linking pin quality on the quality of working life of lower participants. *Administrative Science Quarterly*, 1977, *22*, 491-504.
Holland, T. Organizational structure and institutional care. *Journal of Health and Social Behavior*, 1973, *14*, 241-251.
Hunt, J. et al. Relations of discretionary and non-discretionary leadership performance and satisfaction in a complex organization. *Human Relations*, 1978, *31*, 507-523.
Jansson, B. & Simmons, J. Building departmental or unit power within human service organizations. *Administration in Social Work*, 1984, *8*, 41-56.
Kahn, A. *Social policy and social services*. New York: Random House, 1973.
Kouzes, J. & Mico, P. Domain theory: An introduction to organizational behavior in human service organizations. *Journal of Applied Behavioral Science*, 1979, *15*, 449-469.
Linn, L.S. State hospital environment and rates of patient discharge. *Archives of General Psychiatry*, 1970, *23*, 346-351.
Lipsky, M. *Street level bureaucracy*. New York: Russell Sage Foundation, 1980.
Martin, P.Y. Multiple constituencies, dominant societal values, and human service administrators. *Administration in Social Work*, 1980, *4*, 15-27.
Martin, P.Y. & Segal, B. Bureaucracy, size, and staff expectations for client independence in halfway houses. *Journal of Health and Social Behavior*, 1977, *18*, 376-390.
Moos, R. *Evaluating treatment environments*. New York: Wiley and Sons, 1974.
Morris, R. Persistent issues and elusive answers in social welfare policy, planning, and administration. *Administration in Social Work*, 1982, *6*, 33-47.
Mutschler, E. Evaluating practice: A study of research utilization by practitioners. *Social Work*, 1984, *29*, 332-337.
Newman, J. & Ryder, R. Evaluating administrative performance. *Public Welfare*, Fall, 1987, 45-71.
Patti, R. In search of purpose in social welfare administration. *Administration in Social Work*, 1985, *9*, 1-14.
Patti, R. *Social welfare administration*. Englewood Cliffs, NJ: Prentice-Hall, Inc, 1983.
Pfeiffer, J. & Salancik, G. *The external control of organizations*. New York: Harper and Row, 1978.

Poertner, J. & Rapp, C. Organization learning and problem finding. In M. Dinerman (Ed.), *Social work in a turbulent world*. Silver Spring, MD: NASW, 1983.

Quinn, R. & Rohrbaugh, J.A. A competing values approach to organizational effectiveness. *Public Productivity Review*, 1981, *5*, 122-140.

Steers, R.M. Problems in the measurement of organizational effectiveness. *Administrative Science Quarterly*, 1975, *20*, 546-557.

Vinter, R. Analysis of treatment organizations. In Y. Hasenfeld & R.A. English (Eds.), *Human service organizations*. Ann Arbor: University of Michigan Press, 1974.

Weatherly, R. The micropolitics of madness. Manuscript, University of Washington, 1984.

Welch, G. Will graduates use single subject design to evaluate their casework practice? *Journal of Education for Social Work*, 1983, *19*, 42-47.

Whetten, D. Coping with incompatible expectations. *Administration in Social Work*, 1977, *1*, 379-393.

Moving Clients Center Stage
Through the Use of Client Outcomes

Charles A. Rapp, PhD
John Poertner, DSW

The central issue confronting the field of human service management is moving clients to center stage. Our theory, methods, education, research, and most of all our management practice, must become client centered. Rino Patti and the authors of this paper have argued that client outcomes are the central concern of social work management. The paper will focus on one indispensable dimension to increasing the client centeredness of our human services: the definition and measurement of service effectiveness. It will do so within the context of a performance model of human service management.

MOVING THE CLIENT CENTER STAGE

There are two major elements in what we are referring to as client centeredness. The first focuses attention on the "process" of service provision—the degree to which the practice and the behavior of personnel, and the organizational structures and operating processes reflect a preoccupation with clients and their well being. It includes having the client treated with the highest degree of dignity, respect, and individuality. It involves the design and implementation of intake procedures, service accessibility, courtesy of receptionists, provisions for client input into individual case and programmatic decisions, flexibility to tailor services to individual client needs and desires, etc. The list can be extended tenfold.

The second element of client centeredness is the organizational focus on service effectiveness, client outcomes, results. While the terms vary by author, the central notion is that the centerpiece of agency performance is the benefits accrued by clients as a result of our efforts.

Dr. Rapp is Associate Professor and Associate Dean, and Dr. Poertner is Associate Professor, School of Social Welfare, University of Kansas, Lawrence, KS 66045.

Patti (1985) argues that service effectiveness should be the "philosophical linchpin" of human service organizations. Drucker (1973) claims the first steps in getting human services to perform is to clearly define "what is our business" and to establish clear objectives and goals from this answer. Others have suggested that client outcomes be the centerpiece of human service management (Rapp & Poertner, 1983, 1985).

Overlaid on these two elements is a third factor: the manager must be myopic, single-minded, and obsessed with clients. It is this commitment which Peters and Waterman (1982) found that distinguished between exceptional companies and rest of the field. While the two elements described above provide substance and guidance for management methods and practice, it is this obsession which provides the motivation and allows the managers and organization consistently to pursue increased client centeredness.

There are many indications that the field of human service management is not client centered. The client is either a peripheral concern or is virtually ignored. Perrow (1978), in describing the current dominant model of human service management, suggests that once demystified the goals are to regulate deviants, absorb part of the work force, and provide resources to other organizations. He goes on to suggest that managerial effectiveness is based on:

> the growth of her or his organization, the size of the budget, the contracts with elites, the accommodations it has with other powerful organizations, and the number of programs it has . . . extracting resources from a sometimes stingy environment, delivering goods to interested parties without having scandals, and meeting at a minimal level — the ongoing rate for the locality — the official goals of the agency. (pp. 113-115)

In a similar vein, Carter (1984) states: "Public administrators often consider the measurement of program success irrelevant to their ongoing survival or their expansion" (p. 6). He goes on to argue that the perception is not only that client outcomes are irrelevant but that many managers consider such data as harmful in attracting public support.

Perhaps a few examples of management practice which do not facilitate client centeredness would help make the point. Agency and program goals are almost always stated in terms of what the agency will do or provide rather than on the specific benefits to be accrued by clients as a result of these agency efforts. For example:

To develop a teenage alcoholism program in the community's high school rather than reduced incidence of teenage alcohol and substance abuse in the community's high school. (Weiner, 1982, p. 226)

Similarly, most agency information systems are dominated by productivity data (e.g., amount of service provided, number of clients served) and financial data. It is rather rare for an agency information system to collect and systematically report effectiveness data. Another indicator of the lack of client centeredness is reflected in the agendas of management or staff meetings. A quick perusal would demonstrate that these meetings are dominated or exclusively focused on policies and procedures, staff issues, public relations, funding concerns, etc. The relationship between these issues and clients, or specific discussion of "how well we are doing" in terms of clients is rarely present. These practices and a myriad of others manifest goal displacement whereby achievement of the mission of the agency is preempted by organizational maintenance.

For the last three years, administration and planning students in the University of Kansas School of Social Welfare have been collectively asked to identify indicators of client centeredness in human service programs. The lists vary between 60 and 100 separate indicators. Once completed the students evaluate their field practicum agency against the criteria. Virtually all fields of practice have been represented, as well as about 45 different agencies. The result is that in every case, few agencies meet even a quarter of the indicators to any reasonable extent.

The management literature fares no better. A recent review of the literature in human service management revealed that less than half of the articles contained any mention of an outcome variable (Rapp, Hardcastle, Rosenzweig & Poertner, 1983). In only seven percent of the articles was a dependent variable related to client outcomes, the assumed reason for the agency's existence. Without a model for effectiveness, managers frequently engage in reactive management practice, embrace "sexy" new management practices which consume large amounts of resources before they atrophy and are discarded, and employ problem solving modes which seem to solve problems but which never seem to lead to improved performance.

In terms of the social work profession, Patti (1984) writes:

Administration has never been fully accepted in social work, in part, I suspect, because the goals of this method have been perceived, rightly or wrongly, as either in conflict with, or only tangentially related to, the profession's main business of changing people and social conditions.

The profession continues to be unable to exploit its marginal advantage over other management disciplines (e.g., public administration, business administration) in terms of its knowledge of clients, programs and service systems. The profession is unable to muster the data necessary to suggest that social workers are the preferred leadership for human service organizations. The increasing intrusion of graduates from business and public administration into management positions within the human services reflects a major threat to the profession and to services. The small cadre of MSW students enrolled in management specializations and the continued tension between clinical and management social workers do not auger well for our future (Patti, 1984).

The performance model of social administration has managers define, measure, and focus on five areas. Social programs need to produce client outcomes, acquire resources, maintain high staff morale, generate important products, and do all this with as much efficiency as possible. Performance in these areas can be enhanced or maintained with the skillful use of program design, personnel management, information management and resource management skills.

A critical and indispensable element of this model is the measurement of client outcomes. The manager and other personnel need systematically to monitor the results of their prodigious efforts as a prerequisite to the quest for "always doing it better." Yet, the systematic monitoring of client outcomes is a rare occurrence. In part, this is due to four prevalent myths. This paper will describe these four myths and provide evidence that they are inaccurate.

MYTH #1: THE OUTCOMES
OF HUMAN SERVICES ARE HIGHLY IDIOSYNCRATIC

Like all myths, there seems to be some truth in it. Each program does have to set its own goals based on the underlying program theory (Borich & Jawelka, 1982; Sabatier & Mazmanian, 1979) and expectations from funders. However, this myth has led management scholars to avoid the issue by retreating to the use of such summary terms as results (Lewis & Lewis, 1983), the organization's goals (Mirengoff, 1980), and agency mission or purpose (Drucker, 1973). But if the results, goals, and mission or purpose are stated in service terms rather than in client outcome terms, it is not only not helpful but actually undermines the attempt to increase client centeredness. This myth also unnecessarily separates human services into conceptually unrelated enterprises by assuming that all are different and therefore little cross-fertilization can occur.

The following taxonomy is suggested as applying across human services, and it may provide a unifying framework for human service management. It proposes five types of outcome measures: affective changes, learning, behavior changes, status maintenance or change, and environmental modification.

Affective Changes

Many people seek to change the way they feel about something or their emotional response to a situation. Social workers have a historical concern with this dimension. As examples, people seek to change the grief and sadness they feel after a loss such as a death or divorce. People seek to regain the feelings of love and acceptance which used to accompany a particular relationship. Occasionally society identifies the need for an affective change as in the case of the angry adolescent who is acting violently. A client's feeling of empowerment is central to many human service programs. A special form of affective outcomes is client satisfaction whereby clients are asked to judge their feelings concerning the quality of service provided.

The place of client satisfaction in a taxonomy of client outcomes is in a state of flux. Is client satisfaction an adequate dependent variable for some human service programs? The authors have argued elsewhere, albeit with reservations, that it is worthwhile in its own right (Rapp & Poertner, 1983; Rapp & Poertner, 1984; Poertner & Rapp, 1985). Patti (1985), on the other hand, has viewed client satisfaction as a separate performance area and has combined it with employee satisfaction. The issue is not whether all human services should be concerned with client satisfaction, but whether it can serve as an end in its own right as an effectiveness (client outcome) measure.

Learning

People or society may seek to change the way individuals think about themselves, others, or a situation. The educational aspects of services are quite pervasive. In an extensive review of service outcomes Taber (1980) identified cognitive changes, or the educational aspects, as primary in those services which seem to be effective. The father who uses excessive physical punishment on his young child may think that this is the most effective way to shape the behavior of his child. Society intervenes in situations of this type to help him learn more effective and less harmful methods of discipline. Others seek to learn new ways of relating to one's spouse or boss. For these types of programs, one outcome is the knowledge gained by clients. Do they know more after service than they did upon entrance?

Behavior Changes

Behavioral change is frequently the most desired client outcome. Society has an interest in the parent ceasing to abuse his or her child and the adolescent stopping "ripping off" car stereos. Many people seek social services to learn new behavior or eliminate troublesome behavior. Many programs for the chronically mentally ill and developmentally disabled are focused on teaching daily living and vocational skills. The acquisition of independent living skills by adolescents in foster care or stopping suicidal attempts are other examples.

Status Maintenance or Change

Individuals and society frequently have an interest in the maintenance or change in a person's status. Older people frequently seek services that assist them with daily living activities so that they can maintain their ability to live within one's home and community. Society has repeatedly expressed an interest in certain vulnerable populations such as those with mental and physical disabilities living in the most normal or least restrictive environment.

Environment Modifications

This type of outcome relates to programs which improve living conditions, change policies, or that produce more constructive public attitudes and beliefs. There is some discomfort in placing environmental modification as a separate outcome because it could move the client's well-being from center stage. For example, a change in policy which does not demonstrate subsequent positive impact on clients has not been a success. A policy like the deinstitutionalization of the mentally ill was supported by some of the most client centered people in our field but led to ten to 15 years of pain and suffering by the majority of clients (Basseck & Gerson, 1978). Was this a success? More subtly but more prevalent, if a program improves living conditions within an apartment complex, but those improvements are not perceived by the clients in one of the four previous ways, is it a success? In such situations should client satisfaction be the ultimate test rather than behavior, status, or cognitive or affective changes? We have no intention here of entering into an argument of "if the tree falls in the woods and nobody hears it, did it make a sound" or to even argue that environmental modification itself is an adequate or inadequate criterion. These questions must yet be decided.

MYTH #2:
WE CAN'T MEASURE CLIENT OUTCOMES

"Outcomes for our clients cannot be measured." "Instruments do not exist to measure the outcomes of our clients." "The expertise is not available to develop new measures." "We do not have resources to pay some 'university-type' to develop client outcome measures." Those are just a few of the statements heard when measurement of client outcomes is raised.

That measuring client outcomes is more complex than measuring profit in the business sector cannot be denied. However, a host of techniques and instruments have been developed over the last few years. A brief review of existing measurement techniques for each outcome area follows.

Affective Changes

Various scales that measure attitudes are the primary mechanism for assessing how one feels about something. In the social work context perhaps the best measures in this area are several of those which are part of the Clinical Measurement Package (Hudson, 1982). Scales like the Generalized Contentment Scale or the Index of Self-Esteem contain a series of statements frequently beginning with "I feel." They are to be responded to on a five-point scale from "rarely or none of the time" to "most or all of the time." These particular scales have been carefully developed, are easy to use, and have demonstrated utility in clinical treatment and evaluation.

Client satisfaction as a client outcome has received considerable attention particularly from mental health services. Patti (1985) argues that client satisfaction ought to be a primary outcome of most social services. Clients reporting of their satisfaction is a report on their feelings about the service transactions. Although Lebow's (1983) statement about a definitional muddle was written about client satisfaction, current literature suggests that perceiving client satisfaction as a multidimensional concept is a useful way of learning how clients feel about various aspects of service (Poertner, 1986). The literature is not yet clear on the most important satisfaction dimensions for various services. However, elements such as goal attainment and service provider facilitative behavior, and agency characteristics such as ease of access, seem to be recurrent themes (Poertner, 1985, 1986; Poertner & Wintersteen, 1985). There is sufficient literature on the assessment of client satisfaction that the methodology for scale development is within the grasp of most agencies (Poertner & Wintersteen, 1985).

Acquisition of Knowledge

Assessment of knowledge acquired through a particular intervention is reasonably straightforward with the use of knowledge gained instruments. The tried and true pre-test/post-test is perhaps one of the best known outcome assessment technologies. It is reasonable to attribute improvements in post-test scores and pre-test scores to the educational intervention.

The format of the questions used in such instruments is a consideration deserving additional attention. There are certainly levels of knowing which may be differentially reflected through the format of questions. For example, for an educational service with people who did not exhibit a high level of verbal skills each concept was assessed through a true/false question and a multiple choice question. For this client group this represented two different levels of knowledge and the pairs of items worked well. One could envision a variety of formats that might get at varying levels of cognitive changes.

Sometimes pre- and post-tests are time-consuming and burdensome to both client and provider. The retrospective reporting suggested by Howard for attitude assessment can be used for cognitive change assessment. The inclusion of an item in the form "Before the class, did you know x?" can eliminate the need for a pre-test. This has been tested and was found to be a useful outcome measure (Poertner & Rapp, 1983).

Behavior Change

The primary method for assessment of behavior change is the use of behavioral check lists, which are completed through observation. The observer may be the client, the service provider, or significant other. In a variety of settings there is little reason to believe that the person is not a good reporter on behavior. I did yell at my child yesterday, talk to my father, or go to the employment office. In some situations multiple perspectives may be indicated. When there is a vulnerable third party and society has an interest, such as child protective services, it may be desirable to have the perspective of both the parent and the social worker on the parent's use of physical forms of punishment.

Another frequent behavior change measure is some form of goal attainment. Client and worker mutually define the behavioral change which is the goal of service and periodically review whether or not the goal has been obtained. Goal attainment systems are not exclusively behavior change measures. Clients and workers can set goals about feelings or acquiring knowledge as well. However, many goal attainment systems are focused on behaviors, and this is a useful mechanism for assessment of this class of outcomes.

Status Change

The idea of client status change is an inherent component of many service systems. Examples include: a child is removed from his/her home, a case is opened, a case is closed, a person acquires full-time employment, or a person moves from an institution to a group home. Recidivism is a common concern in areas such as mental health (return to the hospital) and corrections (return to prison). A cursory glance at these examples suggests that they have few of the measurement problems which plague other client outcomes. Gaining full-time, unsubsidized employment is not subject to client or worker perception. There is little danger of inflation of scores from a socially desirable response to a measure such as child is returned home. There is nothing vague about a child removed from his or her home. Status change measures, by their very nature, avoid many of the reliability and validity problems associated with other client outcome measures. Perhaps one of the greatest strengths of status change measures is their availability. Frequently, case files or client data bases already contain the data needed to track client status systematically.

Environmental Changes

Measurement of environmental impacts is the least developed client outcome area. This is not surprising since much of the measurement thrust comes from psychology, which has historically underattended to the environment. However, items which assess the adequacy of a person's residence, food, and finances are included in some scales such as the Oregon Quality of Life Scale (Bigelow, Brodesky, Steward & Olson, 1982) and are good examples of assessment of environmental impacts. Kane and Kane (1984) have identified a set of scales focused on the "person environment fit" which have been developed for long term care clients. Those scales attempt to assess the dimension of

— the degree of perceived control, freedom, choice, autonomy, or individuality permitted by the environment (to the individual);
— structure, rules, and expected behavior imposed by the environment on the individual;
— relationships between individuals and caregivers in the environment;
— perceptions of activity and stimulation levels;
— expressed satisfaction with various aspects of the environment. (p. 192)

Synthetic Measures

Some client outcome assessments are not specific to affective changes, acquisition of knowledge, behavior change, status changes, or environmental impacts. These assessments either operate from a more complex model of change or attempt to synthesize the various changes into one instrument. As our interventions become more multidimensional they attempt to improve the client's situation in several areas. The Oregon Quality of Life (Bigelow et al., 1982) instrument is a current example aimed at assessing the quality of life of chronically mentally ill individuals. The identification of the dimensions of quality of life across populations is not obvious. Relevant dimensions for the chronically mentally ill may be different from those for the elderly or for children. Baker and Intagliata (1984) used a QOL instrument which includes 15 life domains including such areas as housing, food, clothing, health, relationships, leisure time, and finances. This approach of identifying the relevant domains of people's lives and assessing the impact of services across these domains is particularly appealing for a variety of social services. The traditional emphasis of social services on the interactions and reciprocal nature of relationships between people or between a person and their environment is nicely congruent with the ideal of QOL and life domains.

Frequently, a social service transaction is based on a theory of change which brings together or synthesizes several distinct changes. For example, the service model underlying the outcomes for a parent education service was built on the theory that parents' satisfaction with the service, together with increased knowledge of parenting, would converge to produce changed parenting behavior and movement of children through the child welfare system (Poertner & Rapp, 1983).

This model requires four quite different outcome measures which yielded useful results. What might appear as four distinct outcomes assessed independently was in fact a synthesis of these measures where the underlying theory was used to bring the separate indicators together. For any particular parent education group the results very specifically identified points of intervention for service improvement. It was the overall picture which was useful in conjunction with the four different perspectives.

MYTH #3:
WE CAN'T BE HELD ACCOUNTABLE
FOR CLIENT OUTCOMES

This is the political suicide myth: if we reported client outcomes to funders, they would not be likely to continue funding us. "I want funders to continue to base their decisions on their concern with a social problem (e.g., sexual abuse, poverty, mental illness) rather than how well we help clients." The claim is often made that it is up to the client whether the help we provide is used, and the agency cannot be held responsible for this. The implication is that too few of our clients actually do so. Since a large amount of public money goes to these services, it seems irresponsible to claim client outcomes are out of our control. To our knowledge, no one has ever expected human services to cure everyone, prevent all future child abuse or criminal activity, or to employ every mentally ill client. In fact, it seems that in the instances where expectations were overly ambitious, it was the professionals who instigated it:

As social work has begun to formulate its goals, however, it has often tripped itself up by making them overly ambitious. One case in point was the 1962 amendments to the Social Security Act. Increased funding was provided for social services and at the same time goals for the recipients of social services of "self care," "self support" and "strengthened family life" were adopted. For twenty-five years the profession of social work had been trying to convince Congress that "trained social workers" should staff the direct service positions in Public Aid. In the early 1960's a Congress which was alarmed by rising AFDC rolls was ready to buy the NASW argument. President Kennedy proclaimed the amendments as a shift toward rehabilitation, rather than relief. A few short years later, as AFDC rolls rose even

more steeply, social workers hastened to revise their policy position on public aid. (Taber & Finnegan, 1980)

Taber (1980), in a review of the evaluation literature, found several
dozen studies of casework and other social work services showed that
outcome criteria were often couched in terms of reducing delinquency,
getting families out of poverty, and restoring very disorganized individuals and families to harmonious functioning. The social administrator should be the chief educator of realism.
The three points that need to be made are:

1. Client outcomes can be a realistic way of looking at agency performance.
2. Client outcomes can and do lead to increased funding.
3. Client outcomes are a prerequisite for internal agency management.

Program goals can be written in terms of client outcomes and still be
realistic. The technique is that for each goal, a minimum performance
standard is set. For example, the state of Florida has outcome goals
that have standards set from 50% achievement to 90% achievement.
Carter (1986) suggests a standard of 10-20% for the goal of unsubsidized employment for ADC recipients, given the track record in most
locations. The point is that there is every opportunity and necessity to
employ client outcomes in a realistic fashion; it is not a reason for not
using them.
    The second point is that rather than making programs vulnerable,
client outcomes can enhance resource acquisition. Carter (1984) has
begun documenting that when programs have systematically monitored the client outcomes and have used the data in funding forums,
this has led to continued and increased support. This is not to say that
such reporting of effectiveness data will be telling in every case, or
that it is the only type of information which is relevant. In fact, Patti
(1986) has suggested that in some policy forums, effectiveness data
may prove impotent.
    The third point may be the most critical. Regardless of the use of
client outcome data with external constituencies, a social administrator requires such information to manage the internal operation of programs. If, in fact, effectiveness in terms of client outcomes is the
raison d'être of human service programs (and what social administrator would deny this claim), then the systematic monitoring of this
"bottom line" is essential and indispensable. How can a social admin-

istrator keep the program ship on course without such a compass? To not do so is like the business which does not monitor profit or market shares. Would the businessperson assume the company was making a profit if the assembly line kept producing widgets or if workers were obviously working hard? To the authors, not to monitor client outcomes substantially and use that data to improve operations is tantamount to managerial irresponsibility, incompetence, and unethical conduct.

MYTH #4: MONITORING CLIENT OUTCOMES WILL TAKE TOO MUCH TIME AND RESOURCES FOR NEGLIGIBLE GAIN

In most cases, the systematic collection of client outcome data will take a commitment of resources; information systems may need to be revised or new ones purchased, staff may be needed to collect information, and current staff will need to complete more forms. However, in many agencies at least some of the information is already in the computer or file drawer and in other cases small procedural changes would be all that is necessary. The "we can't waste any more time" argument, however, fails to recognize the waste that accrues from not knowing how well the program is contributing to client outcomes. A recent case may help.

One of the authors has been working with a mental health center to develop a monitoring and evaluation system for their partial hospitalization program for the chronically mentally ill. The center operates a modest partial hospitalization program for about 30 clients. The program operates from 9 to 5 five days a week and includes activities focused on recreation and socialization, health, daily living skills, pre-vocational skills, arts and crafts, stress management, meal planning, cooking, music, and interpersonal relations. Counseling services and mediation clinic are a part of the program. The staff is also concerned with the degree to which clients are satisfied with the program and how well the clients are doing when not at the center. The staff is warm and caring and works diligently. It sounds like a very solid program which is doing a lot for their clients.

The only data collected is on rehospitalizations and symptomatology.

Most of the program's efforts were directed at teaching basic living and vocational skills. We jointly developed a series of scales for each domain whereby the staff would make periodic judgments on whether a client had the specific skill in his/her repertoire and the degree to which the client used the skill outside of the program. The instrument was tested on about 10 cases. The result was that the staff assessed the clients as having the ability to do the vocational skills (93%) and the basic living skills (97%). In fact, all but one of the clients had the ability to do all of the skills. Community implementation of the skills, however, was quite varied between specific skills and between clients.

If the issue is waste, this program reaches a new high. The program spends almost all of its efforts teaching skills the clients already have in their repertoires and virtually no time is spent in the community with clients helping them to use the skills in their lives. A major program redesign effort is clearly indicated.

Much has been made of detrimental effects of poor worker morale and job satisfaction on personnel and the organization. Loss of productivity, unresponsiveness to clients, absenteeism, tardiness, organizational sabotage, and burnout have been identified as the results of personnel who do not receive adequate satisfaction from their jobs. Each of these is a major source of waste and inefficiency in organizations. Yet, it is clear that job satisfaction is greatly influenced by such factors as the degree to which one believes his or her job to be important or worthwhile, and the degree to which one receives feedback on the results of his or her efforts (Locke, 1978). The systematic collection and reporting of client outcome data to workers and teams seems to be an indispensable tool for enhancing the job satisfaction of employees and thereby reducing waste.

CONCLUSION

In this paper, it has been argued that client outcomes should be the centerpiece of any model of human service management, but the evidence is that clients are still on the periphery of our management theory, research, education, and most critically, practice. In management practice especially, the lack of client outcome monitoring is in part based on four myths which this paper has sought to deflate. It is hoped that the pages in this volume will contribute to the refinement of the ideas and arguments so that a more powerful and persuasive voice can be used to contribute to the field of human service management.

REFERENCES

Baker, F. & Intagliata, J. The New York State community support system: A profile of clients. *Hospital and Community Psychiatry*, 1984, *35*(1). 39-44.

Basseck, E.L. & Gerson, S. Deinstitutionalization and mental health services. *Scientific American*, 1978, *238*(2). 46-53.

Bigelow, D.A. et al. The concept and measurement of quality of life as a dependent variable in evaluation of mental health services. In G.J. Stohler & W.R. Tash (Eds.), *Innovative approaches to mental health education.* New York: Academic Press, 1982.

Borich, G. & Jawelka, R.P. *Programs and systems: An evaluation perspective.* New York: Academic Press, 1982.

Carter, R. Measuring client outcomes: The experience of the states. Paper presented at the conference Toward a Performance Model of Human Service Management, University of Kansas, 1986.

Drucker, P.F. Managing the public service institution. *Public Interest*, 1973, *33*, 43-60.

Hudson, W. *The clinical measurement package: A field manual.* Homewood, IL: The Dorsey Press, 1982.

Kane, R.A. & Kane, R.L. *Assessing the elderly.* Lexington, MA: Lexington Books, 1984.

Lebow, J.L. Client satisfaction with mental health treatment: Methodological considerations in assessment. *Evaluation Review*, 1983, 7, 729-753.

Lewis, J.A. & Lewis, M.D. *Management of human service programs.* Monterey, CA: Brooks/Cole, 1983.

Locke, E.A. Nature and causes of job satisfaction. In M.D. Dunnette (Ed.). *Handbook of industrial and organizational psychology.* Chicago: Rand McNally, 1975.

Mirengoff, M.L. *Management in human service organizations.* New York: Macmillan, 1980.

Patti, R. In search of purpose for social welfare administration. Paper presented at the Annual Program Meeting of the Council on Social Work Education, Detroit, March, 1984.

Patti, R. In search of purpose for social welfare administration. *Administration in Social Work*, 1985, *9*(3), 1-4.

Patti, R. Managing for service effectiveness in social welfare: Toward a performance model. Paper presented at the conference Toward a Performance Model of Human Service Management. University of Kansas, 1986.

Perrow, C. Demystifying organizations. In R.C. Sarri & Y. Hasenfeld (Eds.). *The management of human services.* New York: Columbia University Press, 1978.

Peters, T.J. & Waterman, R.H. *In search of excellence.* New York: Harper & Row, 1982.

Poertner, J. Measurement of client satisfaction: Development and testing of scale for parent education. *Social Work Research and Abstracts*, 1985, *21*(3), 23-28.

Poertner, J. The use of client feedback to improve practice: Defining the supervisor's role. *The Clinical Supervisor*, 1986, 4(4).

Poertner, J. & Rapp, C.A. Purchase of service and accountability: Will they ever meet? *Administration in Social Work*, 1985, *9*(1). 57-66.

Poertner, J. & Wintersteen, R. Measurement of client satisfaction with social work services. Unpublished manuscript, University of Kansas, School of Social Welfare, 1985.

Rapp, C.A., Hardcastle, D.A., Rosenzweig, J. & Poertner, J. The status of research in social service management. *Administration in Social Work*, 1983, 7(3). 89-100.

Rapp, C.A. & Poertner, J. Organizational learning and problem finding. In *Social work in turbulent times.* New York: NASW, 1983.

Rapp, C.A. & Poertner, J. A human service formulation for management education. Paper presented at the Council on Social Work Education, Detroit, 1984.

38   MANAGING FOR SERVICE EFFECTIVENESS

Rapp, C.A. & Poertner, J. A performance model for human service management. Unpublished manuscript, University of Kansas, School of Social Welfare, 1985.

Taber, M. *The social context of helping: A review of the literature on alternative care for the physically and mentally handicapped.* Washington, DC: U.S. Government Printing Office, 1980.

Taber, M. & Finnegan, D. Realistic program goals and objectives: Outcome of an analytic process. Unpublished manuscript, University of Illinois, School of Social Work, 1980.

Weiner, M.E. *Human services management.* Homewood, IL: Dorsey Press, 1982.

SECTION TWO:
MEASUREMENT
OF CLIENT OUTCOMES

Introduction

This new model of social administration has as its central mission the production of desired client outcomes. It is client outcomes which become the "bottom-line" of human service organizations much like profit is for the business sector. The social administrator's job is to steer the program towards increasingly effective services through program design and the management of people, resources, and information. This simply cannot happen unless the organization systematically defines and measures client outcomes. Not doing so is like the business which does not regularly monitor profit and market share. As Rapp and Poertner state in the preceding article in this volume:

> . . . not to monitor client outcomes systematically and use that data to improve operations is tantamount to managerial irresponsibility, incompetence, and unethical conduct.

The following four papers address the task of measuring client outcomes from different perspectives. The first two papers have been authored respectively by William J. Reid and Walter W. Hudson. These scholars have been major contributors to the fifteen year movement in social work towards empirically based practice and herein extend their thinking to social administration. Reid describes strategies of measurement which balance rigor with the pragmatics of

39

agency life. Hudson addresses philosophical, technical, and educational issues related to effectiveness based social administration.

The paper by Reginald K. Carter seeks to establish the viability of outcome oriented management practice by surveying human service organizations which are currently monitoring client outcomes systematically. From these experiences, Carter identifies six lessons for implementing such systems.

The paper by Anthony J. Grasso and Irwin Epstein describes the dilemmas inherent in moving an organization to an effectiveness model requiring the measurement of client outcomes. Their particular plea is for such monitoring to be an integral part of an organization's staff development effort if improved performance is to result.

Service Effectiveness and the Social Agency

William J. Reid, DSW

Questions about the effectiveness of social programs have long been a source of concern to the human service professions. In social work these questions became especially troublesome in the sixties following a series of experiments that failed to demonstrate the effectiveness of the interventions of professional social workers (Mullen & Dumpson, 1972; Fischer, 1973, 1976; Wood 1978). These studies, and reviews and critiques of them, sparked a continuing "effectiveness controversy" with fingers pointed at the credibility of the research, the adequacy of the services, and in a few other directions. While more recent experiments have given evidence that social work services can indeed be effective (Reid & Hanrahan, 1982; Rubin, 1985), the debate goes on (Fischer, 1983).

In this debate a range of research and practice issues has been examined in considerable detail and often with considerable redundancy. Relatively neglected, however, has been systematic attention to the agency contexts of the service programs examined (Mullen, 1976). Although the typical effectiveness study is conducted as part of an agency program, the focus of the investigator, the report, and subsequent critique is on the particular population and interventions studied. Usually the agency dies an anonymous death in the opening paragraphs of the report as a "medium size mental health facility in a large eastern city," or whatever. The studies from these nameless sites have become part of the body of research that is used to make statements about the effectiveness of social work intervention. These statements may be valid for the world of research experiments but bear only an uncertain relationship to the world of agency practice.

On a different track, agency concern over determining effectiveness has grown in response to increasing stress on accountability from

Dr. Reid is Professor, School of Social Welfare, The Nelson A. Rockefeller College of Public Affairs and Policy, State University of New York at Albany, Albany, NY 12222.

funding and accrediting agencies. The rise of management information systems (MISs) and quality assurance programs have been part of this response. Indeed Patti (1985) has proposed that service effectiveness should be the "central concern of social welfare administration" (p. 4).

This paper attempts to contribute a research perspective to the development of service effectiveness as an agency goal. Its focus will be a number of key issues that arise when service effectiveness is considered from both research and agency standpoints. The issues will concern differing conceptions of effectiveness, measurement strategies and procedures, and utilization of effectiveness research.

WHAT IS EFFECTIVENESS, REALLY?

At a general level there is probably agreement as to what constitutes effectiveness. For example, one would expect little quarrel with Bielawski and Epstein's (1984) definition that "program effectiveness concerns itself with whether the intended goals . . . have been attained as a result of a program" (p. 20). Disagreement arises, however, in respect to what is required to claim that effectiveness has occurred. A hard-nosed researcher is likely to demand that the effectiveness of an intervention be established through a controlled experimental test. By this means one can determine if "intended goals" have been attained by the program or have been produced by extraneous factors, such as natural recovery processes, environmental influences, and the like. Practitioners and managers responsible for program operations are likely to take a much less stringent view, one that may give decisive weight to apparent client change following an intervention. If a depressed client is treated for depression and gets better, the treatment is usually assumed to be responsible and not extraneous factors.

The issue amounts to more than quibbling over semantics. For example, practice wisdom and the favorable results of uncontrolled pilot studies were used as a basis for advancing the claim that professional casework could provide an effective means of rehabilitating welfare families (Bell, 1961). A number of program initiatives resulted. Subsequent controlled experiments found little basis to substantiate this claim (Wallace, 1967; Mullen, Chazin & Feldstein, 1972). On the other hand, insistence that the effectiveness label be reserved for interventions that have passed the test of controlled experimentation seems excessively severe in the present state of both of the research and service arts in social work. There is controlled experimental evidence for the effectiveness of only a modest number of programs. The programs are typically not well enough described to be readily implemented. Only a minority — less than a quarter in one comprehensive survey (Videka-Sherman, 1985) — report data on interventions actually used. Even when it is possible to implement a "proven" program, it is not certain that its effects could be reproduced with different client populations in different settings.

The dilemma is this: If strict scientific criteria for determining effectiveness are applied, we cannot establish much of a basis that routine agency services are effective; if we make effectiveness claims that lack a solid empirical grounding, then our credibility suffers as well as our ability to isolate genuinely effective programs. More work is needed to develop a middle ground in which managers can make defensible claims that a service is demonstrably effective even if strict scientific criteria cannot be met. In this conception of effectiveness, systematic data would be required but standards would be more realistic. For example, use of adaptions of interventions found to be effective in prior tests could provide a basis for an effectiveness claim if results of the modified intervention were in the same range as those formally tested. More emphasis could be placed on a program's surpassing average rates of recovery for particular problems. If data were lacking, expert estimates of recovery rates might be used.

In some programs, changes following interventions bear an obvious imprint of the intervention. For example a program is designed to teach retarded children specific interactive skills — e.g., learning to initiate a conversation. Observation reveals that these skills, absent before the program, are present following it. Such "signed causes," to use Cook and Campbell's (1979) phrase, can be used as a basis for inferring effectiveness of the program. In the example cited, there is probably no satisfactory answer to the question "How else could they have gotten the skills?" In other programs it may be possible to cast doubt on potential extraneous factors through obtaining relevant evidence. Thus spontaneous recovery as a cause for change might be ruled out by obtaining historical data that would show that problems treated had been in a steady state for a substantial period prior to treatment.

However it is done, it may be necessary to develop arguments and supporting evidence for claims of effectiveness that go beyond simple demonstrations that desired changes in the lives of some clients have been realized. Such arguments and evidence may be needed not only to convince the research community but more important constituencies — funding sources, board members, consumers of service, and the like. We live in an era of growing skepticism and savvy about claims to effectiveness of practically everything, from social programs to sleeping pills.

Thus far I have considered effectiveness from the standpoint of service programs that bring about some demonstrable change in the client's problems or functioning. This is the conception of effectiveness used in the tradition of formal research on service effectiveness and, of course, applies to many social work programs, especially those in which some form of counselling looms large. However, much social work actively is focused on attainment of short-term "process" objectives. For example, a hospital social work department may be responsible for helping elderly patients choose the most appropriate health-related facility as a part of its discharge planning function. A probation unit's charge is to secure background data for the court. While such activities may be part of a chain leading to some end goal, the process may not only be difficult to trace but the social work manager and his or her unit may be responsible for only a part of it. Practically speaking the best measures of such "process effectiveness" or "service quality," to use Patti's (1985) term, may be data bearing on whether or not the activity was carried out according to certain criteria and lead to attaining the immediate objective. Recent work on quality assurance approaches (Kagan, 1984; Coulton, 1986) suggest specific procedures for assessing this type of effectiveness that go far beyond familiar but crude process evaluations (e.g., number of client contacts).

HOW MUCH IS ENOUGH?

The establishment of effectiveness, while fundamental, is only the beginning. Managers and their constituencies want to know more than whether or not a program is effective. They want to know "how effective" it is. I shall group together a number of dimensions under the rubric of the sufficiency of a program's effectiveness. Are the effects of adequate size to make a meaningful difference in the lives of the clients? Do they appear in clients and problems of greatest concern? Are they relatively short-lived or durable? Are positive effects complicated or offset by negative effects? Is the scope of change adequate?

These issues have become more pressing in response to some recent developments. First, there has been a growing recognition that client change is multidimensional. Interventions may affect one part of a client system positively without benefitting other parts. For example as Lambert (1983) has concluded from a review of relative studies, even interventions to reduce simple fears may result in behavior change toward feared objects without changing subjective distress. The "how effective" question must then be answered with a discriminating eye to what has been attained and what has not been.

Second, we have seen a growing number of programs that appear to produce genuine but modest effects. These programs, which make up a large proportion of the new wave of positive outcome studies referred to earlier (Reid & Hanrahan, 1982), tend to have specific behavioral goals, such as helping clients acquire certain skills. While such programs may be demonstrably effective in attaining limited goals, they may fall short of attaining objectives that the agency is charged to achieve.

For example, an agency may receive funds for a program to help potentially abusive parents. A service is modelled after an apparently effective program designed to help abusing parents control their anger in interactions with their children. The program appears to accomplish this purpose with parents deemed likely to be abusive. However, the number of clients served and followed up is not large enough to enable one to say that incidents of abuse were actually prevented.

It can be argued that it is better to show clearly effective results in attaining modest goals than ambiguous results in an attempt to achieve ambitious goals. Following the former strategy, one can work incrementally toward achieving effects of desired strength and scope. Following the latter strategy will keep us perpetually mired in uncertainty and ignorance.

However, to focus energy on achieving clearly effective but modest results can discourage more radical but possibly less testable innovations that may be needed to make headway with the serious client problems brought to social agencies. Here again, issues around the genuiness of effects intrude. It is better to make limited but well documented progress or to work toward more important goals with less certainty of what we have attained?

WHEN PERSPECTIVES CLASH

No matter how it is done, assessment of effectiveness comes down to human judgment. Even incontrovertible behavioral data must be interpreted in the light of its significance for program effectiveness. The concept of effectiveness must then be operationalized in terms of who makes such assessments. Different sources of effectiveness data — practitioners, clients, collaterals, research observers, and so on — may have differing conceptions of what is effective. The same applies to different actors who make judgments about these data — managers, staffs of funding agencies, and the like.

Much of this divergence appears due to value differences (Strupp & Hadley, 1977; Bergin, 1980). The notion of effectiveness inevitably incorporates a value component. In the language of the human services to be effective means to achieve a desired effect — "intended goals" to use Bielawski and Epstein's (1984) terms. A program that is designed to reduce delinquency but manages to increase it would not be seen as effective, though we may speak of its negative effects.

It does not stretch one's imagination to see how value differences can complicate assessment of effectiveness. For example, a divorce as an outcome of marital counselling may be viewed as the optimal solution by the husband, a disaster by his wife, as deplorable by the religious organization that funds the agency, and as regrettable but necessary by the practitioner. In addition different sources have access to different information. Clients know details of life at home that practitioners do not have; practitioners may have information about norms of family life that clients lack, and so on. Such differences are revealed in outcome studies in what has been referred to as lack of "intersource consensus" (Lambert, 1983). A common finding is lack of agreement among clients, practitioners and independent observers on effectiveness measures (Bergin & Lambert, 1978; Lambert, 1983). While such disparity is often viewed as a measurement issue, its roots lie in conceptual and value orientations. Although measurement implications will be taken up in a subsequent section, suffice it to say here is that these differences are not always reconcilable or averageable.

Researchers can handle such discrepancies by reporting them and discussing reasons for the variation. For managers the task is not confined to paper. Programs may need to be restructured to accommodate different value positions; often choices must be made between which goals to emphasize or pursue. For example, an adoption program for older emotionally disturbed children was effective from an agency perspective since "good homes" were found for large numbers of children who might otherwise have had to remain in an institutional setting (Reid, Kagan, Kaminsky & Helmer, in press). However, its effectiveness was questioned by many of the adopting parents who found raising the children more than they had bargained for. "How can the needs of such children be squared with those of the adopting parents?" was one of a number of issues raised by divergences in point of view about the effectiveness of the program.

GOOD IS NOT ENOUGH

An intervention may be genuinely effective and quite sufficient from all perspectives yet still not be the preferred one to use. Another intervention may prove more attractive because it can produce stronger and more durable effects with a given population, may cost less, be easier to implement, and so on. In other words effectiveness must be seen in a relative, if not competitive, light. Managers are in the business not only of finding ways to get a job done but to get it done in the best way possible.

However the wise search is not for the one best program. Many approaches achieve modest results with a wide range of clients but few do the job for all. The real task is to select a mix of programs that produce optimal results for different client groups. This is another way of stating a goal that outcome researchers in the human services have for many years been actively pursuing — determination of the most effective intervention for a given type of client or problem.

If the legitimacy of this goal is accepted, then one moves from thinking of the effectiveness of agency services in global terms to developing effective interventions for particular client-problem configurations (Geismar & Wood, 1986). Identification and analysis of these configurations determine what service packages are put together. Thus, an agency would view itself not as offering a particular brand of service but rather in terms of the types of problems and clients served. Granted an agency that is oriented around a particular service modality presumably adjusts treatment to fit the case but the adjustments may be limited by the constraints of that modality. Thus, an agency wedded to a family therapy approach for acting out youngsters may not explore the potentials of school-based interventions, group treatment or other approaches that may be especially effective for certain types of cases. Maintaining an open, flexible position on intervention has the advantage of enabling better matches between client and service.

Efforts to match a problem with the most effective service for that problem has encountered two barriers, however. First, and perhaps the most formidable, is that the programs of many service agencies are defined by particular service methodologies — one might say ideologies — for which staff are trained and to which they are committed. Changing such standard offerings is no simple task.

In addition there is little research-based knowledge to guide the matchmaking. What is needed ideally are studies that demonstrate the relative superiority of certain interventions over others for a given type of client or problem. While a number of comparative studies have been done, few have shown that any one type of intervention is clearly more effective than alternatives for a given situation (Luborsky, Singer & Luborsky, 1975; Smith, Glass & Miller, 1981).

This "tie effect," so often seen in comparative studies, is one of the more perplexing obstacles to developing an empirical basis for choice of intervention. Perhaps the best explanation is that we have not yet developed measures sensitive enough to detect differences in effectiveness that may occur when two interventions are compared. This point becomes more understandable when the following constraints are taken into account: (1) Whether in response to natural processes (e.g., client motivation) or to the nonspecific constants in most forms of intervention (e.g., practitioner attention), many problems brought to social agencies tend to have a high rate of positive change regardless of what intervention they receive; (2) For most classes of problems, a proportion of clients will not respond to any intervention; (3) For clients where intervention may make a genuine difference, the effects, as noted, may be typically modest. Thus, a typical intervention may then show a detectable margin of difference when compared against a "no treatment" control group but not against almost any respectable competitive intervention, given present crudeness of classifying clients and problems and measuring outcomes. It is like trying to decide which horse won in a close race viewed at a bad angle from the grandstand during a cloudburst.

Cost-effectiveness, another variation on the relative effectiveness theme, may provide solution to this dilemma in some situations but any apparent solution needs to be examined with care. In principle, the argument is simple: If two services have the same effects, go with the less costly. Since it is difficult to demonstrate the superiority of one service over another in terms of effectiveness but often easy to do so in terms of cost, the cheaper service is usually the winner. Thus comparative studies have been used to justify using paraprofessionals rather than professionals, short-term rather than long-term counselling, home-based services over institutional care, and so on. The obvious risk in this cost-effective minimalism is that it may be based on unwarranted confidence in our ability to measure the range and variety of effects resulting from intervention. As suggested, tied outcomes mean only lack of demonstrable difference. The more expensive service may have an edge on effectiveness that was not detected. A BMW and a Ford compact may look alike on performance tests, if the tests are simple enough.

Issues concerning relative effectiveness cannot then be easily resolved through empirical research. Little headway has been made in determining optimal problem-intervention matches (treatments of choice) and strict adherence to cost-effectiveness criteria has its risks (Reid, 1984).

In decision-making about relative effectiveness, research can offer some guidance, however. It can be used to argue for favoring programs that have been tested and found to have some measure of effectiveness as opposed to those that have not. Moreover, if comparative studies reveal no differences in effect between two programs that differ greatly in cost and if strong arguments for the superiority of the more expensive program cannot be found, then a rational basis for opting for the less expensive and hence more cost-effective program can be developed.

STRATEGIES FOR DETERMINING EFFECTIVENESS

Whatever conception of effectiveness they may use, managers must face the question: "How effective are the services offered in our agency?" Normally the answer is in a positive vein and is based on a mixture of conventional wisdom and anecdotal data. More empirically oriented managers, however, will attempt to bring systematic evidence to bear on the answer. At a general level, issues concern what kind of evidence to obtain and how best to obtain it. Selected strategies, which can be used singly or in combination, will be briefly reviewed.

Monitoring

Increasingly agencies are turning to some form of routine monitoring of service programs as a means of measuring effectiveness (Rossi & Freeman, 1984; Poertner & Rapp, 1985). Various mechanisms can be used, from a computerized MIS (Rapp, 1984) to audits of case records (Coulton, 1984). Whatever device is used, monitoring is generally limited by data of often dubious quality (e.g., practitioner recording) and by difficulty in isolating the effectiveness of interventions, since extraneous factors cannot be controlled. Measurement can be strengthened by incorporating instrumentation discussed in the subsequent section.

Confidence in the effectiveness of intervention assessed by a monitoring system can be increased if the intervention is adapted from effective programs tested in controlled experiments reported in the literature. While the selection is not exactly breathtaking, as noted, enough tested programs are available to make this option a viable one.

And their numbers are growing. Monitoring of these applications would be designed to provide evidence that service characteristics and outcomes were in line with results of the original experiments. Selected research instruments used in the experiments can be incorporated in the monitoring.

Where "process" effectiveness is at issue, measures can be based on careful recording of process events, such as whether or not a visit between children and natural parents was arranged within a certain period after placement. Recording of exceptions can pin point "negative instances," which can lead to corrective action (Coulton, 1984).

Discrete Evaluations

In this strategy, programs are evaluated through formal evaluations of different programs. Unfortunately, evaluations are more likely to be done on innovative programs although the strategy can and should be extended to periodic evaluations of standard programs. Because of cost and "ethical" considerations, experiments involving control or contrast groups are seldom used. Simple follow up studies or "before" and "after" measures are more the norm (Aaronson & Wilner, 1983). Such evaluations do poorly at isolating effects; they do not build on one another and utilization may be short-lived. On the other hand, they usually generate data of better quality than is yielded by monitoring systems and, if done regularly, can provide significant evidence on the effectiveness of an agency's program.

A variant of this strategy calls for use of single system designs in samples of cases that presumably reflect standard program offerings (Horn & Heerboth, 1982; Briar & Blythe, 1985). Because these designs can be well controlled, strong evidence on the effectiveness of intervention can be obtained. Such rigorous and intensive examination of case samples can supplement or replace larger but softer evaluation projects. This approach may have limited application, however, in programs that do not use the kind of behavioral or highly structured interventions that are best studied through single system designs. Questions concerning sample size and representativeness in such a plan have yet to be resolved as well as questions concerning the aggregation of findings from studies that may vary in design and measurement.

Developmental Research

This strategy makes use of a continuing process of evaluation and feedback to develop service programs (Thomas, 1978, 1985; Blythe & Briar, 1985; Reid, in press). Data from successive studies are used to modify the program and gradually improve its effectiveness. While a progression of designs — from pilot projects to controlled experiments is advocated — adaptation to the realities of social agency resources might limit the approach to some mixture of single case studies and small scale projects without controls. Developmental research may require a considerable investment of time and effort over a series of studies before a pay-off in significantly improved interventions is realized. Moreover, methods for obtaining and utilizing data as a basis for immediate program modification are just beginning to appear (Thomas, 1984; Reid, in press). These limitations not withstanding, a series of evaluations concentrated on developing a single program may still be greater than the same amount of one-shot evaluation effort spread over several programs.

Conclusion

Although these strategies, along with others, can be mapped out, no compelling case at present can be made for the general superiority of any one. Further study of such strategies in actual use is needed before we can say which one or which combination may be best suited to the needs of particular settings.

MEASUREMENT AND DATA COLLECTION

Although questions about optimal strategies remain unanswered, an agency seriously concerned about measuring the effectiveness of its services should be advised to build collection of some evaluative data into routine service operations. Occasional one shot projects won't suffice. In this era of budgetary constraints, most agencies would need to rely on less expensive forms of measurement, such as practitioner ratings, client self-administered instruments, available data, and simple interview protocols that can be administered to client samples over the phone. To get maximum mileage out of its measurement approaches, agencies would want to fashion them to facilitate actual service operations. Service-supportive measurement should be the goal.

Advantage can be taken of continuing developments in low-cost instrumentation. Two examples will be mentioned. One has been the generation of a sizeable number of rapid assessment instruments (RAIs) designed to measure changes of a range of problems, including depression, anxiety, family relations and self-esteem (Levitt & Reid, 1981; Edelson, 1985; Ivanof, et al., 1986). RAIs can be computed in a few minutes by clients and scored by practitioners. For several, normative data and validity evidence have been accumulated. The second example consists of the work in recent years on client satisfaction measures, which like RAIs are usually simple and quickly completed instruments. Client satisfaction norms have been developed for several types of client populations (Lehman & Zastowny, 1983; Lebow, 1984). These norms can be used as bench marks against which to assess client satisfaction with particular agency programs.

How adequately do such measurement and data collection approaches reflect changes associated with agency services? Perhaps the best that can be expected is a partial and hazy picture of program outcomes. For the most part, the kind of data we are considering are generated either by practitioners or clients, who may be both subject to positive biases at assessing the changes they have been working toward. Measuring instruments tend to consist of rather gross categorizations and scales that result in considerable imprecision. Moreover, standardized instruments, which are generally some form of client self-report, are not free from positive biases and may not be sensitive to the specific changes that may result from the program being assessed. Problems of attrition in client samples usually affect collecting data at termination, and particularly in post-service follow-ups. Problems of attrition are especially worrisome in this kind of research because there is reason to suppose that clients who do not do complete terminal or follow-up instruments are likely to be those who have benefitted the least from service.

Collecting data outside the practitioner/client system can introduce much needed elements of independence and objectivity but usually at some cost, since extra effort is needed beyond the requirements of the case. Moreover, they are by no means free of validity problems. Measures obtained from school personnel, child care workers, and so on, have their own biases relating to the outsider's perception of treatment and the client and may be limited by a lack of knowledge of the client's problem or functioning. Measures based on transitional events, such as discharge from or re-entry into service systems may have a high degree of objectivity but their interpretation often poses problems. For example, re-entry into a service system may mean that the intervention has failed, if it was the intent of the practitioner to prevent the client's return, but the same indicator may point to success if the practitioner's goal was to help the client return to the system. Finally, as noted earlier, different data sources are likely to yield divergent readings.

In this world of imperfect instruments, each with its own sources of error, perhaps the best advice to give, and it has been given often, is to use diversified measurements, consisting of multiple instruments and multiple sources. This kind of measurement and data processing load may be a reasonable standard for a research project but is probably unrealistic for routine data collection in an agency of any size. One solution is to use practitioner collected data (ratings and RAIs) that have utility for the service program and to add to this base a brief questionnaire completed by clients at the end of service. The client questionnaire would include not only satisfaction items but also items tapping client perceptions of change in main problem areas.

Measurement at this level would serve monitoring and accountability functions and could provide some basis for effectiveness claims in the case of programs of already demonstrated effectiveness. Even at best, however, such bare-bones measures would provide only data on overall effectiveness. Because of some mixture genuine efficacy, uncontrolled factors and bias, effectiveness measures of the kind described tend to show positive results on the whole. Applying Rossi and Freeman's (1985) "iron law of evaluation" the weaker the methodology, the better the program will look. Such a minimum measurement package would provide little direction for program improvement. This is so because the measures are not usually sensitive enough to discriminate between the effectiveness of different interventions or of the same intervention used with different client types.

It may be advisable, therefore, to augment such "thin" monitoring with more intensive measurement for selected programs, chosen because of their centrality, innovativeness, or other criteria, and evaluated in individual projects or in a developmental research context. In addition to basic monitoring data described earlier, a more intensive package would usually include one or two standardized instruments given before and after service, "individualized" instruments to assess change in target problems from the practitioner and client's perspective, systematic data on program inputs; and provision for post-service follow-up. Regardless of its timing the follow-up assessment should include interviews with clients (which can be conducted by agency staff, volunteers or students) covering client's assessment of change and service.

Individualized instruments are especially important as a means of providing measurement sensitive enough to detect specific changes resulting from the program (Mintz & Kiesler, 1982). For example the problem of most concern to a family may be securing much needed repairs for its apartment. Resolution of the problem would result in a maximum positive rating on such particularistic instruments as goal attainment scaling (Kiresuk & Sherman, 1968) or measures of change in target complaints (Mintz & Kielser, 1982). On a standardized measure of family functioning, the resolution might be just a blip in a general no-change picture. While tailor-made instruments may not correlate well with standardized tests (the example shows why), they are critical to sensitive measurement, especially in the evaluation of social work programs whose strength may be in effecting the kind of problem change that standardized tests do not measure well.

UTILIZATION

The last major set of issues to be considered concerns utilization of effectiveness data in program operations. Like effectiveness, utilization is not a single concept. Early uses of the term in evaluation contexts assumed a straightforward decision-making model in which the utilizer applied research findings to the solution of some practical problem. In studies of utilization it became apparent this kind of "instrumental" utilization did not occur frequently and was perhaps overshadowed by more amorphous but more pervasive type which has been referred to as "conceptual" utilization (Rich, 1977). In conceptual utilization, findings are not directly acted upon but rather are added to the storehouse of contextual information possessed by the decision maker, which may include knowledge from many other sources. The findings may exercise an indirect and delayed influence through complex information processing in which their influence may be impossible to trace. It has been also noted that findings may be used as ammunition to advance a particular point of view, a type of utilization that has been termed "persuasive" (Rich, 1977).

In an effort to provide some grounding and unity to these diverse ideas, Leviton and Hughes (1981) have developed a "bottom line criterion" for defining utilization. Regardless of the type of utilization "there must be evidence that in the absence of the research information, those engaged in policy or program activities would have thought or acted differently" (p. 527). Thus to be considered utilized, findings must have a traceable impact, although the impact may be limited to changes in beliefs or attitudes.

These formulations help clarify two central issues in the utilization of effectiveness research in agency context. One of these issues has concerned the low rate of instrumental utilization and the failure to develop proved means of facilitating this kind of utilization. A second issue concerns difficulties in sorting out the complexities of conceptual utilization and in constructing models to understand and study it. These issues can be combined if we view utilization as essentially "conceptual," at least in respect to a domain as intricate as the evaluation of service effectiveness. One can legitimately view virtually all utilization of effectiveness data by managers in terms of complex cognitive and organizational processes in which the data constitutes one of a variety of inputs. Research information is joined with such other considerations as the manager's own impressions of effectiveness, informal reports of staff, general knowledge, available alternatives, and cost factors. This process may produce new insight but, as Weiss and Bucuvalas (1980) document, seldom produces a clear-cut decision. Rather what is learned may affect the manager as one actor in a collective decision-making process that is responsive to an even wider range of considerations.

Strategies for enabling managers to become better utilizers have emphasized closer working relationships between managers and evaluators. As utilization studies have suggested, managers are more likely to use research that relates to immediate problems, is concerned with the effectiveness of program elements rather than overall effectiveness and fits with his or her own fund of knowledge (Leviton & Hughes, 1980; McNeese, DeNitto, & Johnson, 1983). Such findings support Patton's (1978) approach for "utilization-oriented" evaluations, in which studies are geared to specific utilization decisions. Other proposals have called for training of managers in utilization skills (Rapp, 1984; Pauley & Cohen, 1984) and at least one training model has been tested with encouraging results (Pauley & Cohen, 1984).

If managers become better utilizers, they may be better able to take leadership in facilitating utilization at the service-provider level. Practitioners and supervisors are not simply implementors of decisions about service programs; they are often the primary decision makers, especially concerning specific program options. One of the surest ways to bring about research utilization at this level is to involve staff in some form of developmental research. Program staff essentially utilize their own research if its results are fed back into program development. From many years of involvement in this kind of research, I can attest that processes of utilization are as murky and convoluted as those described earlier. Yet meaningful utilization does occur and

56   MANAGING FOR SERVICE EFFECTIVENESS

does so cumulatively as programs are developed over time (Reid, 1985). More important than which strategies are pursued is the creation of an atmosphere in which the role of effectiveness research and supporting forms of inquiry is understood and valued by the staff. In creating such an atmosphere it is obviously helpful to have staff with a positive orientation to research and some skills in practice research — the kind of practitioner that many schools of social work are now trying to train. Indeed the establishment of a pro-research staff culture may be the key to progress in generating as well as utilizing research. If headway is to be made in using research to document and improve program effectiveness, the staff as a whole must provide the needed motivation and momentum.

REFERENCES

Aaronson, N.K. & Wilner, D.M. Evaluation and outcome research in community mental health centers. *Evaluation Review*, 1983, *7*, 303-320.

Bell, W. *The practical value of social work service: Preliminary report on ten demonstration projects in public assistance.* School of Social Work, Columbia University, 1961.

Bergin, A.E. Negative effects revisited: A reply. *Professional Psychology*, 1980, *11*, 93-100.

Bergin, A.E. & Lambert M.J. The evaluation of therapeutic outcomes. In S.L. Garfield & A.E. Bergin (Eds.). *Handbook of psychotherapy and behavior change: An empirical analysis.* New York: John Wiley and Sons, 1978.

Bielawaski, B. & Epstein, I. Assessing program stabilization: An extension of the differential evaluation model. *Administration in Social Work*, 1984, *8*, 13-23.

Blythe, B.J. & Briar, S. Developing empirically based models of practice. *Social Work*, 1985, *30*, 483-488.

Briar, S. & Blythe, B. Agency support for evaluating the outcomes of social work services. *Administration in Social Work*, 1985, *9*, 25-36.

Cook, T.D. & Campbell, D.T. *Quasi-experimentation: Design and analysis issues for field settings.* Chicago: Rand McNally, 1979.

Coulton, C.J. Approaches to quality assessment in social work. *Quarterly Review Bulletin*, 1980, *6*, 9-13.

Edelson, J.L. Rapid-assessment instruments for evaluating practice with children and youth. *Journal of Social Service Research*, 1985, *8*, 17-32.

Fischer, J. Is casework effective? A review. *Social Work*, 1973, *18*, 5-20.

Fischer, J. *The Effectiveness of social casework.* Springfield, IL: Charles C. Thomas, 1976.

Fischer, J. Evaluations of social work effectiveness: Is positive evidence always good evidence? *Social Work*, 1983, *28*, 74-76.

Geismar, L.L. & Wood, K. *Family and delinquency: Resocializing the young offender.* New York: Human Sciences Press, 1986.

Horn, W.F. & Heerboth, J. Single case experimental designs and program evaluation. *Evaluation Review*, 1982, *3*, 403-424.

Ivanoff, A., et al. Standardized measurement in clinical social work: An annotated bibliography. Paper presented at APM, Council of Social Work Education, Miami, March, 1986.

Kagen, R.M. Organizational change and quality assurance in a psychiatric setting. *Quality Review Bulletin, Journal of Quality Assurance*, 1984, *10*, 269-277.

Kiresuk, T.J. & Sherman, E. Goal attainment scaling: A general method for evaluating comprehensive mental health programs. *Community Mental Health Journal*, 1968, *4*, 443-453.

Lambert, M.J. Introduction to assessment of psychotherapy outcome: Historical perspective and current issues. In M.J. Lambert et al. (Eds.), *The assessment of psychotherapy outcome*. New York: John Wiley and Sons, 1983.

Lebow, J.L. Research assessing consumer satisfaction with mental health treatment: A review of findings. *Evaluation and Program Planning*, 1983, *6*, 211-236.

Lehman, A.F. & Zastowny, T.R. Patient satisfaction with mental health services: A meta-analysis to establish norms. *Evaluation and Program Planning*, 1983, *6*, 265-274.

Leviton, L.C. & Hughes, E.F. Research on the utilization of evaluations, a review and synthesis. *Evaluation Review*, 1981, *5*, 525-548.

Levitt, L & Reid, W.J. Rapid assessment instruments for social work practice. *Social Work Research and Abstracts*, 1981, *17*, 13-19.

Luborsky, L., Singer, B. & Luborsky, L. Comparative studies of psychotherapy. *Archives of General Psychiatry*, 1975, *32*, 995-1008.

McNeece, C.A., DiNitto, D.M. & Johnson, P.J. The utility of evaluation research for administrative decision-making. *Administration in Social Work*, 1983, *7*, 77-87.

Mintz, J..& Kiesler, D.J. Individualized measures of psychotherapy outcome. In P.C. Kendall & J. N. Butcher (Eds.). *Handbook of research methods in clinical psychology*. New York: John Wiley & Sons, 1982.

Mullen, E.J. Specifying casework effects. In J. Fischer (Ed.), *The effectiveness of social casework*. Springfield, IL: Charles C. Thomas Publisher, 1976.

Mullen, E., Chazin, R. & Feldstein, D. Services for the newly dependent: An assessment. *Social Service Review*, 1972, *46*, 309-322.

Mullen, E.J. & Dumpson, J.R. & Associates *Evaluation of social intervention*. San Francisco: Jossey-Bass, 1972.

Patti, R. In search of purpose for social welfare administration. *Administration in Social Work*, 1985, *9*, 1-14.

Patton, M. *Utilization focused evaluation*. Beverly Hills: Sage, 1978.

Pauley, P.A. & Cohen, S. Facilitating data-based decision-making, managers' use of data in a community mental health center. *Evaluation Review*, 1984, *8*, 205-224.

Poertner, J. & Rapp, C.A. Purchase of service and accountability: Will they ever meet? *Administration in Social Work*, 1985, *9*, 57-66.

Rapp, C.A. Information, performance, and the human service manager of the 1980's beyond "housekeeping." *Administration in Social Work*, 1984, *8*, 69-80.

Reid, W. Evaluating an intervention in developmental research. *Journal of Social Service Research* (in press).

Reid, W. *Family problem solving*. New York: Columbia University Press, 1985.

Reid, W. Treatment of choice or choice of treatment: An essay review. *Social Work Research and Abstracts*, 1984, *20*, 33-37.

Reid, W.J. & Hanrahan, P. Recent evaluations of social work: Grounds for optimism. *Social Work*, 1982, *27*, 328-340.

Reid, W.J., et al. Adoptions of older institutionalized youth: A long-term follow-up. *Social Casework* (in press).

Rossi, P.H. & Freeman, H.E. *Evaluation a systematic approach*. 3rd edition. Beverly Hills: Sage Publications, 1985.

Rubin, A. Practice effectiveness: More grounds for optimism. *Social Work*, 1985, *30*, 469-476.

Smith, M.L., Glass, G.J. & Miller, T.I. *The benefits of psychotherapy*. Baltimore: The John Hopkins University Press, 1980.

Strupp, H.H. & Hadley, S.W. A tripartite model of mental health and therapeutic outcomes: With special reference to negative effects in psychotherapy. *American Psychologist*, 1977, *32*, 187-196.

Thomas, E.J. *Designing interventions for the helping professions*. Beverly Hills, CA: Sage, 1984.

Thomas, E.J. Mousetraps, developmental research, and social work education. *Social Service Review*, 1978, *52*, 468-483.

Videka-Sherman, L. Harriet M. Bartlett practice effectiveness project: Final report to the NASW board of directors, January, 1985.

Wallace, D. The Chemung County evaluation of casework service to dependent multi-problem families: Another problem outcome. *Social Service Review*, 1967, *41*, 379-389.

Weiss, C.H. & Bucuvalas, M.J. *Social science research and decision-making*. New York: Columbia Press, 1980.

Wood, K.M. Casework effectiveness: A new look at the research evidence. *Social Work, 23*, 437-458.

Measuring Clinical Outcomes
and Their Use for Managers

Walter W. Hudson, PhD

A new era in the field of social welfare administration was launched with the assertion that "Service effectiveness . . . should be the principal criterion of a model of social welfare administration practice" (Patti, 1985). However, the work ahead for many years will consist of developing and testing the knowledge that we shall need in order to transform this mission into a practice reality. A significant part of that knowledge base will consist of applied measurement theory, and the purpose of this paper is to discuss some of the ways in which formal measurement tools can be used to further the aims of an effectiveness oriented administrative practice. Also discussed are some of the pitfalls that must be avoided if applied measurement theory is to advance the achievement of an effectiveness oriented administrative practice.

While managers and administrators must collect, analyze, and use many different types of information, the principal focus of this paper will be the application of measurement theory to the assessment of client problems and how such measures may be used to examine the effectiveness of interventive efforts. Although the measurement of such clinical or service outcomes is not the only domain to which the administrator must attend, there can be no defensible social work based definition of "effectiveness oriented administrative practice" if it fails to include them.

THE PURPOSE FOR CREATING
AND MEASURING CHANGE

The application of formal measurement theory can be a hollow and useless exercise unless the context and purpose for taking measurements are clearly understood. From an effectiveness perspective, the context and purpose of measurement are very simple. However, the

Dr. Hudson is Professor, School of Social Work, Arizona State University, Tempe, AZ 85287.

behavior of many service workers and administrators in social work and in other professions and disciplines suggests that it is not well understood. It is, therefore, essential to provide a brief comment concerning the fundamental purpose for measuring client problems.

The driving force behind the concept of service effectiveness is the simple notion of change. If some form of change is not created, it is not possible to speak rationally about service effectiveness. Moreover, if administrators and service workers cannot first create and then demonstrate (measure) planned change, all efforts to achieve an effectiveness oriented administrative practice are doomed to failure from the outset. Some, no doubt, will regard this to be excessively dramatic language. It is not. However, it may be useful to elaborate this critical emphasis on change with the briefest of examples.

Consider, for example, an economically impoverished client who needs help in securing transportation to a clinic for the treatment of a chronic disorder. A clearly definable service is needed or requested in this example. If medical transportation is provided to the client, change has occurred. If no such transportation is provided, change that is relevant to the defined problem has not occurred. In the latter outcome any proffered service (attempt to create change) can only be judged as ineffectual. Although this example involves securing transportation, it generalizes to a class of service requests that number into the thousands.

A second example illustrates a different class of client problems for which we presume to render services. Consider a client who is referred for the treatment of severe depression. The worker will presumably provide some form of service that is intended to reduce or eliminate the client's depression. If the client's depression is eliminated or reduced, change has occurred. If the client's depression is neither eliminated nor reduced, change has not occurred and the only rational judgment in this event is that the proferred service was ineffectual with respect to the defined problem.

The matter of assessing the effectiveness of interventive efforts becomes complicated only when desired change takes place. If desired change does occur, it is often difficult to show that it was the proffered service that brought about that change. However, if desired change does not occur, the matter is settled quite simply; the provided service can only be judged as ineffectual in relation to solving the defined problem.

In light of these simple arguments, it follows that all effectiveness oriented practice by service workers and by administrators must ultimately be directed by three fundamental questions regardless of how they may be phrased:

—What is the client's problem?
—What are you going to do about it?
—Did it work?

The first of these questions orients us to the task of clearly and unambiguously defining, for each client, precisely what it is that we are going to change. The second question focuses on interventive technologies. Many are available but our choices among them must no longer be based on their theoretical attractiveness or their congruence with ideological proclivities. We have too long a history of using intervention strategies that have never been shown to be effective. The third question orients us to making judgments about (a) whether desired change occurred, and (b) whether that change arose as a direct consequence of the service that was provided.

Again, the driving force behind the concept of service effectiveness is the simple notion of change. If there is no change in some well defined client problem, there is and can be no such thing as effective service delivery.

THE MISMEASURE OF CHANGE

Given the preceding arguments, it would seem natural to attempt developing a variety of change measures for use in the assessment of service delivery efforts. Often that has been the preferred approach and just as often it has tended to fail rather miserably. Consider, for example, the apparently simple task of capturing information about the extent to which a patient on a psychiatric ward has exhibited growth or deterioration over some period of time. A common approach has been to devise some form of rating scale which is used by one or more professional personnel to record judgments about a patient's progress. Such a scale might be structured as follows:

Rate the patient to reflect your judgment about the degree of improvement or deterioration in primary symptoms by assigning one of the following values.

Severely deteriorated	-3
Moderately deteriorated	-2
Mildly deteriorated	-1
No change	0
Mildly improved	1
Moderately improved	2
Extensively improved	3

There are several implicit assumptions in operation in the use of this type of scale, but they are not obvious. The first one is that the rater can accurately perceive the seriousness of magnitude of the patient's problem at the beginning of the period over which change is to be estimated. Second, it is similarly assumed that the rater can accurately perceive the seriousness of the patient's problem at the end of the assessment period. Finally, it is implicitly assumed that the rater is reasonably effective in executing some mental calculus such that an accurate estimate of the amount of change can be reported.

There is yet another set of assumptions that may be used to drive the use of such a scale. It might be assumed that one need not accurately perceive initial and final magnitudes of the patient's problem and then use those to compute mentally the amount of change. Instead, it might be assumed that a competent rater can directly perceive the degree of· change that has occurred with respect to the attribute in question.

Regardless of the set of assumptions one chooses to believe might be operating in the use of such change ratings, the sad fact is that none of them bears up very well under close scrutiny. That is, such rating scales too often are shown to have notoriously poor reliabilities — and, hence, validities. This is not to suggest that therapists, for example, are a poor class of raters. Instead, it seems that none of us is very good at such tasks and the weakness appears to characterize the species rather than any specific task of its members. In short, the direct estimation of the degree or amount of change in affective or interpersonal relationship disorders is very difficult, it is nearly always done with extremely poor reliability, and as a consequence it is likely that information obtained from such estimates of change will have little or no validity whatsoever.

EFFECTIVE CHANGE MEASURES

Although the use of change ratings is a poor choice for assessing client progress, an excellent alternative is available and there is no longer much doubt as to what constitutes the simplest and most effective means of reflecting change in client problems. It consists of little more than measuring the client's problem at two or more points in time and using the differences in those measures to reflect the degree or amount of change that has occurred. This elementary principle leads to a simple but very powerful means of capturing information about client progress, stability, or deterioration. It consists merely of measuring the client's problem repeatedly over time.

The reason that such a simple strategy works so well arises from the fact that it is not difficult to develop measures of client problems that are both highly reliable and valid. That does not mean that a newly developed measurement tool does not have to be tested rather carefully. To the contrary, the development of standardized measures of client problems can be demanding. However, the task is easy in the sense that we have an extensive technology to guide us in the development of reliable and valid measures of client problems that we wish to reduce or solve (Nunnally, 1978; Allen & Yen, 1979).

DEFINING CLIENT PROBLEMS

Social scientists naturally spend a great deal of time and energy defining and then attempting to measure important theoretical constructs. Many of them use formal measurement theory in the pursuit of those activities, and social workers have largely learned about the fundamentals of measurement theory by studying the social science disciplines. While that has been profitable, it has also tended to mislead us rather severely.

We have tended to emulate the social scientist who invents constructs within a theoretical framework. That is not the business of social workers who have the ambition of engaging in an effectiveness oriented practice for the purpose of helping people "solve problems." Very simply, our attention must be given to the task of defining client problems in specific and measurable terms rather than in terms of high order theoretical abstractions.

This assertion raises some knotty philosophical problems but they are far more trivial than some would have us believe. For example, it is common to hear someone ask, "What do you mean by 'problem'?" They also might retort, and rightly so, that there is no such "thing" "as a" problem out there in the universe. That is quite true. It is also true that "problems" exist strictly and only in terms of the value positions taken by humans in relation to their needs and in terms of their relationships with other humans, groups, organizations, and their environment.

This in no way diminishes the need to focus on the definition and measurement of human problems. It merely recognizes that the use of measurement theory will always be employed within the context of the value positions of the client, the service worker, and the social welfare organization. In this sense, the use of formal measurement is entirely congruent with the humanistic values that drive the profession of social work. Thus, it is quite accurate to say that a problem never exists until someone defines it. Nonetheless, once defined and agreed upon, problems do exists, and they cry out for solutions, and they are measurable.

Our abuse of abstract thinking and formal language has too often led to the definition of a client problem in such high order abstract terms that we become impotent in ever demonstrating that a problem exists, is capable of our solution, or has been solved. Such abuses often lead to the reification of constructs that have no identifiable referents (Hudson, 1985b; Hudson & Harrison, 1986a, 1986b), and it was this phenomenon that led to an earlier assertion that "If you cannot measure a client's problem, then it doesn't exist" (Hudson, 1978). That assertion calls attention to the need for defining client problems, not only in specific and measurable terms, but in terms that render it capable of being treated. That is, a good definition of a client problem leads directly to its measurement, but it should also carry strong implicit clues about what is to be done to solve it.

TECHNIQUES OF MEASURING CLIENT PROBLEMS

In the simplest of terms, there are four, and only four, ways of measuring a client's problem, and it matters not how we define "client" or "problem." Any client problem can be measured in terms of its

1. Binary status (present or absent);
2. Frequency;
3. Duration; or
4. Magnitude (intensity).

Moreover, there are only two ways that a worker can ever determine whether a client has a problem:

1. Direct observation (watch them);
2. Self-report (ask them).

Although the foregoing are cardinal principles that govern and restrict the measurement of client problems, they are only guiding principles. If they are to have practical utility they must be used to devise explicit measurement tools for use in social work practice. The technology for developing specific measurement tools for use in social work practice is discussed in greater detail by Hudson (1985a) and many useful measurement tools are now available from an emerging social work literature that has given attention to this matter in recent years (Hudson, 1982; Levitt & Reid, 1981; Fischer & Hudson, 1983;

Edleson, 1985; Hudson & Thyer, in press; Fisher & Corcoran, in press).

Although space will not allow an extensive discussion of the development of summated scales, it is important to comment on the use of two broad methods of scale development and to consider problems associated with their use. Perhaps the most popular approach to the development of summated scales is to have one or more experts collect or develop a very large number of scale items that presume to play a part in measuring some construct of interest, say, depression. Once a large pool of items has been organized into a questionnaire, the next step is to collect responses from a large number of individuals. When the data are collected the next task is to perform some type of item analysis that is aimed at eliminating poor items and identifying those which are to be retained. Some form of factor analysis is often employed at this stage in order to lift out the one dominant factor that is assumed to measure the construct of interest. The final step is to create a revised and hopefully final version of the desired scale. For ease of identification, we might refer to this approach as the "large item pool" or LIP model of scale development.

There are several potential problems that can arise with the use of the LIP model of scale construction. First among them is a tremendous tendency to include a large number of fringe items that upon close inspection make little if any contribution to the content validity of the final scale. The result could easily be that the final scale does not truly measure the construct of interest. A second objection is the cost and labor involved in working with a very large pool of items and then discarding many of them. It is a common experience to start with 200 or more items and finish with as few as 30 or less. Such an outcome nearly always points to serious problems concerning content and construct validity, but that fact is often completely ignored. Although one often pretends to devise a single unidimensional scale, the factor analysis of a large pool of items will always produce multiple factors. Even when the subsidiary factors are truly meaningless, all but the most ardent and dogged skeptic will fall victim to a temptation to interpret and use them. All of us are extremely clever at finding "meaning" among factors when none really exists, and the probability is far from zero that the "first principal axis" will not be the best or even a good measure of the construct of interest.

An effective alternative to the development of a summated scale is one that is based on a "small item pool" (the SIP model) that is constructed by use of a clear conception or definition of the construct to be measured. In the SIP model the aim is to develop a unidimensional scale and the initial item pool should contain, at most, about 20% more items than the number desired in the final version of the scale. The use of the SIP model forces the scale developer to exercise great care in the creation of the initial pool and each item should be carefully tested for content validity against the definition of the construct that is to be measured. If an item does not conform to the definition of the construct, it is omitted before any data are collected. It is quite easy to use the SIP model and produce a unidimensional scale of 25 or fewer items that has a reliability of .90 or greater and good content, construct, and criterion validity. Indeed, if more items are needed in order to improve reliability, that alone is a signal that validity will not likely be established.

The SIP model is not, however, without its problems. It is often difficult to produce clear definition of the construct to be measured. Questions will also arise as to the content validity of the items, and at worst one might discover that in spite of best efforts to employ a small item pool, the resulting items will fail to produce a reliable and valid scale. Even so, it is still more efficient to discard 30 terrible items and begin anew than it is to discard 170, retain 30, and be misled by the result of statistical artifacts arising from the misuse of factor analysis or other forms of item analysis.

SELECTING USABLE MEASURES OF CLIENT PROBLEMS

Under the assumption that we do have an effective technology for developing or identifying reliable and valid measures of client problems, we still must face the task of selecting appropriate measures for use within social welfare organizations. It is here that we have also tended to be misled by our too-close alliance or identification with colleagues from other disciplines — especially psychology. Thus, our familiarity with the very popular and very large personality batteries can cause us to become entirely too ambitious with respect to the assessment of client problems. The Minnesota Multiphasic Personality Inventory, for example, contains over 500 items and measures many different things. It may be fine for use by the evaluating psychologist, but it and many other similar tools are utterly useless to social workers who choose to define client problems very differently and then try to solve them. We simply cannot ask clients repeatedly to complete long and complex test batteries. They will not do it, and it is not likely that the information will even be useful — to social workers.

Social workers must use an entirely different kind of measurement tool. The measures we must use for the evaluation of client progress must have several additional characteristics beyond the essentials of reliability and validity. They must be short, easy to read, easy to complete, easy to understand, easy to score, easy to interpret, and they must not suffer response decay when used in repeated administrations. These may seem to be stringent requirements but considerable progress has been made in developing and locating such measures (Hudson, 1982; Levitt & Reid, 1981; Fischer & Hudson, 1983; Edleson, 1985; Hudson & Thyer, in press; Fischer & Hudson, in press) and new ones will certainly emerge as more clinical researchers attend to the task of assessing client problems.

While increasing attention will be given to the development and use of scales in accord with criteria such as those listed above, the selection and use of appropriate assessment tools must be guided by still another and far more critical criterion. Namely, measure the "thing" you plan to change. In the context of this discussion, the dictum would be more appropriately stated as "measure the problem that you plan to solve." Many will, no doubt, see this to be so obvious as to scarcely deserve mention or discussion. Not so. Such a simple charge is far more complex than it might at first seem, because it hinges greatly on how we define the client's problem and it hinges as well on the technology that is available for creating planned change. An example might illustrate some of the difficulties.

Suppose, for example, that someone wishes to treat something called a "borderline personality." The first challenge is a technical one of measurement. It has thus far been extremely difficult to measure such a thing. However, assuming a reasonable measurement of something called a "borderline personality," is that what a social worker really wants to change? Do we ever sit down with a client and explain that we shall set about to change, correct, improve or cure their "borderline personality"? If the honest answer is "yes," then one must presume it is appropriate to do so. However, do we have a known treatment technique or collection of techniques that, when applied to clients, will move them from a condition of having a "borderline personality" to a condition of having some other kind of personality? These are not rhetorical questions at all. They deserve far more discussion than can be allowed here, they strike directly as the abuse of abstract language (Hudson, 1985), and they require close scrutiny of our claims regarding intervention techniques that will solve such problems.

The difficulties pointed to by the foregoing example can be avoided to a large degree by more judiciously defining client problems, using measurement tools that measure the thing we plan to change, and using intervention techniques that are known to be at least capable of changing the client's problem. The hallmark of successful measurement for the effectiveness oriented practitioner will always center upon specificity in defining the problem to be solved.

THE USE OF TIME-SERIES DATA BY MANAGERS

Once the effectiveness oriented practitioner defines a client problem in terms that render it capable of being measured, it is a relatively easy matter to measure the problem repeatedly over time and then plot the results in the form of graphs and charts. The technology for using time series data is very well developed for use by a number of readily available sources (e.g., Jayaratne & Levy, 1979; Bloom & Fischer, 1982). However, the use of such data by performance oriented administrators is a veritable untapped gold mine. This is not to suggest there are no problems associated with the task of aggregating time-series data obtained from many clients. To the contrary, there are major problems associated with such a task. Not the least of them concerns the need to use homogeneous problem populations (Hudson, 1976) and the fact of varying baseline and treatment periods across clients poses a genuine challenge.

In spite of the complexities involved in aggregating such data for use by managers, most if not all of these and other problems are capable of solution. During the next several years our researchers and scholars will produce a literature to cope with these problems. In this regard, it would be an oversight of the highest order to ignore some new work that illustrates the power of combining the methodology of nomothetic and idiographic research in the study of clinical outcomes (Nugent, 1986). Once this material is available in our journals it has the potential for changing our entire methodology of evaluating practice.

NEW MEASUREMENT TECHNOLOGY

There will emerge a clear need for developing new measurement techniques and these will surely follow as we become actively involved in the development of performance models of administration. However, there is an old method commonly referred to as as "goal attainment scaling" that still offers great promise but has not yet lived up to it. It is discussed here under the rubric of "new" measurement technology because the potential for such an elegant idea deserves additional attention. The principal failure of goal attainment scaling, to date, arises from the fact that it has too often been employed to capture information about "goals" that have been defined in terms entirely too lofty and abstract. That is not a failing of a rather simple and elegant device. Rather, it is our failure to realize the enormous potential for defining very specific tasks and goals, counting them in terms of whether they have been achieved or not, and using such data as a basis for monitoring the progress of single clients or entire systems. It is likely that this form of assessment will emerge as a far more powerful tool than as currently used, and some initial work has begun in terms of using this tool within a computer based environment (Hudson, 1986c).

Another very promising development for effectiveness oriented administrators is the increased availability and use of microcomputers for assessing client problems. The "Clinical Measurement Package" (Hudson, 1982), for example, has now been incorporated into a computer environment that enables workers not only to monitor client progress over time but manage their entire caseload as well (Hudson, 1985c).[1] Many other computer based assessment systems are available and their potential value as well as problems associated with their use are discussed by Hudson, Nurius and Reisman (in press).

TECHNICAL MEASUREMENT SKILLS

At a very minimum, administration students who are to be prepared for designing and maintaining service effectiveness models of practice must understand the basic ingredients of measurement theory. This minimal content is well represented by the work of Allen and Yen (1979), but a word about "minimum" is in order. Social work educators too often define minimum standards as if they are maximums. We often claim that content is minimally required and we then behave as if it is offensive to ever expect that someone should exceed minimum standards.

In this context, administration students should be caused to master such content as is represented by the above text. However, this is a truly minimal recommendation. A much better recommendation is that performance management students should come to understand the elementary mathematical foundations of basic measurement theory as represented, for example, by Nunnally (1978). Again, mastery should be stressed, and such mastery can be achieved by a three hour graduate level course. This is by no means an unreasonable expectation.

RESEARCH TRAINING

Although social work students pursuing performance models of administration must know the technical literature on measurement theory and its uses in the construction of reliable and valid measurement tools, that alone is insufficient. In addition, they need to understand in what ways that knowledge can best be put to work in the management of social welfare organizations. Thus, they must come to understand how empirically oriented practitioners set about to do their work in monitoring and evaluating direct practice with clients. It is, therefore, essential that administration students master the technology of single subject and single system research design. Since they will be managing the work of their service workers they should, at a minimum, become expert in the technology of courses now routinely offered under the general rubric of "empirical clinical practice."

CONCLUDING REMARKS

This article has focused in the idea that the use of formal measurement technology will play a large and continuing role in the elaboration of an effectiveness oriented model of administrative practice. It has outlined some of the issues and problems that must be considered and it has pointed to some of the small achievements that can presently be used by managers who are concerned with the task of administering effective social services. An effort was also made to suggest a few areas where productive conceptual and technical work can further the aim of producing more effective social services.

The potential for developing a body of training materials that will lead to a generation of effectiveness oriented administrative practitioners is both large and exciting. Such an aspiration may have been with us, in the minds of many scholars, for several years. However, it seems timely for such ambitions to be enunciated so clearly by the works of Patti (1984, 1985) and Rapp and Poertner (1984). The timing is such that we can hope for success in such an adventure because many of the necessary tools and supporting technology are currently available. More will be devised in the future and presently available technology will be expanded to fit new applications, assessment problems, and intervention challenges. It is not likely that the expansion of our measurement skills will dominate the work ahead, but it is likely that the application of formal measurement theory will serve a central and useful purpose.

NOTE

1. The reader may obtain a "free use version" of the "Clinical Assessment System" or CAS program by sending a blank diskette and a stamped self-addressed return diskette mailer to the WALMYR Publishing Co., P.O. Box 3554, Leon Station, Tallahassee, FL 32315. The CAS program administers the "Clinical Measurement Package" scales and runs on any IBM PC, XT, AT or compatible computer that uses DOS 2.0 or greater and has 256K or more memory.

REFERENCES

Allen, M.J. & Yen, W.M. Introduction to measurement theory. Monterey, CA: Brooks/Cole Publishing Co., 1979.

Bloom, M. & Fischer, J. *Evaluating practice: Guidelines for the accountable professional.* Englewood Cliffs, NJ: Prentice-Hall, Inc., 1982.

Edleson, J.L. Rapid assessment instruments for evaluating practice with children and youth. *Journal of Social Service Research*, 1985, *8*(3), 17-31.

Fischer, J. & Hudson, W.W. Measurement of client problems for improved practice. In A. Rosenblatt & D. Waldfogel (Eds.), *Handbook of clinical social work.* San Francisco: Jossey-Bass, 1983.

Fischer, J. & Corcoran, K. *Measuring practice.* New York: The Free Press. In press.

Hudson, W.W. Special problems in the assessment of growth and deterioration. In J. Fischer (Ed.). *The evaluation of social casework.* Springfield, IL: Charles C. Thomas Publishing Co., 1976.

Hudson, W.W. First axioms of treatment. *Social Work*, 1978, *23*(1). 65-66.

Hudson, W.W. *The clinical measurement package: A field manual.* Homewood, IL: Dorsey Press, 1982.

Hudson, W.W. The clinical assessment system. Tallahassee, FL: WALMYR Publishing Co., 1984.

Hudson, W.W. Development and use of indexes and scales. In R.M. Grinnel, Jr. (Ed.), *Social work research and evaluation.* 2nd edition. Itasca, IL: F.E. Peacock, 1985a.

Hudson, W.W. *Future directions in clinical evaluation.* Paper presented at Practitioner as Evaluators of Direct Practice: A Working Conference for Social Work Educators, Practitioners and Researchers. School of Social Work, University of Washington, 1985b.

Hudson, W.W. *Computer assisted management assessment system.* Tallahassee, FL: WALMYR Publishing Co., 1985c.

Hudson, W.W. & Harrison, D.F. Conceptual issues in measuring and assessing family problems. *Family Therapy*, 1986a, *13*(1). 85-94.

Hudson, W.W. & Harrison, D.F. Language, thought and reason in social work practice and education (Mimeo). Arizona State University School of Social Work, 1986b.

Hudson, W.W., Nurius P.S. & Reisman, S. Computerized assessment instruments: Their promise and problems. *Computers in Human Services.* In press.

Hudson, W.W. & Thyer, B.A. Research measures in direct practice. *Encyclopedia of Social Work.* New York: National Association of Social Workers, Inc. In press.

Levitt, J.L. & Reid, W.J. Rapid assessment instruments for practice. *Social Work Research and Abstracts*, 1981, *17*(1), 13-19.

Nunnally, J.C. *Psychometric theory.* New York: McGraw-Hill Books, 1987.

Nugent, W.R. The intended use of group comparison and single case research methods for evaluating the effect of clinical intervention procedures for treatment of situational depression. Unpublished doctoral dissertation, Florida State University, Tallahassee, 1986.

Patti, R. In search of purpose for social welfare administration. *Administration in Social Work*, 1985, *9*(3), 1-14.

Rapp, C.A. & Poertner, J. A human service formulation for management education. Paper presented at the Annual Program Meeting of the Council on Social Work Education, Detroit, March, 1984.

Measuring Client Outcomes: The Experience of the States

Reginald K. Carter, PhD

INTRODUCTION

Arthur Schlesinger recently wrote an editorial entitled "Making Reagan Accountable" (*Wall Street Journal,* April 20, 1984). He observed Reagan's gift for dodging responsibility and concluded his comments in citing previous Presidents Truman and Jackson.

No voter should be permitted to forget where the buck stops. As Andrew Jackson concisely summed up the logic of our democratic order, every president must be held "accountable at the bar of public opinion for every act of his administration."

This same need for accountability exists for all governors, agency directors, program managers, supervisors, and ultimately each worker. Unfortunately, accountability has many meanings and is defined differently by the press, advocacy groups, vested interest groups, and other critics of human service programs. However, most discussions of accountability do not originate within human service agencies but are initiated by oversight organizations. I once believed all public programs needed to regularly collect information on the result of their intervention in the lives of clients. I simply and naively assumed managers of employment programs needed to know if their clients ultimately found jobs, managers of delinquency programs needed to know if their clients continued to be rearrested or sent to prison, and managers of child protective services needed to know if the children continued to be abused or neglected. I also assumed someone would ask the obvious question that is the heart of accountability: Did you make a difference?

After ten years of evaluating social service programs, I am continu-

Dr. Carter is Assistant Vice President, Health Care Association of Michigan, 501 S. Capitol Avenue, Suite 335, Lansing, MI 48933.

ously amazed how seldom the question is raised and how quickly with which it is disposed. My reason for writing this paper, then, is to argue that it is in the best interest of the programs; human service administrators manage to pay attention to the difference they make in clients' lives. This paper presents the experience of several states in measuring client outcomes, defines some successful outcome measures, and identifies strategies involved in creating organizational climates conducive to implementing success measurement systems. Finally, I will outline several lessons learned from two decades of experience working with this approach to true accountability.

RESISTANCE TO MEASURING SUCCESS

About three years ago I was asked to brief welfare program managers from a large state on one approach to accountability — client outcome monitoring. This is the regular collection of impact information after the intervention has taken place and a case is closed. After completing my presentation a manager turned to me and said:

Why should I risk knowing how successful my program is? The legislators already know day care is a good service. Why should I risk finding out if the parent is satisfied with the care provided to their child? If it's lower than expected or assumed, then I lose.

It was clear to this manager that he need not be concerned about the impact of day care on his clients. He was protected from serious review of outcomes because of widespread belief that day care is "intrinsically good" and it is unnecessary to even define an expected outcome, let alone measure it. In managing such a program, there will be little external pressure to know the impact of your program on the lives of the clients served. There are many such managers. They promote a set of values which include:

— It is better not to have clear agreement and understanding of the target population, intervention strategy, or desired outcome, as it causes problems for future resource negotiations. Knowledge of the target population, for example, may lead to a realistic estimate and thus limit the alleged extent of the problem and the staff necessary to resolve the problem. Clarity of current intervention strategy may limit the introduction of new techniques.
— Specification of time frames for impacting on clients acknowledges limitations of a given approach.

— Anecdotal success stories are always more appealing to press and legislators than dull statistics of client outcomes which can never capture the "uniqueness" of cases.

— "Wise" human service program managers never allow anyone (including themselves) to limit the scope of programs because it restricts the autonomy of first line worker who really knows best what should be done for the client.

— It is easier not to know what is expected than to clarify what is expected.

Managers who espouse these values rob their workers and themselves of knowing exactly how successful they are at providing effective interventions. Without adequate outcome measures there is no basis to judge effectiveness. You are left with endless "tinkering with efficiency improvements." Accountability needs to be at the heart of all management decisions and built into management information systems. More importantly it needs to be integrated into the philosophy of service delivery to insure that clients (our customers) are receiving the highest quality intervention possible. In the best programs gifted administrators instill in staff a dedication to quality and to knowing when it is delivered.

THE EXPERIENCE OF THE STATES

In Michigan, the Department of Social Services from 1978-1983 collected outcome information on closed cases. These measures were called "desired program results," were collected on all cases across many programs, and reported in an annual plan. In turn, the desired levels were used to establish appropriate levels for the following year. Oklahoma established a similar approach in 1984. In Robert Fulton's director's statement of priorities to his top management group in the Oklahoma Department of Human Services, he stressed the need to improve public accountability:

Beyond simplifying our own internal and service delivery operations, we should also set our sights on simpler, clearer public expectations of DHS efforts. If we expect widespread public support for our programs, we must do a better job of helping the public understand our purposes, approaches and impacts. Furthermore, as we strive to develop straightforward explanations in these areas, we are apt to find that the process adds to our own insights on how to improve our services. It will help us clear away some of the underbrush that has grown around us and that often blocks our path to better communication and decision making.

In 1979 the Minnesota legislature passed the Community Social Services Act requiring each county evaluate all human services programs. The initiative's intent as interpreted by the Department of Public Welfare was on "developing specific measurable criteria to be applied after the termination of services or periodically during the course of services to determine to what degree the expected results were achieved and at what costs." Minnesota has now created a set of outcome indicators for all its human service programs and is implementing the first statewide accountability system across programs.

In 1981 the Texas Department of Human Resources began an outcome monitoring approach for five program areas. The first was protective services for children. Outcome measures include:

— Percentage of abuse/neglect cases in which there is a reduction in severity or nonrecurrence of abuse/neglect during intervention.
— Percentage of ongoing services cases reinvestigated and reopened.
— Percentage of caretakers providing acceptable parenting after intervention.
— Percentage of children whose permanency plan is achieved.
— Percentage of families in which all children remain with the family.
— Percentage of families who had all their children returned to the home following removal.
— Percentage of non-reunited families in which parental rights were terminated by the courts.

WHAT IS A SUCCESSFUL OUTCOME?

Defining successful outcomes has been done for a number of programs. The following are examples of realistic outcomes for specific programs.

Delinquency Program (Institutionalized)

— 42%-52% of delinquent males will be rearrested 12 months after release.
— 45%-64% of delinquent males will be either in school, training or employed three months after release.

— 21%-23% of delinquent males will be in prison two and one-half years after release.

Foster Care

— 25%-49% of cases entering care will have achieved a permanent placement within six months (returned home, returned to other parent, relative placement, released for adoption, petition filed for termination of parental rights).

Marital Counseling

— 67% of counselors and 66% of clients reported improvement in their presenting problem.

Child Protective Services

— 42% of cases had a reduced propensity to reabuse or reneglect after service was provided according to workers.

A more extensive list is provided in Table 2.1 in *The Accountable Agency* (Carter, 1983). In addition, the appendix to the recently completed Minnesota report provides another set of outcome measures for a broad array of human services. Outcome measures already exist. There is no need for extensive creation of them. There is, however, a need to choose which ones are most appropriate. This need not and should not be an extensive or elaborate process.

CREATING THE CLIMATE FOR SUCCESS MEASURES

Successful implementation and use of any new change is characterized by top management commitment, a detailed sequence of implementation steps, and integration into ongoing operations of the organization.

The Minnesota experience offers a concise set of conditions which are necessary to create a "utilization climate" for introducing such a change.

1. The concern that state and county officials have for exemplary program performance should be visible and clearly evident. This commitment to program excellence can be demonstrated by acts such as making public announcements, adopting written policies, and holding group meetings to discuss the topic.
2. Those who provide services should be given ample latitude to change the way in which services are provided. The general rule

to be adopted is to be less concerned with how services are provided and more concerned with the results that are obtained.

3. Outcomes need to be explicit, measurable and communicated clearly to those who have an effect on performance.

4. Organizations need to reward exemplary performance when it occurs. A program which experiences superior outcomes should be publicly recognized for the achievement. Attention devoted only to those programs that are marginal performers while ignoring those that are superior can discourage the pursuit of excellence.

5. Excellence needs to be pursued on a long term basis.

6. The focus should be on improving impacts and not on having an accountability system. The outcome information system should be seen as one component of a broad effort to improve effectiveness. Without this larger focus the danger is that the accountability data will be seen as a technical product which imposes burdensome reporting requirements.

Staff will resist any new data collection process even if it demonstrates their success in providing effective intervention. They feel unappreciated for their efforts to help clients, but often resist collecting the data necessary to demonstrate their effectiveness. Once collected, moreover, they will resist the "good news" about program effectiveness. Some staff claim to "know" when they have impacted positively on clients, contending that it is difficult to account for outcomes systematically. This is why caseworkers always revert to specific case studies and detail surrounding the unique aspects of a case.

Some supervisors and workers will stress the impossibility of obtaining consensus on outcome measures. Their objections tend to confuse and complicate a relatively straightforward decision:

Tactic or Objection	*Suggested Strategy*
"My clients each have unique needs."	– be patient, persistent and set up time frames to come up with the best possible outcome measures.
	– none will be perfect and each will be arbitrary as all success measures are.
"There are multiple outcomes for clients."	– don't attempt to resolve debate. – simply choose more than one.

"I don't agree with the outcome."

—do not require the worker to agree but simply to seek to influence the desired outcome.

"Why do it if you cannot do it right?"

—set time frames for a less than perfect set of outcome measures which can be revised in light of future information.

Convincing workers of their own effectiveness can best be done by regularly collecting such information on every case and feeding it back directly to them. Besides helping them overcome resistance to good news, there are several other advantages to having workers collect this information:

— knowing the consequences of services delivered in order to correct problems at the lowest appropriate organizational level;
— short feedback loop;
— worker gratification as a result of clients' satisfaction and/or positive change;
— helps workers to think of better ways to provide services;
— reinforces to clients that both the agency and caseworker are interested in knowing their clients' reactions to services rendered;
— does not require yet another agency representative interacting with clients (e.g., special researcher);
— reduces worker burnout (according to Nancy Humphreys, past President of NASW and national expert on worker burnout).

In Michigan, at the Maxey Boys Training School for delinquent youth, Mr. Virgil Pinckney, the director, institutionalized an easy approach to collecting client outcome data. A clerk finds out what happened to closed cases three and 12 months after release from the training facility. The clerk discovers if the youth is in school, work, or training in employment, as well as if the youth has been rearrested. Client specific outcomes and aggregate data are both reported back to the staff. The information is then shared every six months with each of ten operating units and is further broken out by each treatment team within each unit. Every team knows how they are doing relative to every other unit. This feedback, according to Pinckney, "adds a healthy element of constructive competition not only with other units but more importantly with last year's results for their own unit."

Pinckney now has had several years of experience with outcome information and uses it to reinforce or change current operating policies:

— The productivity status (school, training, or work) at three months after release is the best predictor of rearrest. This has been our best intervention strategy to insure a delinquency free lifestyle.

— We use the fact that over 40% of the youth will spend some time in the Michigan prison system as a deterrent. We tell delinquents that unless they get some type of education and/or skill training while at Maxey they have a much greater chance of ending up in prison.

— Outcome information allows us to defend our programs in budget appropriation hearings with data clearly showing our effectiveness. We are not as vulnerable to impulsive decisions or recommendations by budget analysts because we have better data than most programs by which to argue for continued funding.

— There is always a risk with collecting outcome data. The risk is that you don't know how it's going to come out nor how it is going to be interpreted. This is true of all information, but it is particularly true of outcome data. Over the years, however, the range is relatively small and there are few really surprising deviations from the rates which were experienced in the first few years.

— The best outcome measures are not perfect. However, they are our best estimators at this time. Not everyone is completely content with them and occasionally the rate of expected outcome or the wording needs to be renegotiated. It is important that managers not try to establish the "perfect" outcome measure but only the best ones.

What Pinckney has done can be done in any agency committed to collecting client outcome data. It is not an elaborate system. It doesn't use a computer. It does, however, give the director the kind of information needed to adequately defend the budget each year.

A second example is the Milwaukee County Department of Social Services which wanted to know how effective various purchase of service agencies were in providing day care, work assistance and homemaker services. The Milwaukee County Board of Supervisors also was convinced that it was necessary for the good management of these $11 million programs.

> . . . at least once a year, the Department (of Social Services) shall offer qualified recipients receiving care or service from an agency, or their respective guardian, a questionnaire regarding

their impressions as to the adequacy and quality of the care or service provided to them by the agency. Results of these questionnaires shall be tabulated annually by the Department according to agency. (Milwaukee County Ordinance 46.09)

It costs approximately $25,000 per year to draw a two percent per month client survey, mail the questionnaires and tabulate results. Subsequent reports by service agency are shared with each agency. Consumer information is utilized by the Department of Social Services to draw conclusions on client satisfaction with specific services and provider agencies. Where problem areas are noted, the information is used to improve the situation. Where major problems prevail this information is used to support a decision to terminate a purchase of service contract. Additional positive consequences of the consumer satisfaction data are:

— Many clients use the survey to express appreciation and to say thank-you for help given.
— Social workers take encouragement and motivation from favorable client survey reports.
— The survey alerted the department to sarcastic short-tempered social workers. Agencies, after further investigation, have terminated or reassigned such employees.
— Survey data results help reassure planners that programs are or are not responsive to client needs. The survey indirectly provides consumers with a voice in the resource allocation process.

IMPLEMENTING SUCCESS MEASUREMENT SYSTEMS

Many managers, supervisors, and workers attempt to define the collection of client outcome information as a unique and somewhat mystical procedure, as if contacting closed cases is totally beyond workers' skills. Some will even get "blank" looks on their faces as if they cannot imagine how such a process may be implemented.

Inevitably there will be long discussions of such esoteric statistical topics as reliability and validity of outcome data, elaborate sampling designs, worker bias (as if there is not bias in all other reporting), client bias, extensive mobility of closed cases (as if open cases were stable), conditions necessary for inferring causality, external factors influencing closed cases (as if external factors do not influence open cases). These issues should be viewed as legitimate concerns common to all reporting systems and largely dismissed for ongoing information systems.

A success measurement system needs to be implemented just like other information systems:

— You decide what you want collected.
— You develop a form to capture the information.
— You write manual material detailing how to fill out the form.
— You tell workers or clients to complete the form.
— You collect the data and store it in a computer.
— You summarize the information on monthly management forms.
— You give staff feedback.
— You look at the data and interpret it in light of everything else you know about the program.

THE LESSONS

Several lessons can be drawn from the last 15 to 20 years of experimenting with institutionalizing success measures in public programs. Future managers may be able to learn from these observations in customizing their approach to true accountability.

Measuring Client Outcomes Requires a Critical Mass of Committed Administrators

In each state that has implemented regular client outcome monitoring there has been a critical mass of key administrators who have believed in and promoted the concept of systematic collection of client impact information. There is no secret number or necessary organizational position insuring the acceptance of this type of management.

In Michigan, I was the director of Planning and Evaluation within the budget office of the Department of Social Services from 1974 to 1984. Dr. John Dempsey was the director and began promoting outcome related management. He used this approach largely for public relations purposes with the release each year of an annual plan clearly outlining expected levels of outcomes for each program. He did not use it for making internal resource commitment decisions. He realized, correctly, that most politicians at that time (and today) would not understand nor appreciate making decisions based on client outcome results.

In Texas, the key administrators have been Dr. Murray Newman, Assistant Commissioner, Office of Research, Demonstration and Evaluation for the Texas Department of Human Resources and Merle

Springer, Deputy Commissioner for the same organization. They initiated in 1981 a "Master Plan for a Texas Department of Human Resources Impact Evaluation System." Its purpose is to provide on-going client outcome monitoring for Texas Department of Human Resources, focusing on service effectiveness. The evaluation system will be designed to assess the impact of services upon clients. Its goal is to design a user-oriented system by identifying potential users and their information needs, ranging from caseworkers to executive level staff. User-orientation ensures that relevant information will be collected and that the system will be used to its fullest potential.

These key administrators are located in leadership positions which allow a commitment of resources. In addition, they have and use influence to introduce and sustain necessary changes. Introducing this change in management philosophy requires the same steps as any other innovation; an idea or concept needs to be promoted by opinion leaders and institutionalized with a commitment of resources.

Outcome Oriented Leaders and Resources Need to Be Continually Acquired

In any organization there is a limited time frame for an idea to move from a conceptual level to an accepted institutionalized approach. This time frame is limited to five to ten years because the individuals who believe in and promote the idea will move to other jobs, die, become involved with other projects, etc. Other opinion leaders and resources need to be secured to continue the effort.

In Michigan, Dr. Dempsey was the director of the Department of Social Services from 1975 until his death in 1981. For six years he tried to define and institutionalize the collection of client outcome information. His successor had her own concept of accountability and did not continue this approach. Without strong support within an organization, any new concept will not survive.

Consensus Is Possible

There are many differences among managers and workers regarding appropriate indicators of client outcomes. However, for any given program there seems to be a limited number of indicators selected by agencies to represent their impact on clients' lives.

The Florida HRS list of outcomes is relatively representative of the kinds of outcomes likely to be selected by human service agencies. The Strategic Plan directs the resources of this large umbrella agency to attain twelve goals. Goal five is to "ensure the quality of care and treatment in HRS operated and purchased community programs." To meet this goal HRS adopted standards and outcome measures for all programs and implemented a plan for application of outcome measures by July 1, 1986.

HRS developed a goal, target population, and list of services for each program area. In addition, an outcome measure was selected along with an indicator and a minimal target and ideal attainment level. HRS also identifies which program client population is targeted, what data elements are necessary to measure each indicator, the method of collecting the data elements and the timetable for collection.

Florida created these accountability levels for the following programs:

Sub-Program	Targeted Value
1. Community Care for the Elderly	—90% of total unduplicated clients served who will remain in their own home during the year
	—60% of Community Care for the Elderly target group who will maintain or improve their functional status.
2. Adult Protective Services	— 75% recidivism rate of Adult Protective Service complaints within six months of original complaint.
3. Community Mental Health Services	— Not more that 50% of the persons stabilized in a Baker Act facility will subsequently be readmitted for Baker Act treatment within 90 days.
4. Community Drug Abuse Services	—At least 60% of clients graduating from drug abuse residential treatment programs will either be employed or enrolled in and attending an educational program.
	—At least 70% of the criminal justice system referrals for drug treatment who participate in the TASC Program will not

subsequently be arrested within 90 days of discharge from treatment.

5. Child Protection Team
  — 80% of children will not be reabused or neglected after receiving CPT services.

6. Foster Care
  — 60% of cases with reunification as the case goal will be reunited.

7. Rehabilitation
  — 75% of clients will indicate improvement according to program data.

  — 75% of clients will use skills without assistance in actual situation.

  — 90% of severely handicapped clients who have been provided substantial rehabilitative services will be successfully employed in a suitable employment situation for a minimum of 60 days.

8. Family Planning
  — 75% of IPO (maternity) postpartum clients will adopt a method of Family Planning.

  — 60% of family planning clients will maintain a method of family planning for a minimum of one year or until a pregnancy is desired.

9. Employment and Training
  — 80% of ADC clients will obtain unsubsidized employment for 30 days.

  — 65% of ADC clients will obtain unsubsidized employment for 90 days.

  — 50% of ADC clients will obtain unsubsidized employment for 180 days.

Florida devised an integrated decision making information system comprised of three main elements: compliance (with process requirements), outcomes, and costs. It is one of the most developed conceptual accountability systems across a wide spectrum of social service programs.

Computer Technology May Make it Easier

As computer technology allows the manager to link outcome information with process and cost data it is more likely that managers will ask more appropriate accountability questions. In Florida, Nancy Ross, Senior Management Analyst for the Office of Evaluation and Management Review, believes that the availability of these linkages in 1985 was largely responsible for the initiation and acceptance of their outcome oriented quality of care project.

In Nacogdoces, Texas, the Regional Office staff obtained a grant from the T.L.L. Temple Foundation to acquire a computer system in 1984. This acquisition allowed the outcome monitoring system to be introduced with minimal impact on worker time and maximum turnaround time to provide feedback to workers and supervisors regarding the impact of services to clients.

This technological advancement diminishes a major obstacle of additional paper requirements which restricted some attempts to measure client outcomes. The less dependent outcome monitoring systems are on additional worker input, the more likely it will be implemented. In short, the best measure should be generated by an information process already in existence or one that does not require more input from first line workers.

Success Is Difficult to Accept

Outcome measures provide workers with rare feedback on the success of their professional intervention. In the absence of objective systematic information on their own success most workers assume they are less successful than clients perceive them to be. Family Services Association of America does a follow-up survey of clients of its member agencies. FSAA found that "clients in a followup sample reported global ratings of 'much better' considerably more often than did their counselors (32% versus 17%)." Clients reported considerably more change after one, two or three interviews than did counselors (Carter, 1983). One of the biggest barriers to accepting client impact information are workers themselves. They want to know what the realistic levels of impact are, but are afraid to ask. If they knew on a regular basis, they could begin to acknowledge the incredible difficulty of the task of changing an individual or their environment. Without such feedback workers are destined to low self esteem because we are harder on ourselves than any objective feedback could ever approximate.

A Model for Service Effectiveness

The Service Effectiveness Model links managerial skills with five performance areas: productivity, effectiveness, resource acquisition, efficiency, and staff morale. I believe attaining the first four should, in turn, cause staff morale to improve. Social service managers are assessed, and prefer to be assessed, through improvements in productivity, efficiency and resource acquisition. "More is better and faster is better." Seldom are managers or workers assessed in terms of effectiveness and because there is no feedback of their impact on clients, staff morale will predictably never rise above relatively low levels.

This model also correctly recognizes the need to acquire resources from the external environment:

Minimally, it (every social program) needs to acquire funds, per sonnel, clients, and goodwill. Top level managers devote the majority of their time to activities focusing on acquiring these resources. In the current political climate, these activities assume increasing importance.

Throughout the Reagan Administration there has been heightened awareness of the need to measure the consequences to clients and providers of the cuts in resources to human service programs. The major objective is to document how fewer services are being provided with less funding and how much more difficult it is for clients to survive with less benefits.

What is not being recognized is the need for administrators to demonstrate a positive impact on the lives of clients regardless of the amount of resources available. If we articulate clear outcomes and document how our intervention strategies result in improvements in the quality of life for our clients and communities, we win the ultimate "goodwill" of the taxpayers funding our programs. More importantly, we increase our own sense of accomplishment and ensure our clients they are being provided the most effective programs possible with the level of resources available to us.

Without success measures no one can know if spending more or less on human services will result in an increase or decrease in the quality of our society. Now is the time to invest in the future of human service programs by publicly articulating, measuring, and sharing our results so that we, and everyone else, can share in our progress towards a more effective use of the resources committed to us.

REFERENCES

Carter, R. *The accountable agency*. Beverly Hills: Sage Publications, 1983.

Fulton, R. *Director's statement of priorities*. Norman, OK: Department of Human Services, 1984.

HCFA. *PACS survey process: Draft procedural guidelines*. HHS. Washington, DC: U.S. Government Printing Office, 1986.

Magura, S. & Moses, B. Outcome measurement in child welfare. *Child Welfare*, 1980, *59*, 595-606.

Michigan Department of Social Services. *The institutional centers*. MDSS, 1983.

Minnesota Department of Public Welfare. Evaluation: A total approach. HHS Grant 90PD10028, 1984.

Newman, M. *Master plan for Texas*. Austin, TX: Department of Human Resources, 1981.

Schlesinger, A. Making Reagan accountable, *Wall Street Journal*, April 20, 1984, p.14.

Management by Measurement: Organizational Dilemmas and Opportunities

Anthony J. Grasso, MSW
Irwin Epstein, PhD

Although organizational sociologists have warned us against over-reliance on effectiveness models (Etzioni, 1964; Hasenfeld, 1983), the accountability movement, the advent of the computer, and the fiscal attraction to business administration techniques in times of scarcity have led human service organizations and their funding sources to place great emphasis on statistical measurement of effectiveness and efficiency. For agencies and programs, life and death decisions are often based on statistical indicators such as number of client contacts, number of units of service delivered, number of closed cases, average length of stay, and the like (Bielawski & Epstein, 1984; Conrad, 1985).

This emphasis on quantitative measures of effectiveness and efficiency has resulted in a number of different types of goal distortion and displacement. So, for example, in discussing the phenomenon of "overmeasurement," Etzioni (1964) points out that

> Frequent measuring can distort . . . organizational efforts be-
> cause, as a rule, some aspects of its output are more measureable
> than the others. Frequent measuring tends to encourage over-
> production, of measureable items and neglect of less measure-
> able ones. (p. 9)

To illustrate this point, Conrad (1985) has shown that the Program Assessment System (PAS) applied to New York City foster care work-

Mr. Grasso is Director of Management Information and Evaluation, Boysville of Michigan, 8744 Clinton-Macon Road, Clinton, MI 49236. Dr. Epstein is Professor, Hunter College School of Social Work, The City University of New York, 129 East 79th Street, New York, NY 10021. He serves as Research Consultant to Boysville of Michigan.

ers encourages them "to put more emphasis on accomplishing a certain number of parental visits, for example, or the placing of a child in an adoptive home by the required date, rather than on the way it is accomplished" (p. 643). At the administrative level, she shows how the same measurement system puts pressure on the foster care administrator "to displace the goal of family reunification because of the very procedures devised to achieve this goal" (p. 642).

Elsewhere, Hasenfeld (1983) has warned of "the tendency by the organization to reify these measures as true indicators of effectiveness." In so doing, "the organization allocates its resources and concentrates its efforts to score well on these criteria," despite their real limitations (p. 212). Whether or not the criteria are inherently valid, organizations may seek clients that most approximate "output" criteria at intake (Dale, 1983/84). If they cannot control intake, programs may jettison unpromising clients before they can show up as indicators of program failure (Lerman, 1968). Finally, Walker (1972) has observed the "strain towards falsification" whereby staff are pressured to lie with statistics in order to make their programs and themselves look better in the eyes of external evaluators and internal superiors.

The underlying causes of these dysfunctions in human service organizations are, among others, "the multiplicity and ambiguity of organizational goals, the indeterminacy of the service technologies, and the inherent difficulties in observing and measuring human attributes," such as client change (Hasenfeld, 1983, pp. 10-11). Moreover, in contrast with industrial organizations where the orientations of staff are highly instrumental and focused on outputs, workers in human service organizations tend to stress professional autonomy, humanistic rather than instrumental objectives, and professional "process" (Kouzes & Mico, 1979). Nevertheless, it is probably safe to predict that effectiveness models and statistical assessment are here to stay.

In social agencies, the most commonly used measures involve number counts of staff activity (e.g., client contacts, services provided, etc.), client outputs (e.g., cases closed, type of program completion, satisfaction with service, etc.), and client outcomes (e.g., recidivism, post-treatment adjustment, etc.).

In the study of human service organizations, Patti (1983) has identified four levels for analysis. These are: the executive management level, the program management level, the supervisory management level, and the program staff level. It is no surprise that the problems associated with measuring service effectiveness and efficiency impact on each of these levels. Thus, in discussing PAS, Conrad (1985) comments:

Whether the primary motivating force behind these . . . is to improve services or reduce costs, their imposition has created as many problems as it has resolved. Thus, the sheer number and complexity of these requirements pose an enormous problem for administrators, supervisors, and workers alike. (p. 640)

And, despite their common organizational base, these difficulties get played out in different ways at different program levels. This is because each level is likely to have different criteria for assessing its own effectiveness and efficiency, different organizational loyalties, different informational needs, and different central tasks. On the latter point, Patti (1983) remarks:

Yet while there are essential similarities this should not obscure the fact that the relative emphasis given to tasks and thus the activity configurations of management practices varies significantly with the organizational level in which the practice occurs. (p. 43)

In this paper, we describe some of the dilemmas that effects-measurement poses for staff at different program levels. In small agencies, a number of different dilemmas may simultaneously confront the same individuals, i.e., those with multiple roles and responsibilities. In large, highly differentiated agencies, these dilemmas confront different staff levels in singular ways. The examples that we draw are from the field of residential child care though they are readily applicable to other areas of human service provision and measurement.

Irrespective of the type of agency and the level of analysis, management by measurement assumes that staff should be held "accountable for specific service outputs and . . . rewarded according to their ability to attain them" (Hasenfeld, 1983, p. 174). Our central assumption, however, is that a reward system based solely on performance indicators encourages dysfunctions such as "falsification." The consequence of this dysfunctional response is an illusion of quality performance rather than actual quality performance.

The introduction of an effects management system into an agency causes one additional problem that has its roots in basic human learning behavior. For persons to learn they must be free to doubt. When pressured to perform they no longer feel that freedom. Instead, they feel they must now know how to do what it is they are being asked to do by the agency. The introduction of a measurement system alone places pressure on staff to conceal their practice problems and to hide their professional doubts from themselves as well as from their superiors. Clearly this inhibits professional growth.

Hence, our final point is that to improve actual performance, management has to invest resources into staff skill development. To illustrate the importance of skill development in conjunction with effectiveness measurement, we conclude with a case example of an innovative research/practice collaboration at Boysville of Michigan where the first author is the Director of Management Information and Evaluation and the second is Research Consultant.

PROGRAM STAFF LEVEL

The point in the human service organization where the exchange between the technology and resources takes place, also referred to as the transformation process in industrial analysis.

In studying human service organizations, researchers have found that social workers are often caught in a conflict between a desire for more supervision and, conversely, for more professional autonomy (Scott, 1966; Aiken & Hage, 1969). This is particularly apparent when social workers complete their formal education. Upon leaving school and joining an organization, social workers are likely to embrace supervision as a means of improving their skills in helping clients. However, since technological models for client change are indeterminate, whereas agency rules are not, workers may experience supervision as a means of control rather than as a means of further education. Commonly, the more questioning and creative new program staff do not experience supervisory support and their newly acquired methods are challenged as their work is scrutinized by higher level organization staff. As a result, line workers frequently feel pressure to comply with existing agency norms and sense that clients' needs become secondary to standard organizational procedures.

Exacerbating this problem further is a structurally based ideological conflict between managers and direct service deliverers. The line social worker, who identifies with interpersonal practice, generally views social workers in administration as not part of "practice" (Patti, 1983). In addition, the direct service practitioner is likely to focus on helping individual clients, whereas the social worker in administration tends to be concerned with the values of organizational effectiveness and efficiency. While these sometimes coincide, they often conflict.

The informational needs at the program staff level are related to meeting individual clients' needs. For line workers, effectiveness is informally assessed by their ability to help clients who come to them in pain. These clients test the very limits of their workers' emotional capacities as well as their technical skills. For the social workers, their being effective is not reducible to how many phone calls they have made in a month or where the client will be twelve months after discharge; but rather it relates to whether they were able to help relieve the pain and suffering of their clients. Under such conditions, direct service workers resent applying quantitative systems of measurement to their work and have often responded angrily that number counts do not really tell the story of what they do. Furthermore, from a technical point of view, emphasis on quantitative measurement of client contact often reflects an, at best, assumed relationship between activity and effect. This "hypothesis" is rarely tested. And, even if such a correlation exists, questions about causation are likely to remain unanswered (Kadushin, 1976; Smith, 1976).

Another type of effectiveness measurement, where the client is after program completion, rarely provides more than superficial information about adaptation. Because of this, such measures do not contribute much to the quality of the service technology. Finally, practitioners resent these systems because they do not take into account the difficulty of the case or level of skill required to achieve desired outcomes. Nevertheless, direct service workers see these measurement systems being used by administration for individual performance evaluation as well as program evaluation.

Weissman (1977), in looking at this problem, asserts that evaluation must provide operating staff directly with information, not only on how well or how poorly they are doing their job but much more significantly with information that will offer guidance on how they can improve their work. If human service professionals are merely held accountable for result, but not given the kind of information that will help them improve performance, the strain towards falsification is increased. Or, over-conformity (Merton, 1952) and excessive caution may result. Weissman further states that in order to mitigate the defensive perception of staff that they, rather than their program are being evaluated, program evaluation or effects measurement must be separated from individual staff evaluation.

Client outcome, i.e., condition at a future date, is another often used measure of program effectiveness. In industry, where effects management originally started, it is assumed that once a product is completed and ready for marketing, no further alterations will be made on the product. By contrast, the final product of the human service agency, a changed client, will continue to make independent choices and will experience other changes caused by their constant exchange and interaction with the environment. In this context, client outcomes are often judged without regard to conditions over which the agency or service professional or client has no control.

In residential child care, recidivism is a perfect example of this. Bloedorn's (1970) writings suggest that problems arise when social service programs make claims that extend far beyond their ability to control as well as document. He argues that agencies should measure effects on contracted program outcomes at time of program completion. He uses the example of an employment agency being judged by its ability to make clients more employable as opposed to being judged by whether or not clients actually became employed. In so suggesting, he views employment as a condition determined by economics, not by employment programs.

SUPERVISORY LEVEL OF THE ORGANIZATION

The level in the organization at which technology is preserved and disseminated and the first level of responsibility for implementation of the technology is assumed.

At the supervisory level of the organization there are three main areas of organizational stress related to effects management. In relationship to organizational hierarchy, the supervisory level is the first point in the structure where hierarchy places strain on role identification from above and from below. The commitment of the supervisor is more likely to be with the preservation and implementation of the professional technology than with the maintenance of the organization, per se. Because of this, supervisors are more often identified with the direct service professionals in an organization than with those at higher levels of administration. Additionally, the supervisor is responsible for imparting skills that have no demonstrated cause/effect relationship, although they are ultimately responsible for outcomes or effects. Supervisors also serve as the buffer between accountability pressure on the one hand and client demands on the other. Ultimately, however, their informational needs involve quality control and improvement of program technology rather than direct service outcomes. Role conflict at this level is often a consequence of being held responsible for service effects without having the information necessary to teach the intervention and technological resources to secure these outcomes. For supervisors, there is a constant struggle with line workers over control of the treatment process and line worker autonomy. As the measurement of "process" is formalized, it is most often translated into activity counts of some kind (number of phone calls, number of client sessions conducted, etc.). Consequently, the service practitioner often complains that paperwork gets in the way of helping clients, while supervisors pressure for completed reports and high scores on activity measurements.

PROGRAM MANAGEMENT LEVEL

The point in the organization where the service technology becomes secondary to accountability.

Identification of individuals at the program management level is more often associated with maintenance of the organizational hierarchy than with professional autonomy. Middle level managers are committed to the primary value of accountability but have not yet found viable methods for implementing that value. As a result, the middle level manager finds her/himself caught between the supervisor's commitment to professional skills and the need to report or control. Thus, the middle level manager often experiences conflict over how to know the difference between ritualized compliance versus really good work. Often identifying with business or corporate models of management, staff at this level have the most tenuous identification with the field of social service. Instead, they tend to see themselves as corporate managers.

As stated earlier, however, the inexactness of the technology in human service organizations severely limits the applicability of corporate, effects management systems. This results in a dilemma for middle level managers who are drawn to corporate models of evaluation which have limited applicability in social service settings. Frustration at this level is associated with the lack of appropriate assessment approaches that provide accountability structures as well as systems for human service management and administration. Still, the greatest impetus to look at program effects comes from this level of the organization. Program managers have to report on program outcome to the executive level and thus need systematic and reliable information. As a result, staff at this level identify directly with management information systems. The informational needs and pressure to perform at this level inevitably conflicts with the informational needs of the practitioner and supervisor.

EXECUTIVE LEVEL

The level in the organization at which policy is made, performance relates primarily to broadbase concerns of the organization, and interpretation is made beyond the boundaries of the organization.

The role of the individual at the executive level of the organization is most often concerned with the external environment of the organization, such as, procuring funds, overseeing the overall operations of the total agency, dealing with fiscal accountability, recruitment of personnel, agency advocacy, and program evaluation in the broadest sense. Individuals at this level in the organization are more concerned with general operations rather than with day to day management. In relation to service technology, their primary concern is on demonstrable results as opposed to professional "process." Executive level staff often experience conflict, finding themselves defending "the good work that their organization does" to the greater community, while at the same time dealing with information from middle level managers about far from perfect programs. Consequently, the designer of an effects management system finds her/himself in a very difficult dilemma. Thus, if you create a system giving top authority too much information about staff effort and effectiveness you may reduce the potential for an internal environment that encourages improvement in the service technology. In other words, empowering the top level of an organization with information on accountability, without empowering the line staff with the ability to improve skills, creates a profound conflict of authority inside the organization causing greater strain and further dysfunction.

The kind of measurement this level of the organization is most interested in relates to client outcome. Executives frequently find themselves responding to the questions of board members and funding bodies about recidivism rates, post-treatment adjustment, etc. The organizational strain which their information needs create inside the agency further limits the potential for an internal learning environment. This is the primary dilemma that needs to be addressed in designing an effects management system. One such attempt is described below.

THE INTEGRATED MANAGEMENT INFORMATION, PROGRAM EVALUATION, AND APPLIED RESEARCH MODEL

Boysville of Michigan is the state's largest private residential agency for troubled adolescents. Since its founding in 1948 with fifteen boys, the agency has grown to where it now serves two hundred and seventy boys and girls. Treatment facilities are its main campus in Clinton, a smaller campus in Saginaw, and group homes in Detroit, Ecorse, Mt. Clemens, Redford, Saginaw, and Alpena. The Boysville treatment program is based on a modified version of Positive Peer Culture in which the natural influences of the adolescent peer group are enlisted to bring about change in behavior and attitude. Over the last few years, Boysville has also implemented an intensive family therapy program on the main campus for all youth in placement, specialized family foster care for youth unable to return to their natural family, and a metro area emergency placement program. While a growing number of the Boysville youth are neglected/abused, most are adjudicated delinquents with serious behavioral, social, and educational problems. Most come from the tri-county Detroit area. This year, in response to needs from both the public and private sector, Boysville expanded its mission to include service to girls. Girls are served at St. Vincent Center in Saginaw, which merged with Boysville in February 1985, and at our new group home, Carbini Center in Redford Township.

In contrast with the externally designed compliance oriented (PAS) system described by Conrad (1985), the Management Information and Program Evaluation system designed at Boysville of Michigan (BOMIS) was based on the assumption that if you simultaneously improved the service technology of the organization when you measured accountability or when you measured effects, the actual performance of the organization would improve as well as the measured performance. In developing this model, heavy emphasis was placed on providing useful information to the direct service professionals so as to improve their helping skills. The common value that runs across all levels of the organization is related to helping Boysville's clients. With the line staff, we emphasize that by participating in this management information system they can improve their skills and, thereby, provide more effective services to clients. Further, it was believed that an information system that improved the delivery of services to clients could also assess program effectiveness in ways required by the three other levels of the organization. In looking at organizational design, administration, program operations, and service delivery this assumption is central. The needs of the line-level practitioner were seen as primary in the operation of program at Boysville and, likewise, in the development of the effects-management system. We further felt that most other models, which have had serious difficulties, have not been able to integrate management, research, training, and social service delivery into one system. In order to have such an integrated system, the management information/research department needs to be providing information to each level of the organization that is useful for decision making appropriate to that particular level. The executive office needs information on broader base policy, the middle level management needs information on contract compliance, the supervisory level needs information in order to enhance staff development, and the service delivery level needs information to facilitate the treatment of clients. In most management information systems, the needs of supervisory and service delivery levels have been neglected. Consequently, management information systems in social services have been effective at providing information to top level management and middle level managers on broader base policy issues and contract compliance, but have failed to promote an improved service technology. This difficulty is magnified because these information systems are most dependent upon the lower level of the organization for reliable and valid data. As a result, they typically go through a cycle of failure and falsification because practitioners do not see these systems as useful. Instead, as we stated earlier, they are viewed as excessively controlling or punitively judgmental of staff efforts.

In the system designed at Boysville, we are using four different family and client coping instruments developed by McCubbin and Olson (1982) at the University of Minnesota. Staff administers these instruments in a time series to clients and receives in return easily understandable graphic print-outs on subdimensions related to family and client change. Boysville also gathers information on staff activity and through the supervisory process, trains staff on the use of interventions directly intended to impact change on these subdimensions in client and family dynamics. Supervisors in this process receive information which then can be used to improve the implementation of the group work and family systems technologies that are used at Boysville. Consequently, program staff routinely receive information concerning client problems and client change; middle level managers routinely receive information from the system on performance as it relates to contracting issues in their area; and executive staff routinely receive information which can then be used at the state and national level in influencing public policy and procuring additional funds. Staff at all levels actively participate in both the gathering and utilization of information because they can see it as a valuable part in the development of their skills in working with clients.

In testing the assumption that by improving staff skill you can improve effectiveness at different levels of the organization, we decided to look at an issue that was extremely salient to funding sources, to the executive and program management levels, to line staff, and to clients as well. The issue of length of stay was important for ultimate agency survival because cost containment in providing services to clients was being strenuously encouraged by the Michigan Department of Social Services. We felt that if we could show how improved family treatment skill shortens length of stay, the agency administration and the state would continue to support this mode of intervention. Since family work was the area in which most recent staff training had taken place on the main campus, we decided to look at the relationship between family work contacts and length of stay, over time in that setting.

In 1983, at Boysville in general, family work was not viewed as an individualized service specialty and was functioning only as an auxil liary to the residential treatment program. In 1984, Boysville hired a family work trainer and initiated, on the main campus, the use of the applied research model intended to improve family worker skill.

Our evaluative strategy was to look at differences between 1983 and 1984 in family worker contacts in relationship to length of stay. In studying these relationships, we found that on campus in 1983 the family work contacts were primarily associated with "critical events" in the agency (i.e., truancy of clients, clients acting out on campus, etc.) and not related to length of stay. As stated earlier, in 1983 family work at Boysville was secondary to residential care and not viewed as an individual treatment program in its own right. In 1984, when family work came into its own on campus, we no longer found any statistical relationship between family worker activity and client acting out. In 1984, we further found that for program successes (i.e., clients released to less restrictive settings) the greater the number of family contacts, the shorter the length of stay. This finding contravened the common sense expectation that those clients who remained in the program longer would quite naturally have more family contacts. And, since the previous on-campus patterns prevailed off-campus in 1984, we had further validation of our assumption.

The issue of length of stay was important to both the executive staff and also the program manager level of the organization since they were being asked to reduce the cost of care by reducing length of stay. By improving family treatment skill and effort, Boysville was able to reduce the cost of care by reducing length of stay and, at the same time, increase effectiveness. Clearly, this was viewed positively by all levels of staff and by clients as well. This finding supports the contention that an improvement in the skill of the service practitioner can have positive effects on the actual and measured performance of the agency.

In summary, the primary issue is not what specific instrument or what research strategy is used to measure effectiveness. Rather, it is a question of the integration of measurement and service delivery systems. This integration requires a full understanding of organizational dynamics. At the very least, the systems designer must be sure that the measurement of effectiveness does not hinder the ability of staff to improve their skill levels. At best, measurement should promote professional development. Nonetheless, even the most sophisticated information system and computer technology will fail to produce beneficial effects without concurrent commitment to improving staff skill.

REFERENCES

Aiken, M., & Hage, J. Organizational interdependence and interorganizational structure. *American Sociological Review*, 1968, *33*, 912-930.
Bielawski, B. & Epstein, I. Assessing program stabilization: An extension of the differential evaluation model. *Administration in Social Work*, 1984, *8*, 13-23.
Bloedorn, J. Application of system analysis approach to social welfare problems and organizations. *Public Welfare,* 1970, *28*, 280-284.
Conrad, K. Promoting quality of care: The role of the compliance director. *Child Welfare*, 1985, *64*, 639-649.
Dale, N. The new foster care system: A procrustean bed. *The Childrens Village Bulletin*, Winter, 1983-84.
Etzioni, A. *Modern organizations.* Englewood Cliffs, NJ: Prentice-Hill, Inc., 1964.
Hasenfeld, Y. *Human service organizations.* Englewood Cliffs, NJ: Prentice-Hill, Inc., 1983.
Kadushin, A. Children in foster families and institutions. In H. Maas (Ed.). *Social services research.* Washington, DC: National Association of Social Workers, 1976.
Kouzes, J. & Mico, P. Domain theory. *Journal of Applied Behavioral Science,* 1979, *15*, 449-469.
Lerman, P. Evaluative studies of institutions for delinquents: Implications for research and social policy. *Social Work*, *13*, 55-64, 1968.
Merton, R. *Bureaucratic structure and personality.* In R. Merton et al. *Reader in bureaucracy.* Glencoe, IL: The Free Press, 1952.
Patti, R. *Social welfare administration.* Englewood Cliffs, NJ: Prentice-Hall, Inc., 1983.
Scott, R. Reactions to supervision in a heteronomous professional organization. *Administrative Science Quarterly*, 1965, *10*, 65-81.
Smith, M.A. Question about parental visiting and foster care. *Social Service Review*, 1976, *50*, 525-526.
Walker, R. The ninth panacea: Program evaluation. *Evaluation*, 1972, *1*, 45-53.
Weissman, H. Clients, staff, and researchers: Their role in management information systems. *Administration in Social Work*, 1977, *1*, 43-51.

SECTION THREE:
SOCIAL PROGRAM DESIGN

Introduction

Program design is both a product and a method. As a product, program design is a written document which prescribes the minimum sets of behaviors of multiple actors required for the program to achieve its goals. As a method, program design is a framework by which critical management decisions are made. It is a process which makes explicit the decisions and provides analytical tools for making those decisions.

It is through the social program that clients benefit and workers attempt to find satisfying and fulfilling work. Social workers have long known that, at times, even herculean efforts in the trenches cannot overcome a poorly designed program. Inadequate program design contributes to:

1. Staff not being clear about what the program expects of them, so that critical products and desired client outcomes do not result;
2. Other agencies, professionals, clients, and public not being clear as to your program, leading to conflicts and failure to perform the behaviors required for proper success;
3. Funders not knowing what it takes to do the job, and producing unrealistic expectations;
4. The latest "hot idea" being selected for program interventions, avoiding a careful exploration of potentially more powerful alternatives.

101

A casual approach to program design has meant that critical decisions were either not made or were implicitly delegated to front-line workers with its inevitable inconsistency. For social administrators to take responsibility for program performance, these decisions must become administrative decisions.

The field, however, has not produced any set of procedures or analytic tools to guide the design of our social programs. The selection of papers which follow provides the beginning of attention to this critical administrative function.

Edwin J. Thomas draws on principles of social research and development, model development, and organizational innovation to create concepts of program design and development. Methods of design and steps in the design process are outlined. Thomas' concept of design and development can help managers control the design process so that programs produce intended benefits.

Merlin A. Taber's theory of accountability provides a specific model of program design. Taber's five program design elements provide managers with a framework for specifying the components of a program, identifying client benefits, and keeping the program operating as intended. Placing program design within a proactive definition of accountability puts the social administrator in charge rather than subject to accountability.

Andrea Savage's study examines the relationship between technology and client outcome in heroin addiction treatment program. Matching clients with program technologies is a key to producing intended outcomes. This matching requires managers to develop a repertoire of technology with proven effectiveness as well as intake and assessment tools that produce accurate matches.

Design and Development
in Organizational Innovation

Edwin J. Thomas, PhD

Managers, administrators, and other practitioners in human service organizations regularly encounter problems calling for planful change and innovation yet, as Patti (1978) and others have indicated, relatively little attention has been given to the developmental requirements of these roles. Design and development (abbreviated hereafter as D&D) is an emerging area related to social R&D (Rothman, 1980), developmental research (Thomas, 1978a, 1978b, 1980, 1984, 1985, in press) and model development (Mullen, 1978; Reid, 1979; Paine, Pellamy & Wilcox, 1984) that may make many contributions to organizational management. Among the advantages of employing the contributions of D&D in organizational innovation are that they can provide for more control of managers and others over the innovations evolved and developed, help prevent indiscriminate borrowing from other fields, make the process of innovation more systematic and orderly, and increase the likelihood of generating better innovations to meet organizational goals.

Although relatively new, D&D is already a large, complex subject to be found scattered in the literature and practices of diverse fields. Whole books and more, plus practice training in D&D would be required to begin to do the subject justice. Only selected topics can be touched on here. These are innovation in organizations, design, development, and the model development approach.

INNOVATION IN ORGANIZATIONS

Social service organizations are typically human service organizations whose primary purpose is to provide social, welfare, or health services to people. As Hasenfeld (1983) has indicated, human service

---

Dr. Thomas is Professor, School of Social Work, The University of Michigan, Ann Arbor, MI 48109.

103

organizations have a human service "technology" that has been broadly defined ". . . as a set of institutionalized procedures aimed at changing the physical, psychological, social, or cultural attributes of people in order to transform them from a given status to a new prescribed status" (p. 111). The human service technology consists more specifically of such factors as the selection and processing of clients, the techniques of intervention and the knowledge of causal relations, and the interaction, client control, and operations that pertain to staff activities in the process of service delivery (Hasenfeld, 1983). Seen most generally, innovation consists of selected changes introduced in these aspects of the human service technology and the organizational factors that support and relate to that instrumentality.

The Concept of Innovation

The word "innovation" is generally understood to mean the introduction of something novel. However, the change need not be entirely new to qualify as an innovation, as many writers on innovation have indicated (Delbecq, 1978; Eveland, Rogers & Klipper, 1977; Pelz & Munson, 1982; Rice & Rogers, 1980). The innovation may range from an *invention* of a novel tool (e.g., creating new hardware for a management information system) through *adaptation* by modification of existing tool (e.g., altering the software of an existing management information system so that it is compatible with the user needs in a particular organization), *novel application* for different purposes of an existing tool, often called technological transfer (e.g., application of a computerized information system developed initially for clients to be used with organizational employees) to *adoption* of an existing tool by a different group for the same purposes for which it was developed (e.g., agency A may take over in its entirety an existing management information system currently used by agency B) (Thomas, 1984).

Domains of Organizational Innovation

Although innovations in principle can be made in any or all aspects of the human service organization, it is useful to distinguish the domains particularly relevant in organizations designed and developed in the context of a performance model. These domains are organizational objectives, constituent services, service objectives, outcome objectives, outcome indicators, the technical subsystem (consisting of such factors as the intervention methods, service delivery and related technology), the social subsystem, and implementation. These domains are presented above in the approximate order in which they should be

addressed. This sequence is proposed because any change in the domain preceding others in the above ordering can and generally does have implications for subsequent domains. The domains are largely self-explanatory except for the technical subsystem, the social subsystem, and implementation, which are elaborated below.
As Munson and Pelz (1982) have indicated:

We view the organization as a socio-technical system in which the "technical" components are procedures for performing activities or delivering services, and the "social" components are organizational arrangements and human capacities that support the performance of these operations (individuals or groups, their skills, beliefs, and norms, and the arrangements for coordinating their activities). As emphasized in the literature on sociotechnical systems, changes in the technical subsystem will require changes in the social subsystem, and vice versa. (p. 8)

The technical subsystem may be conceived as consisting of at least three components. These are particularly applicable to human service organizations that provide some intervention as broadly conceived. The first is the interventional component which involves one or more aspects of a helping strategy. A helping strategy, in turn, can include at least the following: change objectives, targets of intervention, participants (target persons and helping persons), roles (helping person roles and client roles), context of helping (helping situations and service settings), adjuncts and props, assessment methods, a method of planning intervention, intervention methods (techniques of intervention and program format), implementation procedures, maintenance methods, termination procedures, monitoring methods, evaluation methods, follow-up procedure, behavior theory, and intervention theory (Thomas, 1984). Each of these involves a number of options for D&D, and needs to be attended to in any restructuring of an interventive approach. Further, each aspect of a helping strategy must be evolved in light of the other components.
The second component of the technical subsystem is the means by which the service or intervention is given. As the work on the Teaching Family Model of Blase, Fixsen and Phillips (1984) has so clearly indicated, the delivery system must also be designed to be consistent with the treatment program. The delivery system of the Teaching Family Model, for example, included staffing by professional teaching parents, family-style living, community involvement, and the Teaching Family site affiliation.

The third component consists of related technology, such as a management information system, personal computers as decision supports, and methods of aggregating and processing data for purposes of evaluation.

The social subsystem, in contrast, may involve any or all aspects of leadership, authority and control systems, rewards, informal systems, organizational culture and climate and, among others, the tasks, jobs, and the division of labor as they serve to support the technical subsystem (Galbraith, 1977; Gerlof, 1985). The technical and social subsystems need to be properly linked, one important aspect of which is structuring the social subsystem to provide proper support for innovations introduced in the technical subsystem.

While it is possible to design aspects of the technical or social subsystems as separate entities, it is not possible to make the changes operational in organizations without their implementation. Implementation involves all those activities required to put innovations into action (e.g., hiring different personnel, training staff members, preparing guidebooks and training manuals) (Munson & Pelz, 1982). Any given socio-technical system may be implemented in diverse ways, depending upon the particular organizational and contextual conditions. After it has been evolved, however, the implementation procedures are often incorporated as an extension of the innovation (Munson & Pelz, 1982).

DESIGN

As used here, design is ". . . the planful and systematic application of relevant scientific, technical, and practical information to the creation and assembly of innovations appropriate in human service intervention" (Thomas, 1984). As one of the series of phases, it is important to emphasize that design should not be carried out without prior analysis, a set of activities that will determine whether design is appropriate and what to focus on. In this analysis phase, there are preliminary activities of identification and examination of the problem, a state-of-the-art review, and a feasibility study. The activities of design, in turn, necessarily precede those of development, to be discussed below, and those of evaluation, an important topic but one already familiar to most readers and one which goes beyond the scope of this paper.

Steps of Design

Design consists of a number of constituent activities, each of which may be viewed as a step to be carried out in the design process. These activities include (1) determination of the objective of the innovation (2) identification of the requirements of the innovation (3) identification of design problems (4) selection of such sources of information as basic and applied research, scientific and allied technology, legal policy, indigenous innovation, practice, and professional and personal experience (5) gathering and processing information (6) generating and selecting alternative solutions (7) the assembly of the components of the design (8) real world representation of the innovation, and (9) proceduralization (Thomas, 1984). Each step is an essential activity in the design process which, if completed properly at the appropriate point, reduces the problems to manageable size and increases the likelihood that a subsequent activity will be carried out successfully.

Proceduralization

Further illustration of what is involved in the steps is provided by the last step of design, proceduralization.

> Proceduralization, as applied to the design of interventions, is the process by which the desired activities of the helping process are described, explicated, and made into procedures that persons involved in the helping process may follow. Without proceduralization, much of the methodology of interventions in the helping professions would be in the memory and habits of interventionists and would not progress beyond what has often been called "practice wisdom." Proceduralization makes it possible to formulate methods of intervention into suitable procedures, thereby facilitating the systematic and cumulative advancement of theories of intervention and the helping methods that are so essential to the human services. (p. 52)

Further, in regard to the process of proceduralization:

> . . . procedures should be utilized as an ongoing product and tool. Considered as a product, procedures consist of a series of successive approximations with revisions and extensions based on a systematic interplay between the actual intervention activity, its description and explication, and the subsequent reformulation of the procedures. The resulting procedure, in turn, is then

used as a tool to direct the intervention when it is next carried out. Every time an intervention is used in this way, it provides an occasion for description, explication, and procedural reformulation — a process that should result in cumulative refinement of the procedure when repeated. The successive revision of procedures is part of developmental testing in trial use for which there are empirical and analytic techniques that are useful for specifying and explicating procedures. (pp. 52-53)

Techniques

Throughout the phases and steps of D&D, the manager may find it useful to draw on selected techniques to address one or another of the specialized tasks of D&D. Task analysis, for example, is a technique to analyze complex behavioral repertoires for purposes of isolating the constituent activities and behavioral components required to accomplish given objectives. Task analysis has many uses in D&D.

. . . it can be employed to specify (a) the elements of competent and incompetent performance of clients, practitioners, or others; (b) the behavioral objectives of intervention; and (c) the tasks for which clients or practitioners may be trained. When appropriate elements of the task have been isolated, task analysis can facilitate pinpointed intervention, standardization of intervention, replication for purposes of practice and research, as well as documentation and codification of the behaviors involved. Through isolating the components of a task, task analysis can also facilitate study of the underlying psychological processes and organization of skills and knowledge. (Thomas, 1984, p. 232)

Among other empirical techniques having application in D&D are the critical incident technique and needs assessment. Some analytic techniques are flow charting, latticing, decision tables and PERT. Practice techniques include neutral interviewing, determining probably controlling conditions, the assessment experiment, individualized data based intervention planning, and empirically-based practice.

User Participation

The activities of D&D can be greatly enriched by including potential users of the innovation in the design process (Benn, 1977; Hussain, 1973; King & Cleland, 1975; Poertner & Rapp, 1980). Potential users include interventionists who might adopt the innovation, their supervisors and administrators, as well as potential clients. Among the possible advantages are the likelihood that user participation will result in innovations that are more acceptable to users, more compatible with existing methods, simpler, easier to sustain in the adopting organization and, in general, more contextually appropriate. There are also disadvantages to user participation (e.g., compromising technical sophistication) that must be weighed when composing the design team.

DEVELOPMENT

As to the companion to design, development has distinctive activities and is best viewed as a separate phase that is largely different from that of design which precedes it and from evaluation that it follows. Development is defined here as " . . . the process by which an innovative intervention is implemented and used on a trial basis, tested for its adequacy, and refined and redesigned as necessary and to meet new design problems that may arise." The steps of a development include (1) formulation of the development plan, which embraces determination of the scope of development, the proper role of evaluation and research in the development, and the type of setting to be employed; (2) operational preparation, including such factors as determining the staffing and development skills required, supervision and project management, and selection of sites to be sampled in the development; and (3) trial use and developmental testing. Although all these steps are important, trial use and developmental testing are briefly elaborated here to underline the fact that development is a systematic process.

Trial Use and Developmental Testing

Trial use, of course, entails the implementation of innovations with the clientele for whom the innovations were intended (Rothman, 1980; Thomas, 1984). Although it is similar to plot testing in social research, that which is tested is different. Trial use in D&D involves examination of the reliability of the innovation, the conditions under which it works, and whether it functions as it was intended to. As applied to organizations, trial use would be the provisional and contingent introduction of the innovation for purposes of pilot testing and obtaining necessary information concerning the adequacy of the innovation. There would not be the introduction of change on any long-term or ongoing basis unless earlier the innovation had been adequately tested developmentally, thus providing a basis for the developmental validity of the innovation (Thomas, 1985). The testing process may be characterized further as follows:

> Developmental testing is an appropriate concept for the process in trial use in which an innovation is systematically tested, revised, or redesigned. It is similar to performance testing in industrial and scientific research and development in that the focus is on the reliability of the innovation, the conditions under which it works, and whether it functions as intended. Developmental testing may yield such critical information as the appropriateness and feasibility of the innovation, whether the practitioner-researcher can carry out the intervention, how satisfactory the implementation is for the clientele involved, the adequacy of the innovation, aspects of the innovation that need to be redesigned, and whether enough replications of the innovation have been conducted. Considered more generally, developmental testing yields three principal types of outcomes, each of which is critical in the developmental process. These outcomes are (1) the redesign of innovations for which limitations have been discerned in developmental testing (2) the initial design of the components of the intervention occasioned by encountering problems in practice for which the existing intervention has been found to be inadequate, and (3) the replicated use of interventions that do not need to be revised when they are utilized in essentially the same way as they were on prior occasions. (Thomas, 1984, p. 53)

Developmental Practice

Trial use and developmental testing can be facilitated by conducting practice to provide service as well as to evolve and test innovations related to a given D&D objective.

> Developmental practice differs from conventional practice in that, in addition to the use of relevant practice methods, methods of design and development are followed cases and selected according to the criterion of developmental relevance, innovations are introduced and developmentally tested in practice, the outcomes of the testing are monitored in the context of a larger design-and-development process of which the particular practice endeavor is a part, and the outcomes of such practice include innovative interventions as well as possible gains in service. Developmental practice may be carried out individually, without

project or team affiliation, or with others functioning together in a coordinated effort. An important direction for further work is to evolve procedures to enhance the developmental gains that may be achieved in developmental practices. (Thomas, 1985, p. 54)

Although the above comments refer to direct practice with individuals and families, they apply equally to practice and management in human service organizations.

Evaluation of the innovation is vitally important but should not be undertaken until development has been completed. All too often, unfortunately, programs and other organizational innovations are evaluated before the steps of development have been completed, thus risking investment of resources in evaluating innovations that have been insufficiently developed and that accordingly may lack developmental validity.

THE MODEL DEVELOPMENTAL APPROACH

In the model developmental approach of Paine, Bellamy and Wilcox (1984), a model of human service is developed founded on prior basic and applied research, standardized for the clientele to which it applies, field tested and evaluated in settings to which it applies, and disseminated to relevant consumers. An example is the Specialized Training Program which is a structured employment model focuses on benchwork assembly tasks to provide community based vocational training and employment for adults with severe handicaps (Boles, Bellamy, Horner & Mark, 1984). As the authors indicate

. . . the model integrates the best available technology of training and behavior change with individualized programming, small business procedures, management advances, and established workshop practices to form a program blueprint that can be applied and followed in a variety of local service contexts. (Paine et al., 1984, p. 182)

Components of the Specialized Training Program Model are habilitation and skill training in the benchwork tasks, a commercial operation to sell the products made, management and finances, and information gathering and disseminating procedures to provide reliable data for program-related decisions. In the evaluation the program has been found to relate to many positive outcomes and has been disseminated to and implemented in may diverse sites.

Model development, social R&D and developmental research more generally are much stronger paradigms for D&D than are those of planned change and should be adopted for organizational D&D when appropriate and feasible. It is recognized, however, that it is not always possible to follow all aspects of the model development approach in organizations. Even so, this approach is itself and exemplar, and when all aspects of the approach cannot be implemented, relevant methods and techniques can be applied so that D&D can be carried out consistently with the model development approach. In so doing, the innovations thus generated should be more general, standardized, developmentally valid, and capable of wider dissemination than those that might be forthcoming from contemporary models of planned change.

THE D&D PERSPECTIVE

As should be evident in the above presentation, D&D contains within it a distinctive point of view regarding how problems in human service are to be conceived and may be resolved. Thus, in this perspective, organizational problems are viewed in terms of their potentialities for D&D, the needs for change are thought of as presenting possibilities for innovation, and the implementation of change is seen as an occasion when it might be suitable to use one or more of the contributions of D&D. As D&D matures, it is to be hoped that the D&D perspective will be adopted by more and more managers, practitioners, and researchers in human service and that the contributions of D&D are more widely used.

REFERENCES

Benn, C. *Attacking poverty through participation*. Melbourne, Australia: Preston Institute of Technology, 1981.
Blase, K., Fissen, D. & Phillips, E. Residential treatment for troubled children: Developing service delivery systems. In S.C. Paine, G.T. Bellamy & B.L. Wilcox (Eds.). *Human services that work: From innovation to standard practice*. Baltimore: Paul H. Brookes, 1984.
Boles, S.M., Bellamy, G.T., Horner, R.H. & Mark, D.M. Specialized training program: The structured employment model. In S.C. Paine, G.T. Bellamy & B.L. Wilcox (Eds.), *Human services that work: From innovation to standard practice*. Baltimore: Paul H. Brookes, 1984.
Eveland, J.D., Rogers, E.M. & Klipper, C.M. *The innovative process in public organizations: Some elements of a preliminary model*. Final Report, NSF Grant RDA75-17952. Ann Arbor: Department of Journalism, University of Michigan, 1977.
Galbraith, J.R. *Organizational design*. New York: Addison-Wesley, 1977.

Gerloff, E.A. *Organizational theory and design: A strategic approach to management*. New York: McGraw-Hill, 1985.

Hussain, K.M. *Development of information systems for education*. Englewood Cliffs, NJ: Prentice-Hall, Inc., 1973.

King, W.R. & Cleland, D.I. The design of management information systems: An information analysis approach. *Management Science*, 1975, *22*, 286-297.

Munson, F.C., & Pelz, D.C. *Innovating in organizations: A conceptual framework*. Ann Arbor, MI: Institute for Social Research, University of Michigan, 1982.

Mullen, E.J. The construction of personal models for effective practice: A method of utilizing research findings to guide social interventions. *Journal of Social Service Research*, 1978, *2*, 45-65.

Paine, S.C., Bellamy, G.T. & Wilcox, B.L. (Eds.). *Human services that work: From innovation to standard practice*. Baltimore: Paul H. Brookes, 1984.

Patti, R. Toward a paradigm of middle-management practice in social welfare programs. In R.C. Sarri & Y. Hasenfeld (Eds)., *The management of human services*. New York: Columbia University Press, 1978.

Poertner, J. & Rapp, C.A. Information system design in foster care. *Social Work*, 1980, *25*, 114-122.

Reid, W.J. The model development dissertation. *Journal of Social Service Research*, 1979, *3*, 215-225.

Rothman, J. *Social R&D: Research and development in the human services*. Englewood Cliffs, NJ: Prentice-Hall, 1980.

Rothman, J. *Planning and organizing for social change: Action principles from social science research*. New York: Columbia University Press, 1974.

Schaefer, M. *Designing and implementing procedures for health and human services*. Beverly Hills: Sage Publications, 1985.

Thomas, E.J. Research: The developmental approach. *Encyclopedia of Social Work*, New York: National Association of Social Workers. In press.

Thomas, E.J. The validity of design and development and related concepts in developmental research. *Social Work Research and Abstracts*, 1985, *21*, 50-55.

Thomas, E.J. *Designing interventions for the helping professions*. Beverly Hills: Sage Publications, 1984.

Thomas, E.J. Beyond knowledge utilization in generating human service technology. In D. Fanshel (Ed.), *Future of social research*. Washington, DC: National Association of Social Workers, 1980.

Thomas, E.J. Generating innovation and social work: The paradigm of developmental research. *Journal of Social Service Research*, 1978a, *2*, 95-115.

Thomas, E.J. Mousetraps, developmental research, and social work education. *Social Service Review*, 1978b, *52*, 469-483.

A Theory of Accountability
for the Human Services
and the Implications for Social
Program Design

Merlin A. Taber, PhD

This paper introduces a framework for the design and description of
social work programs. This framework differs from others chiefly in
that interpersonal helping activity is made the center of management
planning; budget, organization, personnel, and information systems
are all designed to support that activity. Careful design and implementation of programs can provide social work with a viable mechanism
of accountability to society. Social work has suffered unfairly from a
combination of its exalted goals, soft technology, and difficult target
groups. With a better codified and widely used program design technology appropriate to social work, we can be accountable for reasonable progress through human technologies, with clients who represent
major social underinvestment.

ACCOUNTABILITY AND PROGRAM DESIGN

The accountability problem of social work has been misconstrued.
In the past two decades, accountability has most often been viewed as
a requirement to satisfy our sponsors that we are doing what they
want. This formulation leads to concerns over effectiveness and cost,
which are useful but premature. This formulation also obscures the
fact that our sponsors may be more realistic than we are; they know we
have society's most difficult problems. Our sponsors expect earnest,
intelligent effort and visible amelioration, not striking results.
    A more useful notion of accountability that I have sought to develop

Dr. Taber is Professor, School of Social Work, University of Illinois, Urbana-Champaign,
Urbana, IL 61801.

is that accountability is a measurable property of systems of action, not a normative standard. A system is accountable to an actor if that actor has both the information and the mechanism to influence system outcomes. Thus, an annual report in four colors mailed to board members who cannot vote on policy is not accountability. A brochure on client rights, written in English and handed to a client who cannot read English, is not accountability. In short, my definition of accountability is one where all key actors are accountable to all others in terms of their joint action, where information required by actors is available to them in time, and where each person with responsibility for the joint outcome has appropriate power to intervene. The accountability problem for social work programs, in this view, stems from the inability of these programs to effectively communicate relevant information so that the various audiences can meet programmatic responsibilities.

This framework makes the program of social work central. The program of service calls on individuals' skills but is something more; it is a prescription for action by people with different roles and responsibilities. It does not belong to the worker; it lays out the means and norms for client-worker interactions which produce benefits. The program is not a creation of one professional and cannot be renegotiated away with some clients; it is developed and legitimated through a formal organization. Most important of all, the program is the means by which the worker commands societal resources to help the client. The program of social service, in contrast to many other programs, is played out between worker and client. But the client is helped by more than efforts of the worker alone. Through the program the larger society is not simply a silent partner or perplexed observer of interactions but a contributor of resources, approval, and structure for the helping process.

This paper sets out a framework for providing a description of program operations. It provides a basic frame of reference for this theory of accountability. It outlines what information needs to be conveyed and how it should be provided in order to assure a program's accountability.

MODEL FOR DESIGN OF ACCOUNTABLE PROGRAMS

The main terms and concepts for design of accountable programs are briefly summarized in Figure 1. Each concept however requires additional exposition which is supplied in the following pages.

Figure 1: A Summary of Terms and Concepts for Program Design

1. Problem Definition: A description of the personal and societal aspects of a problem and an analysis of factors contributing to a problem's existence or severity.

2. Program Goal: A statement of the benefits intended for society and individuals from the program, developed from the problem analysis and reflecting a normative theory of problem amelioration.

3. Target Population: A description of the target population and mechanisms for client targeting.

4. Program Objectives: A statement of specific measurable indexes of change, developed from program goals and client population description.

5. Program Hypothesis: A succinct statement of the social intervention and resulting effect.

6. Service Plan: A description of the interactions between clients and workers which create the proposed program benefits, using the following typology:

   a) Setting - The physical and social situation in which clients and workers relate to each other.

   b) Natural History - The usual process or typical episode of service from the client's viewpoint.

   c) Key Actors - Those whose collaboration in service transactions is necessary for effective helping.

   d) Legitimate Expectations - A description of reasonable expectations of client and worker for each other.

   e) Actual Behaviors - A description of typical behaviors performed by client and worker in the course of helping.

   f) Affective Involvements - A description of the emotional responses usual for client and worker in this helping program.

Problem Definition

The first step in this approach to developing goals and objectives is a problem definition. A clear description of the consequences of the problem for society and for individuals lays the groundwork for establishing goals and justifying the need for the problem's amelioration. The following typology illustrates the various bases for the judgment that a social problem exists. The typology is intended to assist social workers in specifying why a given situation is a problem and what needs to be changed.

Social work problems are problematic for society in one of the following respects:

— resource cost to society;
— threat to the health and safety of members of society;
— threat to societal values or social integration.

These situations or conditions also represent problems for individuals in one or more of the following ways:

— deprivation of a minimal standard of health and decency;
— threat of abuse or exploitation;
— barrier to full social participation.

Social welfare programs are enacted by society out of concern for continued integration of society and protection of dominant groups, not from concern for the individual victims of social disorganization. This claim is debatable, but in my opinion is largely true. To acknowledge its truth does not in any way deny social altruism or lessen social work's responsibility to make programs work for the most disadvantaged. This claim is stated, however, to underline the point that we owe society a clear justification of our program, in society's own terms. At the same time we owe clients a clear definition of how the program we propose will authentically relate to, and relieve, individual suffering and dislocation.

I have found it useful in analyzing a problem to ask: How is the problem maintained and perpetuated? What are the key factors which might be changed to interrupt a problematic situation? From this approach, goals for a social work program may be specified in a way which recognizes both the individual and societal aspects of the problem.

A useful problem definition need not be wordy or extensive. The main utility of the problem definition is to focus on exactly the conditions or the behaviors which are to be changed (or in some cases maintained) by a social work program. Above all, the problem definition needs to be stated in terms that are generally understandable. Use of legal, medical, or psychiatric terminology is not useful. To know that members of a target group for a social work program are "schizophrenic" is not helpful. On the other hand, if the goals of the program are based on the observation that most adults diagnosed as schizophrenic have difficulty in establishing and maintaining intimate social relations, then the problem definition should describe what these difficulties are.

Program Goals

What is the purpose of social work services? Social integration? More effective personality functioning and coping ability? Reduction in rates of deviant behavior? More widespread satisfaction and happiness? Surely most social workers would agree that all of these are goals for social work services. But all of these goals have the same difficulties. First they are vague; it is not clear what is meant by social integration or happiness, or deviant behavior. Second, the goals are very ambitious. Happiness and social integration have been the object of humankind's struggle for thousands of years. Why does the infant profession of social work, less than one hundred years old, believe it can achieve these long standing goals of mankind? A third difficulty with these statements is that they do not differentiate social work from other professions and disciplines. All of the human services strive for better social functioning and satisfaction of individuals in a smoothly functioning social order.

Vague goals make it difficult to manage a program. One can never be sure whether goals for the clientele are approaching or receding. Goals should provide a reference point for feedback and correction but vague goals do not do so. Overly ambitious goals may help obtain funding but ultimately they open social work programs to criticism; results are never good enough. This problem has been as acute for social workers, I believe, as for our sponsors. Social work seems unique among human service professions in its self-deprecation, which I think has come from exalted goal-setting.

My approach to setting goals seeks to set goals which are clear and meaningful for the society and for the professional and for the client, which are feasible; and which are based on an understanding of the problem processes.

Goal-setting is a cyclical process in which goals are considered in relation to problem definition and successively better definitions of the target population. The following standards for developing goals are recommended.

First, goals are for the client, not for the worker; goals need to specify desired outcomes for clients, not program activities. Second, goals must be realistic for the target group and the social work problem of interest. The fiscal, technological, ethical, and legal constraints surrounding social programs must be considered in setting goals. Third, goals need to be stated in terms generally understandable to most people. Professional jargon tends to confuse rather than enlighten programs' missions. Additional aids to goal setting include specifically mentioning the client population in the goal, writing goals in ways that the outcomes are observable and measurable, stating goals in terms of what will be accomplished rather than in terms of absence of something, and finally, deriving goals directly from the problem statement.

In short, it would be well if social work could desert its heritage of overpromising and underproducing. Legislators and the public are quite ready, I believe, to support social services which have reasonable goals for clearly disadvantaged groups. If social workers portray clearly what they expect to do — when, for how long, with whom, toward what modest goal — I believe that adequate support will be forthcoming.

Target Population

The target population is the people with whom the program can be effective. It is the group of people experiencing the problem in a way that justifies societal concern and also is a group which the professional believes can reach program goals.

Politics, according to one aphorism, always concerns the question "who benefits?" Social work programs by definition are socially sanctioned and social workers cannot substitute their own judgment for that of legislators and other elected officials in determining who should be served. Therefore, any program design must define carefully and fully who benefits.

Some simple terminology is useful for narrowing the definition of a target population. First it is important to define a *general population*. The general population is the geographical or demographic group (Californians, or teenage mothers, or frail elderly) among whom the problem is developed and maintained and hopefully ameliorated. The characteristics of that general population are important in determining the nature of a program. What is the age distribution? What are income levels? Are there unusual features in terms of minorities, sex distributions, or ethnic and religious groupings? How large is that population?

Among the general population there is a smaller number of persons who are particularly vulnerable to the problem of interest. This group may be called the *at-risk population*. For program design the key question is, how does the at-risk population differ from the general population? At this point a model for problem development is crucial; one needs to identify in terms of personal or social characteristics the nature of this at risk population as well as its size in relation to the general population.

The term *target population* introduces still another distinction. Not all persons at risk of the problem of interest will be targeted for a particular social work program. Size limitations, legal requirements, and considerations of time and distance, are examples of constraints which may eliminate subgroups of those suffering from, or exposed to, the problem. The most important factors for the program are those factors which determine ability to make effective use of the service. There is a tension between society's desire to help the most disabled and the professionals' desire to have capable clients; the only solution is careful delineation of factors in targeting. Again, the designation of a group having specific characteristics is most useful when accompanied by an estimate of numbers.

The concept of *client population* introduces still a fourth important distinction. Social work has a tradition of setting up programs to try to serve large problem groups; at best these programs are bellwethers and at worst they are tokens. We need to hold society responsible for programs of a scope to meet the problem, not just make a gesture. Further, we now know that worker discretion and organizational procedures can be more important than stated policy in selecting a caseload from a population. For example, if a mental health counseling service is not open in the evening, then the number of factory workers served will be low, regardless of how devoutly the counselors may wish to work with this target group. The client population is the group of individuals who will actually receive service. To describe and to estimate that population, one must indicate how intake decisions will be made.

Program Objectives

Program goals are invaluable for general orientation and planning but for specific feedback and correction program objectives are also needed. A program objective is an easily observable, measurable index of goal achievement. As with program goals, objectives must be formulated so they are outcome-oriented, clear, positive, and realistic. Ideally, each objective sets a single standard, such as a number or percentage that defines adequate performance. The most useful objectives are those which can be collected repeatedly, with minimal interruption of the service process. Objectives should not be thought of as showing success or failure; they are readings to indicate whether things seem to be moving in the right direction. The most useful objectives, then, are readily and repeatedly observable, yield a clearly understandable index value, have an unmistakable meaning as to goal achievement, and are widely disseminated.

It is assumed that reaching objectives is indicative of progress being made in reaching a program goal. In this regard the function of specific objectives for interpreting general goals is like the function of the hypothesis in relation to scientific theory. A testable hypothesis permits one to nullify a specific hypothesis implied by a broad theory and thus throw the entire theory into question. In exactly the same way, the adoption of specific measurable objectives makes it possible for program operators and social work professionals to determine the degree to which program goals are being reached, thus showing possible areas for program revision.

A Service Plan

By service plan is meant the prescription, or the scenario, for personal interactions between professionals and clients. Social work benefits are unusual in that they are created by the interaction between clients and workers. The individualized service process does not merely involve the delivery of the benefit; the process creates the benefit. Therefore, a clear description of the service plan is central to accountability for social work.

Setting

A setting for service is the typical situation, both physical and social, in which interaction takes place. The physical situation may be the counselor's office, a street corner for meetings with a juvenile gang, or the offices of community professionals for an advocacy service. Particular space requirements should be indicated clearly. Privacy is essential for some programs but openness and accessibility may be equally essential for services such as organization of tenants in a low-income neighborhood or a social activity program for the frail aged.

The social aspects of the service setting are equally as important as the physical aspects. How many people are usually present? What is the meaning of the location or the situation for different participants? Is it desirable that the setting be home ground of workers? Setting the stage for client-worker interaction may include definition of values, as much as it may include adjustment of the lights or closing of the door.

Natural History

The natural history of interactions is the overall pattern of interaction from the client's viewpoint. Pattern and not content of the interaction is wanted. Average length of calendar time for a service episode and deviations from the average are important. Phases may vary in intensity of interaction which might be very high in the beginning for example, and then gradually be reduced over a period of six to eight months.

It is usual to think of intake being followed by treatment and eventually by termination. If possible, it is helpful to individualize a particular program and discern the usual and minimal stages and time frames for effective service. Calendars or flow chart techniques can be used to advantage, but the important step is to conceptualize the changing nature of the helping relationship.

Key Actors

Social work services depend for their success on the client but also on a secondary cast of characters, or key actors. Here is where social work is different from psychotherapy; while psychotherapy focuses attention on the two persons in dialogue, social work always involves others. Effective social work programs produce changes in social functioning, and program design cannot pretend that worker and client are alone on a desert island.

In describing other key actors it is the role relationship (parent, closest friend, employer) and not the personal identity which is of interest. There is no general rule for determining which people in the social world of the client may be important. The criterion for determining which persons to identify is the question: Can the program service reach its objective without cooperation of this person?

In all program descriptions it is important not only to identify the "key actors" but to show the collaboration and behavior on their part which is essential for program success. In this way the program developer can determine personnel requirements, resource requirements, and service elements necessary to enlist, to neutralize, or to inform these other key actors.

Legitimate Expectations

The program description should indicate what reciprocal obligations are reasonable and normal in their relationship of worker or clients. In our society certain role behaviors are widely known and accepted. One learns how to act toward the doctor when one is the patient; how to be a parent toward a child; the behaviors usual for a student in relation to a teacher. We all master these roles and in addition have a keen understanding of what we can expect from the other person in these relationships. Without precise knowledge of legitimate expectations there will be breakdowns of communication and strong feelings of resentment at being let down.

The social work profession is maturing and becoming more open about its expectations. The social case worker in mental health expects the client to keep appointments and the client should expect the social worker counselor to keep their conversation private, at least outside the work situation. In programs for alcoholic drivers and for abusive parents the expectation of better client performance may be written down and enforced by the court. Recent methodologies of social work include the defining of legitimate expectations as a standard method. Task-oriented counseling makes the definition of immediate tasks or activities by each person a first part of counseling. Behavior modification techniques require identification of consequences attendant on certain types of behavior. Presumably, these positive or negative consequences are as clear in the mind of the client as the mind of the worker, and therefore define mutual expectations. If the "schedule" of consequences are known only to the worker then the procedure would not be social work, by my definition.

The particular value of identifying legitimate reciprocal obligations is that the worker and client roles are seen as mutual, interacting and reciprocal. The powers and duties that each person carries when acting toward the other becomes clear. Clear designation of these powers and duties is not an imposition on the client; the reverse is true, when powers and mutual duties are unclear the worker is not accountable to the client.

Actual Behaviors

In addition to the history or typical sequence of events and in addition to expectations or mutual responsibilities, it is vital that a program description show representative actual behaviors of both worker and client. Behavioral description is difficult. Still one can indicate certain patterns of communication, of conduct, and show typical actions.

Probably the use of selected examples is the most efficient means of indicating typical behavior. For example, the therapist in play therapy may physically restrain the child who is violent so that neither may be injured. The mentally retarded adult in a sheltered workshop will increasingly exhibit proper grooming, prompt reporting for work, and performance of assigned tasks. The group therapist with delinquent girls may shout and show anger in repudiating antisocial activities. The social worker with a rape victim will listen closely, will exhibit warm, supportive behavior, will be factual, and will not destroy evidence.

Affective Involvements

The motives and emotions of client and of worker for each other — affective involvements — may be crucial to the success of a service program and if so, should be clearly outlined. With some goals, for example, acceptance by terminal cancer patients of approaching death, or resolution of chronic guilt on the part of the mother of a developmentally disabled child, may be virtually impossible to achieve without deeply affecting experiences in the helping process. If this is the case, then the nature of the involvement and its usual course should be made clear.

I believe that the ideal of professional neutrality, coming to us from psychiatry and medicine, is highly dubious for social work. Social workers involve themselves in the life space of clients in a way which physicians do not. Social work services do in fact stimulate strong emotions. For program design, the point is to discern what kinds of responses are typical and to be expected and in some cases essential for effective service. Then make the necessary organization support and safeguards available for both worker and client, as a necessary part of the program and not as an afterthought.

CONCLUSION AND IMPLICATIONS

My theory of accountability is based on a philosophy of social work which emphasizes communication among all actors. Program design specifications are key accountability mechanisms. I believe that social work practice has been radically misperceived as an individualistic and personal helping activity. This misconception is understandable on the basis of our roots in religious and medically-oriented helping. The nursing, medical and social service professions (including social work) are rooted in a tradition of the capable helping the incapable.

Hospitals, almshouses, prisons and other social and health institutions share an aura of altruistic beneficence. As such one did not expect to be required to be accountable. The professional was viewed as responsible for having the right feelings, for trying hard, and for being kindly. Clients were expected to be cooperative and, perhaps, to be properly appreciative of help. Programs were justified by the good intentions and right feelings of the workers, not by how money was spent and what happened to the clients as a result of program activities. But good intentions are no longer enough to ensure public support. Our failure to develop a framework for coherent and intelligible descriptions of our programs has prevented us from gaining the continued public acceptance and support essential to help our clients.

In closing I would like to note a few ideas which I have found especially seminal in ten years of developing this framework. If the ideas are not new, then at least my working out of their implications may be new. First, the idea that social work helping involves three parties—client, helper, and society—rather than two parties. Second, the idea that social work benefits are created in the service process and cannot be designated clearly in advance. Third, the idea that social workers help clients through the program not solely through a relationship. Fourth, that clear targeting of our programs may be more important for accountability than clear goal-setting. Fifth, that social work has lost more than it has gained from overpromising.

Each of these ideas has important implications for our thinking about social work and about social administration as well. If benefits come from interaction, for example, much of our outcome research is flawed since it has ignored process in general and input from the participants in particular. Many of our management borrowings from business and industry may be dubious or even pernicious for good social work. If social work is always a three party activity, then is private practice of social work really social work? Probably not. I have found some clinically-oriented social workers to embrace these ideas, others to detest the implication that the worker is "only" a functionary. My own interpretation is that the capable social worker uses programs as a tool, but also fashions and reshapes tools as needed. And it is for the fashioning and reshaping of social work programs that I have found this frame of reference effective.

Maximizing Effectiveness Through Technological Complexity

Andrea Savage, PhD

A confluence of internal and external forces press managers and their organizations to increase routinization and narrow the scope or complexity of their service technologies. Increased routinization and decreased complexity have been favored by funding and regulatory agencies. The accountability requirements of these funding organizations and regulatory and accreditation bodies have promulgated standards for service accountability which tend to reward a program's most routine and "measurable" efforts at the expense of the more complex, less easily counted efforts.

In response to funding constraints human service managers may try to simplify their programs' technologies through specialization or to routinize their organizations' technologies in order to cut costs. Such simplification and routinization cuts staff recruitment, wage, and training costs by limiting the organization's use of multifaceted professional staff in favor of staff with more limited training and job functions. By pairing a consonant ideology with routinization managers may decrese task uncertainty, limit staff discretion and decrease the necessary intensity of supervision thereby reducing the costs of supervision. It becomes possible to utilize standard procedures, and more extensive rule-based control systems. As complexity decreases the costs of coordination, communication, and control also decrease.

Even clinical research has the unintended consequence of intensifying the simplification and routinization trend. The use of more measureable concepts of practice interventions and outcomes may inadvertently result in the devalueing of the complexity of clinical interchange.

In essence, it is common wisdom that the most routine technology will reduce uncertainty and yield optimal cost-effectiveness. The cen-

Dr. Savage is Assistant Professor, Hunter College School of Social Work, The City University of New York, 129 East 79th Street, New York, New York, NY 10021.

127

tral thesis of this paper, however, is that the effectiveness of a human service organization, in this study, opiate addiction treatment programs, is largely determined by the organization's capacity to match its technology to its clients' service needs. It is posited that this capacity to match clients' needs is dependent primarily on the size and complexity of its technological repertoire and its flexibility of use. Contrary to common wisdom, the routine or uniform implementation of its technology with clients, if the clients are varied, or have multiple or poorly understood problems, may in fact limit effectiveness and increase costs.

ORGANIZATION TECHNOLOGY: BRIEF REVIEW OF THE LITERATURE

Clinical research provides some assistance in the selection of effective technologies and in assessing clients' needs. The repertoire of tested, reliable, and effective clinical interventions is growing slowly. In opiate addiction treatment the effectiveness research has moved to medical-style clinical trials. The focus is on trying to isolate the impact of specific interventions often ignoring the treatment context in which the technique is being employed. Though an important step in knowledge building, such work may be ultimately less useful to managers than research which studies the interventions, the context in which they are applied and the constellation of other therapeutic interactions with clients.

The manager seeking knowledge to aid in accomplishing the fit of resource allocation, structure, and process to the requisites of technology will find that the logical source, the sociological literature on organization technology is a mosaic of diverse research and conceptual material reflecting a preoccupation with the issues of uncertainty reduction, routinization, and their structural correlates.

Much of the literature has centered on the relationship between organization technology and structure. Some work asserts that technology is a key determinant of organization structure (Woodward, 1958, 1965; Zwerman, 1970; Marsh & Mannari, 1981). Others conclude that size is a far more powerful predictor of structure (Hickson et al., 1969; Blau & Schoenherr, 1960). The diversity of definitions and operational measures of technology and of structure utilized in these studies may explain the conflicting results reported. It is also likely that the interaction of technology and structure is not a static occurrence but a dynamic process. At times in a program's development, structure determines technology while at other points technology and technological innovation become the source of structural adaptation. The dynamics of such a process are beyond the cross-sectional research methods generally employed to study these relationships.

Though industrial organizations (Marsh & Mannari, 1981) and human service organizations employ a multiplicity of individual technologies, in the past an organization's technology was usually defined as the single or dominant process or activity which the organization used to transform its raw materials. The early work on technology either ignored the existence of multiple technologies in one organization (Harvey, 1968; Rushing, 1968; Hickson et al., 1969), dropped organizations with multiple technologies from the study (Woodward, 1959) or developed scales for averaging several technologies (Khandwalla, 1974). Such approaches have been a source of distortion and overabstraction in the literature. Since each technology employed may be quite unique, an accurate view of a program's technology requires the examination of the whole repertoire of technologies rather than merely characterizing the organization in terms of a single dominant technology.

The components of technology most often identified are (1) the raw materials, (2) the operations or transformation processes, and (3) the knowledge of both the raw material and the processes. While different aspects of each component have been studied, those focusing on the degree of uncertainty are the most frequent: the stability, uniformity, and predictability of raw material (Perrow, 1965; Scott, 1972), task routineness (Hage & Aiken, 1969; Lynch, 1974; Perrow, 1967), and predictability (Comstock & Scott, 1977) of operations or task technology; the determinantness, efficacy and sufficiency of knowledge have also been noted (Hasenfeld & English, 1977; Lynch, 1974; Scott, 1972). Structural features which are associated with lowering costs such as lengthened span of supervisory control, increased formalization and standardization appear to be associated with technology which is routine, repetitive, and/or predictable. This suggests that reducing technological uncertainty and increasing routineness will permit concurrent structural shifts such as increased unit size, expansion of written procedures, greater dependence on rule centered control systems, and a decreased reliance on supervisor-supervisee face-to-face interaction. Such shifts can cut administrative costs.

There has been very little exploration of the relationship of technology and client transformation or outcome. This is a central concern of human service managers. However, the preoccupation with technology as a determinant of structure and with uncertainty reduction as well as the failure to examine the full range of technologies employed in an organization makes most previous approaches to technology of limited usefulness for the study of technology and client outcome.

CONCEPTUAL FRAMEWORK AND CENTRAL HYPOTHESIS

The central premise of the model of technology employed in this study is that all programs have a repertoire of service technologies which may be employed in varying combinations and sequences in order to transform clients. The concepts in this model are drawn from the product mix/task scope stream of literature on program technology (Dewar & Hage, 1978; Harvey, 1968), Perrow's work on task routineness (1970), and the client-organization relations literature (Rosengren & Lefton, 1970). These repertoires vary on several dimensions. The first key concept is *scope,* the number of different service technologies in the repertoire and in the areas of clients' lives and problems on which the technologies are to impact. A program with a narrow scope repertoire will have a small number of technologies targeted at only a few aspects of a client's life. Such a program might offer individual counseling focused on the client's drug use, dispension of methadone and physical examinations. By contrast, a high scope program might provide general counseling on drug taking, the dispension of methadone, physical examination, specialized counseling focused on intrapsychic difficulties, structural family therapy, various vocational services, child care services while parents are involved in program activities, legal and medical advocacy, and recreational activities. In essence, such a program has many different technologies which more comprehensively address the various aspects of the client's life.

The second key concept is that of *uniformity.* Programs may implement what Perrow might label "nonroutine" technologies in a highly uniform fashion. His notion of routineness rests on the organizational actor's perception of the frequency of exceptions and the analyzability of the task. The concept of uniformity refers to the extent of uniform or standardized use of service technologies with clients across the organization. This is an indicator of the extent to which programs implement similar patterns of service technologies for most of their clients or at the other extreme, choose unique combinations for each client based on an assessment of the particular needs of that client. The variables of *scope* and *uniformity* become the base for a typology of technology used to examine the relationship to technology and client outcome. As noted earlier, though multiple forces press organizations toward limited scope and increased uniformity it is expected that complexity, i.e., high scope, would be positively related to successful client transformation.

ORGANIZATIONS OF INTEREST: OPIATE ADDICTION TREATMENT PROGRAMS

The usual classification scheme for opiate addiction treatment programs is modality. The dominant types of addiction treatment programs are methadone programs and therapeutic communities. By 1976 an estimated 75,000 clients were being treated in methadone programs while an additional 15,000 clients resided in therapeutic communities (DeLeon & Beschner, 1977). Though very few systematic and comparative studies of these programs are available, it is possible to develop a general portrait of each modality type from case studies and program descriptions (Sugarman, 1974; DeLeon & Beschner, 1977, Weppner, 1983); crossmodality reports (Glasscote et al., 1972; Lieberman, 1972), effectiveness studies (Pin, Martin, & Walsh, 1976; Collier & Hijazi, 1974; Cuskey, 1979; DeLeon et al., 1979; Gearing, et al., 1974; Dole & Joseph, 1979; Sells & associates, 1976; Simpson & Sells, 1982), and federal manuals and funding guidelines. Neither of the program forms is monolithic, but the literature sometimes handles them as if all programs of each type are identical.

The residential drug free therapeutic community is the older form of treatment originating in 1958 with Synanon and followed by several other types of therapeutic communities within the next five years. These programs varied in their planned duration of treatment and in their connection to the existing human service network. The common thread among all therapeutic communities is their residential nature, their emphasis on self-help and the healing effects of the community, their extensive use of ex-addict staff, and their use of a standard, sequenced stage or phase model of treatment.

The use of methadone, a synthetic analgesic, as a central tool in addict rehabilitation began extensively in 1965. Initial experiments used methadone in conjunction with an initial, short inpatient stay followed by a long-term outpatient regime which included substantial services. By eliminating the hospital stay and limiting the other services, methadone treatment became an inexpensive alternative to the other modes of treatment. It was possible to serve the large numbers of addicts in need who could not be otherwise accommodated. By 1971,

1,300 licenses to use methadone in agency or hospital sponsored programs had been approved by Bureau of Narcotic and Dangerous Drugs. Because methadone was an investigational drug, federal authorities had substantial control in its utilization and influence in the programs employing it. The initial federal emphasis was on cost-effectiveness and volume. This resulted in the program model which is still considered typical: methadone dispension, initial physical examinations, regular periodic screening of client urine for the continued use of opiates, basic medical screening, and counseling. Despite this minimalistic model, a wide range of programs developed incorporating various mixes of service technologies. Some programs developed a service array which reflected the resources and interests of the mental health centers, hospitals and other types of parent or umbrella organizations with which they were affiliated.

There was a shift in the federal approach in the early 1970s, with a new emphasis on lower dose and shorter course methadone treatment paired with a modicum of ancillary services, particularly health and vocational services and a minimum of one half hour each week of counseling. Some have suggested that this thrust for more service did little to alter the preeminent minimal service model which still characterizes methadone programs (Attewell & Gerstein, 1976).

Because the therapeutic community is a residential program with a self-help focus, it is usually viewed as more intense than outpatient programs. It seems to involve itself in all facets of its clients' lives. By contrast, methadone programs are most often portrayed as minimal, highly routine, mass production programs providing little service beyond methadone maintenance while one might classify the therapeutic community as utilizing indeterminant or nonroutine technology. In fact, many therapeutic communities employ technologies which one might think of as being nonroutine in a highly uniform, almost ritualistic way with all clients, allowing little or no variability to match client needs.

Opiate addiction treatment programs provide an excellent model system for the study of human service technology, routinization and environmental interchanges because what is best known about these programs is their modality, in essence, technology. Environmental interchanges are particularly developed as such programs operate in environments in which regulatory and funding agencies are numerous, complex in requirements and quite demanding. The concept of technological repertoire has particular utility in addiction treatment programs. These programs usually combine a number of individual technologies of different degrees of determinantness, in variably rigid and flexible combinations and sequences. Rarely does a single service technology adequately characterize all the others.

METHODS

The work presented here employs a dataset originally gathered under the auspices of Women's Drug Research Project (WDR). The study was envisioned as an exploration of many aspects of treatment programs as organizations with particular emphasis on treatment of women clients. The design included two waves of data collection within a twelve month period (November 1976-1977) planned to maximize the volume, reliability and validity of the data obtained. Structured interview schedules were employed as the central data collection method in both waves. Program directors and managers were the primary organization respondents. In addition, in each wave field workers collected program documents for later perusal and utilized a structured outline for program observation and recording of field notes. Programs were generally receptive to providing copies of operating manuals, reports, newsletters, client data forms, and other material which provided cross validation of data provided in interviews and additional information on ideology and climate.

SAMPLE DESCRIPTION

A purposive sample of 24 programs from 7 cities covering most areas of the country except the Southwest was assembled. All 24 programs are (1) engaged in the treatment of addiction to heroin, to the exclusion of other drugs of abuse, (2) attempting to transform addicted persons directly from illegal drug use to abstinence, and (3) serving either women only (single sex program) or both men and women (co-sex program). Five programs are single sex programs, 4 of these are NIDA funded, special women's demonstration programs.

The sample programs were selected from a group of programs cooperating with other studies conducted by WDR and a study based at Rutgers University in Newark, the Dynamics of Therapeutic Communities Study.

The patchwork assembly and the size of the sample limits the external validity and generalizability of the findings. It is clearly adequate to the exploratory goals of this study. It is likely that more stable and environmentally competent programs are overrepresented and programs more marginal in survival status or in capacity or willingness to interact with professionals are probably underrepresented in the sample.

Twelve of the 24 programs in the sample are drug free residential therapeutic communities. The remaining 12 are outpatient methadone employing programs. The sample programs ranged in age from less than 1 year to 9 years of operation, with an overall mean of 4.46 years. Though 2 of the programs were less than 1 year old, the remainder were old enough to suggest that patterns of interest to this study would have been relatively stabilized at the time of data collection. Several measures of size were computed. Methadone programs were larger on all measures than therapeutic communities. This was true of static capacity, the number of clients which a program is designed to serve at any one point in time. Methadone programs report a range from 60 to 280 clients, with a mean static capacity of 177 while therapeutic communities report a range of 12 to 100 clients with a mean static capacity of 57.

The mean number of staff for methadone programs is 18.8 and the mean number for therapeutic communities is 13.3. However the ranges for each modality are quite similar. Methadone programs report a range of from 8 to 32 positions and therapeutic communities a range of from 5 to 33 positions. In view of the far larger number of clients served in methadone programs it is clear that the staff to client ratio in them is less favorable than in therapeutic communities.

FINDINGS

A typology of program technology was empirically derived using the variables of composite scope, a measure of size and complexity of the technological repertoire of the program, the actual uniformity of application of service technologies (see Savage-Abramovitz, 1985 for index construction details). Table 1 presents the results.

Type 1 programs are those which pair low scope with low uniformity of service. Their technology can be characterized as *Limited.* As indicated by the scope level, the age and complexity of service technologies is minimal. The level of actual uniformity suggests that not all clients are subjected even to the minimal scope of transformation available.

Type 2 programs are those which can be characterized as having *Specialized* technology. Such programs specialize in a few key biographical areas such as intrapsychic adjustment or parenting, hence

TABLE 1

Basic Typology of Program Technology

ACTUAL UNIFORMITY	COMPOSITE SCOPE	
	Low	High
Low	(1)	(3)
	LIMITED	INDIVIDUALIZED
	(2)	(4)
High	SPECIALIZED	ENCOMPASSING

their low scope and they expose all or most of their clients to these specialized service technologies in a uniform fashion.

Type 3 programs, labeled as *Individualized,* are programs which offer a large scope or menu of service technologies paired with an individualized approach to clients, as indicated by the low uniformity level. The classic social work approach to clients, "starting where the client is" and assessing individual client needs is most likely found in this program type.

Type 4 programs, called here *Encompassing,* are those programs with scopes covering large areas of their clients' biographies to which clients are uniformly exposed. Such programs envelop their clients completely.

Table 2 presents the classification of the sample programs and the breakdown of each cell by modality.

The two extreme cells of the typology are modality specific, that is the Limited technology programs are all methadone programs and the Encompassing technology programs are all therapeutic communities. These results are very consistent with the match of the type with the stereotypes of the respective modalities. The model methadone program is limited in scope, providing chiefly pharmacological treatment in a medical model emphasizing some degree of individual diagnosis.

TABLE 2

Type of Program Technology by Program Modality

Technology Type	Modality		
	Total	Methadone Programs	Therapeutic Communities
	n=24	n=12	n=12
Limited	7(29.2%)	7(58.3%)	0
Specialized	6(25%)	3(25%)	3(25%)
Individualized	5(20.8%)	2(16.7%)	3(25%)
Encompassing	6(25%)	0	6(50%)

The model therapeutic community is an all-embracing environment which attempts to transform all clients in the same fashion. The remaining methadone programs and therapeutic communities are about evenly divided between the Specialized and Individualized types. These 11 programs are among programs identified as deviating from the typical modality profiles. The typology appears to provide a more sensitive classificatory scheme for programs than the categorization by modality per se.

TECHNOLOGY, STRUCTURE, AND ENVIRONMENTAL FORCES

As noted earlier a number of studies have established a link between structure and technology (Comstock & Scott, 1977; Dewar & Hage, 1978; Hage & Aikern, 1969; Marsh & Mannari, 1981; Woodward, 1958, 1965; Zwerman, 1970). Dewar and Hage (1978) established a link between task (technological) scope and resource and structural complexity. They posited that the more ambitious and complex the planned tasks of an organization (the greater its task scope) the more specialized its staff and complex its structure. As anticipated they found that increased technological scope was related to greater diversity of job titles (an indicator of staff specialization), increased horizontal differentiation, i.e., greater numbers of distinct department with specialized functions within the organization and greater professionalization.

Similar measures of horizontal differentiation, occupational diversity and professionalization were employed in this study with an additional measure: the proportion of total staff in the generic title of "counselor" with generalist rather than specialized functions. It was reasoned that organizations with greater diversity of job titles paired with smaller portions of staff in generic counselor positions could be viewed as more structurally complex and specialized than those with less occupational diversity and a large segment of staff in generic counseling positions.

Table 3 displays the mean values for each measure by technology type. Though horizontal differentiation (number of departments) did not appear to be related to scope, the remaining measures are positively related to scope among the Limited, Specialized and Individualized program types. In comparison with the high scope Individualized programs, Limited and Specialized programs, the low scope types, report less diversity of job titles, twice as large proportions of staff in generic counselor roles and notably smaller proportions of staff who are professionals. Individualized programs report the highest level of

TABLE 3

Measures of Complexity by Type of Technology

(Mean Values)

Measure	Technology Type			
	Limited	Specialized	Individualized	Encompassing
* of Departments	3.14	4.0	3.7	4.16
* Diverse Job Titles	1.7	1.83	3.2	**
%Generic Counselors	36.9	32.1	16.4	47.6
% Professional	26.9	30.7	43.9	19.2

**INSUFFICIENT NUMBER OF PROGRAMS REPORTING ANY SPECIALIZED TITLES TO COMPUTE MEAN

occupational diversity and professionalization and the lowest presence of generic counselors among all program types.

The apparent absence of comparable complexity in Encompassing programs is inconsistent with the pattern in the data for the other program types but quite consistent with the strong self-help, anti-professional ideology characteristic of some of the classic therapeutic communities. All of these programs are therapeutic communities. Less than 20% of the staff, on the average, possess more than a bachelors degree while 52.6% on average, possess no more than a high school diploma. Nearly 50% of the staff positions, on the average, are generic counselor positions and in all but two of these programs no specialization of position was reported at all.

Addiction treatment programs are excellent illustrations of the significance of environmental forces on technological choice and on organization structure. These programs are responsible to five regulatory agencies on the average with a range of three to eight. More than 60% of these agencies were rated as having extensive to very extensive reporting requirements. In addition, these programs are dependent on an average of more than five funding sources with one program dependent on 16 separate sources of funds. Each source requires a degree of programmatic interaction and energy and, to varying degree, compliance with required service, staffing pattern, and accountability systems.

Both the technological repertoires and staffing patterns of these programs bear the imprint of environmental forces. No program reports less than the minimum technologies required by the National Institute on Drug Abuse, Food and Drug Administration, and Drug Enforcement Administration (at the time of data collection the Bureau of Narcotic and Dangerous Drugs). It is not possible to prove that this match is the outcome of regulation but this seems quite likely. A number of the Limited programs provide no more than the minimum FDA requirements, one half hour per week of counseling, a medical examination, medical screening and access through referral or direct service to vocational assistance and additional medical care.

The staffing patterns reflect the general regulatory standards for vocational services. Eight programs report specialized vocational staff positions such as job counselor or vocational counselor. Despite the presence of specialized vocational staff none of these programs offered extensive vocational services. The presence of the job title makes these organizations isomorphic with the institutional environment (Rowan, 1982); they appear to fulfill staffing and service requirements and this provides protection from further environmental scrutiny. This pattern is present with respect to medical staff as well. The structure and resources appear consonant with environmental standards but are not necessarily indicators of the services actually provided.

TECHNOLOGY AND EFFECTIVENESS

It was speculated that high scope and low uniformity programs, the Individualized type, would be the most successful in fitting clients needs and maximizing their progress. It seemed likely that Encompassing programs might also yield positive outcome because of their high scope. Positive outcome in Specialized programs was expected to be a function of the screening and pre-entry matching of client needs with program specializations. Since these programs paired low scope with high uniformity the best possible outcomes would likely be achieved by screening out those clients who were not well fitted for the specialized focus of the programs. For example, one of the special demonstration programs specializes in services in child, family, and health areas to the nearly complete exclusion of vocational concerns. While it may be successful in assisting women with a means of support, the absence of vocational services will make it of limited assistance for many women with insecure sources of income. In view of the well-documented multiple needs of women, positive outcome for them in Limited programs was felt unlikely. It is possible that Limited programs may be helpful to very well functioning clients whose only need is for heroin replacement.

An aggregate measures of graduation is used as a crude measure of program effectiveness Table 4 shows the relationship of program technology and graduation rates.

Examination of the rates of successful program completion demonstrate the woefully low rates of client progress, i.e., "success" in all of these programs. Only three programs report more than 21% of clients are successful. The data shows that client progress as measured by successful program completion is significantly related to the typology of program technology. (The relationship attains significance at the .01 level.) Greater levels of scope of technology are related to more favorable client progress. Encompassing programs report a mean percent of women graduating of 14.22% that is double the graduating rate in the Individualized programs, the next highest average percentage of successful completions. This confirms the hypothesis that in-

TABLE 4

Women Who Successfully Completed Treatment as a Percentage of Women
Clients Served by the Program During the Year by Type of Program
Technology

Type of Program Technology

% of Women Served Who Successfully Completed Program	Limited n=7	Specialized n=6	Individualized n=5	Encompassing n=6
none	0	3(50%)	2(40%)	0
less than 5%	5(71.4%)	1(16.7%)	1(20%)	0
6-10%	1(14.3%)	1(16.7%)	1(20%)	1(16.7%)
11-20%	0	0	0	3(50%)
21% +	1(14.3%)	0	1(20%)	0
Missing data	0	1(16.7%)	0	2(33.3%)
Range	1%-24.4%	0-10.8%	0-22.6%	9.8%-19.2%
Mean	6.8%	3.08%	7.28%	14.22%

creasing complexity of a program's technology will, under certain
conditions, increase program effectiveness. The apparent low success
achieved in Specialized programs may point to the folly of uniformly
employing a simple or specialized technology without substantial client screening and when such technologies have not as yet been proven
to be effective. Programs with high uniformity when paired with broad
scope, i.e., complex technology may be successful because the broad
spectrum of service technologies increases the probability that some of
the technologies will be successful with all of the clients. The wholesale move to specialization and routineness is contraindicated by this
data.

For several reasons caution must be exercised interpreting this data.
First, these are programmatic reports of their own success and even
though based on statistical information, they are likely to be subject to
some distortion. Second, missing data cases might easily shift the pattern of the relationship obtained. Despite these concerns, the data support the notion that greater program scope will yield better client out-

come. Clearly, more precise data on the treatment technologies implemented with specific clients and their treatment careers would provide much stronger support for this finding.

DISCUSSION AND IMPLICATIONS

The results of this exploratory study support the presence of a linkage between structure, resources, and technology. They also demonstrate the extreme interpretation of the opiate addiction treatment program by its environment. Of most importance, this data support the view that when clients' needs are diverse or poorly understood the scope of a program's technological repertoire will be positively related to successful client outcome, and important indicator of programmatic effectiveness. A narrow scope technological repertoire paired with uniformity will be effective only when technologies with proven effectiveness are employed and reliable instruments and processes for screening are available to match clients to the organization's technology. Such technologies and instruments are not yet available for opiate addiction programs.

Though the study is exploratory, several suggestions for managerial actions emerge. First, managers would do well to invest in program evaluation and clinical research as a means to develop a repertoire of service technologies with proven effectiveness. Such research efforts must not only assess the impact of any one technology but rather examine the impact of various technological mixes on client progress. Second, in the same vein, managers must encourage the development of effective and reliable intake and assessment tools. The availability of such tools would enable programs to improve their effectiveness by enhancing their capacity to match clients to technologies without the expansion of the program's technological set. Third, managers have to develop accountability mechanisms which go beyond the count of the simplest, most easily measurable program efforts. Instead, internal accountability approaches must document the very complex range of program interactions with clients. This step is crucial in an effort to influence funding and regulatory accountability requirements. Fourth, managers must resist the temptations to implement industrial, mass production approaches to human services. The narrowing and routinizing of organizational technology are not associated with positive outcome, particularly when the clients are not well understood, and when proven technologies are not available. The routinization and simplification of technological repertoire will limit the program's capacity to adhere to the social work principle of "starting where the client is" and will create unacceptable costs for the organizations, its workers, and its clients.

REFERENCES

Attewell, P. & Gerstein, D. F. Government police and local practice. *American Sociological Review*, 1979, *44*, 311-327.

Blau, P. M. & Schoenherr, R. A. *The Structure of organizations.* New York: Basic Books. 1971.

Collier, W. V. & Hijazi, Y. A. A follow up study of former residents of a therapeutic community. *International Journal of the Addictions*, 1974, *9*, 805-826.

Comstock, D. E. & Scott, W. R. Technology and the structure of subunits: Distinguishing individual and work group effects. *Administrative Science Quarterly*, 1977, *22*, 177-201.

Cuskey, W. R. et al. *Specialized therapeutic community for female addicts.* Washington, DC: National Institute on Drug Abuse, 1979.

DeLeon, G. et al. Therapeutic community dropouts: Criminal behavior five years after treatment. *American Journal of Drug/Alcohol Abuse*, 1979, *6*, 3, 253-271.

DeLeon, G. & Beschner, G. M. *The therapeutic community.* Washington, DC: National Institute on Drug Abuse, 1977.

Dewar, R. & Hage, J. Size, technology, complexity and structural differentiation: Towards a theoretical synthesis. *Administrative Science Quarterly*, 1978, *23*, 111-135.

Dole, V. P. & Herman J. *The long-term consequences of methadone maintenance treatment.* New York: Rockefeller University and the Community Treatment Foundation. Final Report under National Institute of Drug Abuse Contract 5 H81 DA 01778-02, December 1979.

Dole, V. P. & Nyswander, M. E. A medical treatment for diacetyl morphine heroin addiction: A clinical trial with methadone hydrochloride. *Journal of the American Medical Association*, 1965, *19*, 80-85.

Fabricant, M. The industrialization of social work practice. *Social Work*, 1985, *30*, 389-395.

Federal Register. *Methadone, 27*, 242: 26790-26807.

Gearing, F. R. Methadone maintenance treatment: 5 years later—where are they now? *American Journal of Public Health Supplement*, 1974, *64*, 44-50.

Glasscote, R. & Sussex, J. M. The treatment of drug abuse. Joint Information Service of American Psychiatric Association, National Association for Mental Health, Washington, DC, 1972.

Hage, J. & Aiken, M. Routine technology, social structure and organizational goals. *Administrative Science Quarterly*, 1969, *14*, 366-375.

Harvey, E. Technology and structures of organizations. *American Sociological Review*, 1968, *33*, 247-259.

Hasenfeld, Y. & English, R. A. (Eds.). *Human service organizations.* Ann Arbor: University of Michigan Press, 1974.

Hickson, D. J. et al. Operations technology and organization structure: An empirical reappraisal *Administrative Science Quarterly*, 1969, *14*, 378-397.

Lefton, M. & Rosengren, W. Organizations and clients: Lateral and longitudinal dimensions. *American Sociological Review*, 1966, *31*, 802-810.

Lieberman, L. Current trends in the rehabilitation of narcotics addicts. *Social Work*, 1967, *12*, 53-59.

Lynch, B. P. An empirical assessment of Perrow's technology construct. *Administrative Science Quarterly*, 1974, *19*, 338-356.

Marsh, R. M. & Mannari, H. Technology and size as determinants of the organizational structure of Japanese factories. *Administrative Science Quarterly*, 1981, *26*, 33-57.

Patti, R. Managing for service effectiveness in social welfare. Paper presented at the NASW Symposium, Chicago, November 1985.

Perrow, C. A framework for the comparative analysis of organizations. *American Sociological Review*, 1967, *32*, 194-208.

Perrow, C. Hospitals: Technology, structure and goals. In J. March (Ed.), *Handbook of organizations*. Chicago: Rand McNally, 1965.

Perrow, C. *Organizational analysis: A sociological view*. Belmont, CA: Wadsworth Publishing, 1970.

Pin, E. J., Martin, M. M. & Walsh, J. F. A follow-up study of 300 clients of a drug free narcotics treatment program in New York City. *American Journal of Drug and Alcohol Abuse*, 1976, *3*, 397-407.

Rosengren, W. R. & Lefton, M. (Eds.). *Organizations and clients*. Columbus, OH: Charles E. Merrill, 1970.

Rushing, W. A. Hardness of material as related to division of labor in manufacturing industries. *Administrative Science Quarterly*, 1968, *13*, 227-245.

Savage-Abramovitz, A. Opiate addiction treatment organizations. Doctoral dissertation, University of Michigan, 1985.

Scott, W. R. Professionals in hospitals: Technology and the organization of work. In B. S. Georgopoulos (Ed.), *Organization research on health institutions*. Ann Arbor: Institute for Social Research, 1972.

Sells, S. B. & Simpson, D. D. *Effectiveness of drug abuse treatment*. Cambridge, MA: Ballinger, 1976.

Simpson, D. D. *Evaluation of drug abuse treatment effectiveness*. Washington, DC: National Institute on Drug Abuse Treatment, Research and Assessment Branch, 1982.

Special Action Office for Drug Abuse Prevention. *Residential drug free manual*. Washington, DC: Office of the President, October, 1974.

Sugarman, B. *Daytop village*. New York: Holt, Rhinehart and Winston, 1974.

Weppner, R. S. *The untherapeutic community*. Lincoln: University of Nebraska Press, 1983.

Woodward, J. *Management and technology*. Problems of progress in industry. Series #3. London: Her Majesty's Stationery Office, 1958.

Woodward, J. *Industrial Organization: Theory and practice*. London: Oxford University Press, 1965.

Zwerman, W. L. *New perspectives on organizational theory*. Westport, CT: Greenwood Press, 1970.

SECTION FOUR:
MANAGING PEOPLE

Introduction

Service effectiveness is a direct outcome of quality interaction between people — the client and the worker. As such, the ability of social work administrators to manage people in ways that enhance this human interactional process is critical to organizational performance.

Reframing traditional approaches to personnel management, some of which are borrowed from the private business sector, is a necessary step to creating organizations that support and enhance, rather than hinder, client-worker interaction. From this perspective of service effectiveness, traditional views of workers as components of a technical production system typified by rigid hierarchies and excessive control need to give way to management based on social work values and ethics. From a social work perspective, creating work environments that promote service effectiveness involves designing organizations in which workers are treated as assets, and organizations become learning environments nurturing the development of clients and workers alike.

Drawing on previous scholarship, Myron E. Weiner addresses the issue of linking worker performance to client outcomes through identifying actions that enhance both job satisfaction and client change. Asserting that the act of blending organizational goals with workers' personal goals is paramount to managing people effectively, the author links four core elements in this process — job design, staff development, rewards and incentives, and performance evaluation.

145

The second paper in this section outlines concrete strategies for managers to use in redesigning social service organizations according to the profession's value base. Drawing on considerable research regarding quality of work life (QWL) projects from the private sector, Elizabeth A. Gowdy presents nine primary interventions for transforming human service organizations into more humane work environments for both clients and workers. The author provides illustrations of applying QWL change strategies in a variety of social work practice settings.

Managing People for Enhanced Performance

Myron E. Weiner, MGA

THESIS

This paper focuses on linking worker performance (job satisfaction) with organizational performance (client outcomes). It is a classic human services management issue: Workers complain that managers are only interested in productivity and efficiency; managers complain that workers ignore the problem created by limited resources, which reduce effectiveness in achieving client change. The process of blending worker performance with organizational performance is a very delicate one. On the one hand, it holds the key for mutual enhancement of organizational performance measured in terms of effectiveness (client outcomes) and staff morale (work satisfaction). But on the other hand, it has the potential for an ever present conflict in human services organizations between workers oriented toward personal-professional goals and managers oriented toward organizational goals. The human services manager consistently has to deal simultaneously with a large number of equally viable, but opposing, value tensions. This is very apparent in managing people when it is necessary to blend and link two sets of goals that are not necessarily congruent: organizational performance goals and the worker's personal and performance goals.

Organizational goals are articulated in a way that they can be measured in terms of such criteria as:

- greater effectiveness of services;
- increased productivity;
- expanded acquisition of resources;
- increased staff morale;
- greater staff efficiency.

Mr. Weiner is Professor, School of Social Work, University of Connecticut, Greater Hartford Campus, West Hartford, CT 06117.

147

Employees' personal and professional goals are measured in such terms as:

— extrinsic rewards from their work;
— intrinsic rewards from that work;
— more effective impact of services on clients;
— challenging and growth enhancing work;
— greater autonomy and self-determination in shaping work.

One can quickly present the thesis that the primary talent for managing people in human services organizations is skill in *blending and linking* organizational with personal/professional goals (see Figure 1). In its most simplified form, such a set of skills requires:

1. clearly establishing organizational performance goals and communicating them to all employees;
2. ascertaining employees' personal and professional goals and providing opportunities to continuously acquire updated information on such goals;
3. using every opportunity and method possible to blend and link these two sets of goals.

Figure 1.

BLENDING: The Critical People Management Skill

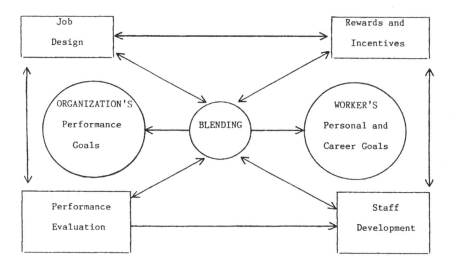

These coincide with the "Congruence Hypothesis" of organization behavior. Nadler and Tushman (1983) define several different types of congruence or fits necessary for effective organizational functioning:

- individual-organization: to what extent individual needs are met by organizational arrangements;
- individual-task: to what extent the needs of individuals are met by the task; to what extent individuals have skills to meet task requirements;
- individual-organization: to what extent individual needs are met by the organization;
- task-organization: whether organizational arrangements are adequate to meet the demands of the task.

BASIC PEOPLE MANAGEMENT

What serves to support and strengthen the "blending" role-conception of people managers is the fact that the job serves to link the individual and the organization. This is the starting point for our discussion of people management skills. J.D. Thompson (1967) indicates that the individual-organization linkage through the "job" is the basis for the "inducements/contribution" theory of Barnard (1938), Simon (1957), and March and Simon (1958). This theory asserts that the individual organization linkage is based on a formal or informal inducements/contributions contract. This type of contract sets into motion developmental processes in which individuals invest energy and effort in developing careers, and organizations try to influence the development of individuals. "When there is a convergence between the individual's career goals and the organization's development plans, an effective integration of the individual and the organization can take place" (Porter, Lawler & Hackman, 1975, p. 190). These processes are the basis for four core elements of people management skills: job design, rewards and incentives, staff development, and performance evaluation (see Figure 1.) While these four cornerstones to personnel management are generally understood by those involved in human services management, I will briefly summarize current thinking on each.

JOB DESIGN

The design of jobs, for individuals and for groups, has received a great deal of attention in recent years, concentrating heavily on concepts and techniques of job enlargement, enrichment and rotation, and work design in general (Hackman & Suttle, 1977; Abels & Murphy, 1981: Lewis & Lewis, 1983; Naylor, Pritchard & Iigen, 1980; Porter, et al., 1975; Hackman, Lawler & Porter, 1983). Hackman and Suttle (1977) suggest five principles for enriching jobs: forming natural work units; combining tasks; establishing client relationships; vertical loading (giving employees some responsibilities and controls generally reserved for other managers); and opening feedback channels (pp. 136-142). The principle dealing with direct relationships between worker and clients is particularly important for a performance model since it increases opportunities for direct praise or criticism from clients on work outputs as well as increasing employees' skill variety and autonomy. But job enrichment is complex and subtle, and not without critics, Fein (1983) notes that "the simple truth is that there are no data which show that restructuring and enriching jobs will raise the will to work. . . . The intrinsic nature of the work is only one fact among many that affect worker satisfaction" (p. 276).

Traditionally, jobs were analyzed and designed to maximize organizational productivity and effectiveness and the person/organization blending was approached by adapting people to jobs. Currently, however, there is consensus that optimizing individual-organization relationships is a mutual effort: adapting jobs to people as much as adapting people to jobs.

While there are several new suggested approaches to worker behavior and job design, Hackman and Oldham (1980) have a model of particular importance. Very simply stated, the Hackman-Oldham model indicates that organizational and worker outcomes are dependent upon "Critical Psychological States" which can be shaped in turn, by "Core Job Characteristics." These are modified by three sets of variables that take into account for differences among people (see Figure 2).

The "Final Criteria of Work Group Effectiveness" (Hackman & Oldham, 1980) are identified as follows:

—output of the group meets and exceeds organizational standards of quantity and quality;
—members' needs are more satisfied than frustrated by the group experience;

— the capability of members to work together on subsequent group tasks is maintained or enhanced. (p. 170)

In effect, not only is it important for human services managers to link worker outcomes with organizational-client outcomes, but also to create a process by which linking itself is an outcome.

Figure 2.

Job Characteristics Model

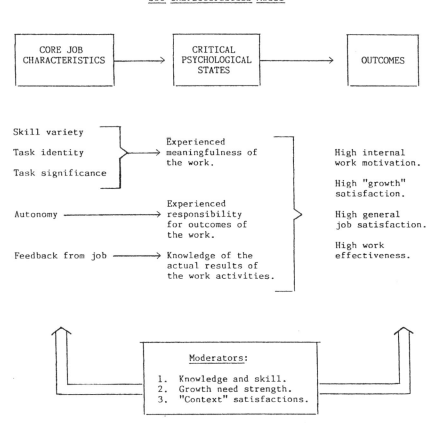

SOURCE: Figure 4.6, Work redesign. J.R. Hackman & G.R. Oldham.

REWARDS AND INCENTIVES

Currently, research suggests that in organizational settings, workers' incentives and rewards (outcomes) are based on "Expectancy Theory" defined by Davis (1972) as:

A person's motivation toward an action at a particular time is determined by the anticipated values of all the outcomes (positive and negative) of the action, multiplied by the strength of a person's expectation that the action will lead to the outcome sought. (p. 60)

Nadler and Lawler (1983) view the following concepts as basic to expectancy theory:

— Performance-Outcome Expectancy: the individual believes that if he or she behaves in a certain way, he or she will get certain things;
— Valance: Each outcome has a valance (value, worth, attractiveness) to a specific individual. Outcomes have different valances for different individuals;
— Effort-Performance Expectancy: Each behavior has associated with it, in the individual's mind, a certain expectancy or probability of success. (pp. 67-78)

These concepts form the basis for design of pay, reward, and incentive systems. The supervisor's role, thus, becomes one of defining clear goals, setting clear reward expectancies and providing the right reward for different people, both organizational rewards and personal rewards dealing with recognition, approval, and support. Lawler (1973, 1977) has undertaken a great amount of research dealing with worker satisfaction and reward system, which deserve more examination for our purposes; for as he notes: "Tying rewards to performance contributes to motivation. It can also contribute to satisfaction because people only feel equitably treated when rewards are based on their contributions, one of the most important of which is job performance" (1977, p. 173). Figure 3 provides Lawler's overview of reward system requirements.

There are a number of new techniques of rewards and incentives which are important for people management. Two deserve noting in passing, namely incentive pay and flexible (cafeteria) benefits.

Incentive pay, in the form of performance contracts, has become an increasing phenomenon for managers in public organizations and as

Figure 3.

Overview of Reward System Requirements

Quality of Work Life

---

a. Reward Level	A reward level high enough to satisfy the basic needs of individuals.
b. External Equity	Rewards equal to or greater than those in other organizations.
c. Internal Equity	A distribution of rewards that is seen as fair by members.
d. Individuality	Provision of rewards that fit the needs of individuals.

Organizational Effectiveness

---

a. Membership	High overall satisfaction, external equity, and higher reward level for better performers.
b. Absenteeism	Important rewards related to actually coming to work (high job satisfaction).
c. Performance Motivation	Important rewards perceived to be related to performance.
d. Organization Structure	Reward distribution pattern than fits the management style and organization structure.

---

such has affected human services managers indirectly. But, for the most part, incentive pay is rarely if ever found in human services organizations. Recently, however, some practitioners are experimenting with the setting of productivity and client outcome measures and providing workers with incentive pay if these measures are met or exceeded (Queisser, 1985). Among other factors, the pressure for this flows out of the changing human services funding patterns. In the Holyoke-Chicopee (Massachusetts) Community Health Inc., the slack resources accumulated from increased worker productivity is paid to the workers in the form of "incentive-rewards," with the surplus channeled to support services for clients who do not qualify for third-party of public agency support. This new approach warrants sufficient experimentation to assess whether or not it meets the criteria set forth by the performance model.

On the other hand, what has become increasingly an acceptable practice in people management skills is the development of "flexible" or "cafeteria" employee benefit systems (Milkovich & Glueck, 1985) in which workers can select the specific benefits they wish to have depending on their specific needs at any one time (e.g., day care support for workers with infants; long-term care support for employees with older parents who need care). This marks the beginning of an approach to people management which ultimately will see personal systems individualized for each employee. It is not unlike efforts to provide individualized service packages for clients and flows out of the flexible-systems approach to the production of goods and services which were first designed and implemented in the late 1940s by the automobile industry (Gannon, 1982). With the rapid spread of the electronic technologies worldwide, we have the ability to individualize societal institutional services, people management systems included. The speed of such spread is dependent upon overcoming built in resistance in current institutional patterns, including those within our own professional and academic settings.

STAFF DEVELOPMENT

Sarason (1972) has noted that creating an environment in which workers continue to grow personally and professionally is in the long run the most important approach to the mutual enhancement of client-oriented organization outcomes and worker satisfaction. From this perspective, staff development and training is a subset of human development.

Staff development can be viewed broadly as career development of more specifically as training and professional development.

> The fundamental purpose of management is to be able to predict and control human behavior in pursuit of organizational goals. Staff development programs are vital to meeting that purpose. The major function of the staff development manager's role is to ensure that training resources are used to enhance the agency's mission and its staff's capabilities. (Austin, Brannon & Pecora, 1984, p. 139)

To accomplish this, Austin (1981) indicates that staff development requires several ADMINISTRATIVE roles (analyst, planner, program designer, implementor, and evaluator) as well as four INSTRUCTIONAL roles (translator, orchestrator, facilitator, and change agent). Most of the "traditional" staff development, training and career development techniques are fairly well-known (Austin, 1981; Austin et al., 1984; Milkovich & Glueck, 1985). During the past two decades, two new techniques have evolved which have the potential for linking client outcomes with worker job satisfaction. They are assessment centers and career planning.

Assessment Centers

A process that involves a series of exercises and group activities administered by trained assessors for a group of workers. The assessment can be used as a method of evaluating candidates for promotion. The process is also used to help workers identify their strengths and weaknesses. Working with career counselors and trainers, this data can then be used by workers to build on their strengths and identify bodies of knowledge and skills which can be acquired through the additional investment of time and effort (Cleare, 1984).

Career Planning

Both on a formal and informal basis, this involves the initiation of processes by which employee development managers work with individual workers to develop a career plan. Initially a manual process, the state of the art has moved to interactive computer programs which help workers explore career options. In addition, organizational "success planning" has been automated to indicate the career paths open for workers as senior employees are promoted or opt for retirement.

Before leaving the subject of staff development, training and career development, it is important to note a "traditional," but often neglected, technique which is a fundamental prerequisite for linking worker performance and satisfaction to client outcomes – orientation. I would suggest that one measure of a human services administrator's people management performance is the extent to which formal and informal orientation of workers is a continuous activity in a human service organization. It is a vital independent variable that has direct impact on both client change and worker satisfaction.

PERFORMANCE EVALUATION

Performance evaluation traditionally has concentrated largely on a process by which individual workers are evaluated in terms of the effective performance of their jobs. As a systematic process for human services management, however, performance evaluation is concerned with assessing both the performance of the organization as well as that of the employee. A performance model emphasizes the essential interdependence of both types of performance evaluation, as noted by Figure 4.

Figure 4.

Interdependency of Organizational and Worker Performance Evaluation

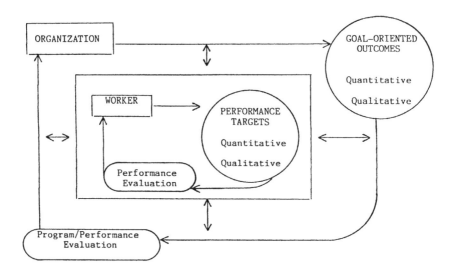

Though client outcome monitoring systems are more the focus of program management skills of human services managers, than skills in people management, the issue of how to measure outcomes is vital for people management if the linkage between job and satisfaction, worker performance, and client outcome is to be effective. Patti (1985) has set forth a number of suggested client outcome measures. The Urban Institute's Client Outcome Monitoring System (1981) also details client outcome measures as well as a system for monitoring such outcomes. It is obvious such a system is vital for people management since it can be used for:

— motivating employees to improve performance:
    — discuss feedback on client outcomes to encourage improved performance and corrective actions;
    — performance targeting, to encourage better performance; be the basis for monetary or nonmonetary incentives, linking pay to performance;
— enhancing quality assurance;
— obtaining client feedback;
— comparing performance in different time periods;
— comparing actual performance to targets;
— comparing different outcomes, in terms of treatment modalities.

The Urban Institute's Client Outcome Monitoring System also includes feedback from clients themselves, which raises an interesting variable. To what extent should human services managers' evaluation of organizational outcomes and performance be shaped by clients' feedback? Maluccio (1979) forcefully argues the need for obtaining feedback from each client, both in terms of monitoring workers' performance and improving their skills and as an "essential component of program evaluation and planning" (pp. 202-203).

While it seems tangential to the main thrust of people management skills, one cannot ignore competency-based social work, a body of thought and literature which focuses on creating an organizational and work environment in which the focus is on the relationship between the worker, client and organizational managers, for the purpose of mutual enhancement.

Maluccio (1981) calls for the redefinition of the roles played by the clients and social workers, with clients viewed as partners in the helping process, redefined primary in terms of a resource rather than the carrier of pathology. Maluccio sets forth the features of competence-oriented practice:

- redefinition of the client and practitioner roles, with clients viewed primarily as RESOURCES and workers as ENABLING AGENTS;
- redefinition of the client-worker relationships, particularly in terms of MUTUALITY AND AUTHENTICITY;
- regular use of CLIENT FEEDBACK. (pp. 10-11)

For our purposes, the feature of client feedback is very important. "It is perhaps the most glaring deficit in the helping relationships that professional counselors, clinical psychologists, psychiatrists, social workers and others rarely, if ever, are given systematic feedback of their effects on clients" (Traux & Mitchell, 1971, p. 339). In essence, the competence-orientation redefines both client and worker roles.

Performance appraisal is a fundamental element of people management skills. It is the basis not only for improving an employee's abilities, training, pay increases, and promotions, it is vital for linking worker performance with organizational outcome-performance evaluation. The technology of performance appraisal is widely known and available (Milkovich & Glueck, 1985). But the process of appraisal in many human services organizations is perfunctory and not fully exploited. It is often viewed negatively because pay increases tend to be automatic and in a merit system career service, linking rewards and incentives to performance is difficult. Effective performance appraisal still remains a challenge for human services managers.

Perhaps the concept of "performance contracts," which thus far has mainly been applied to managers, should be used for individual workers. Perhaps the focus of worker-performance contracts should be that each employee develops his or her own annual contract to improve their own performance in a way that they can measure the degree to which they have contributed to more effective client outcomes while achieving intrinsic and extrinsic rewards.

LINKING WORKER PERFORMANCE TO CLIENT OUTCOMES: ENHANCEMENT OF JOB SATISFACTION AND CLIENT CHANGE

This paper has focused on the interdependency between effectiveness and staff morale — and the people management skills needed to improve the linkage between worker performance, job satisfaction, and client outcomes. In isolating variables that differentiate human services management from other management environments, the following sets of people management skills are critical:

1. goal clarification — defining clear organizational goals measurable in terms of client outcomes;
2. goal blending — blending organizational goals with workers' personal goals and aspirations;
3. performance linkage — linking worker expectations with organizational goal achievement;
4. performance feedback — continuously feeding back to workers on their individual and group performance in terms of goal-outcome achievement;
5. job design — blending work content (tasks, functions, and relationships) with intrinsic-extrinsic job rewards and job qualifications (skills, knowledge, and abilities);
6. job-role linkage — shaping, challenging, and growth-enhancing roles for workers that generate self-responsibility toward achieving more effective client-organizational outcomes;
7. job training — providing for worker career growth through orientation, professional development, and training;
8. worker participation — involving workers in processes that will mutually enhance job satisfaction and client outcomes.

Social workers begin to acquire people management skills when they are thrust into a supervisory or leadership position. In addition to focusing on skill acquisition, they must maintain a set of values which are distinctive to our profession, values which emphasize working with people over "managing" people, values which stress human development over human manipulation.

But, I would suggest that there are also a number of irreconcilable value tensions in which there is no desirable value, only the tension between legitimate values: governance of self by self versus governance of self by others; equal access versus human dignity; the universal versus the particular (Weiner, 1982). Management is both an art and a science; dealing with values and value-tensions is largely the former. The distinctiveness of human services management lies in the former also, and conveying this to our field, and to the general field of management, presents us with our primary professional challenge.

REFERENCES

Abels, P. & Murphy, M. *Administration in the human services*. Englewood Cliffs, NJ: Prentice-Hall, Inc., 1981.

Austin, M.J. *Supervisory management for the human services*. Englewood Cliffs, NJ: Prentice-Hall, Inc., 1981.

Austin, M.J., Brannon, D. & Pecora, P.J. *Managing staff development programs in human service agencies*. Chicago: Nelson-Hall, 1984.

Barnard, C. *The functions of the executive*. Cambridge: Harvard University Press, 1938.

Cleare, M.J. *The assessment center*. Storrs, CT: University of Connecticut, Institute of Public Service, 1985.

Davis, K. *Human behavior at work*. New York: McGraw-Hill, 1972.

Fein, M. Job enrichment: A reevaluation. In J.R. Hackman, E.E. Lawler, III & L.W. Porter (Eds.). *Perspectives on behavior in organizations*. New York: McGraw-Hill, 1983.

Gannon, M.J. *Management: An integrated framework*. Boston: Little & Brown, 1982.

Hackman, J.R. & Suttle, J.L. (Eds.) *Improving life at work: Behavioral science approaches to organizational change*. Santa Monica, CA: Goodyear Publishing, 1977.

Hackman, J.R. & Oldham, C.B. *Work redesign*. Reading, MA: Addison-Wesley, 1980.

Hackman, J.R., Lawler, E.E., III & Porter, L.W. (Eds.) *Perspectives on behavior in organizations*. New York: McGraw-Hill, 1983.

Lawler, E.E., III. *Motivation in work organizations*. Monterey, CA: Brooks/Cole, 1973.

Lawler, E.E., III. Reward systems. In J.R. Hackman & J.L. Suttle (Eds.) *Improving life at work*. Santa Monica, CA: Goodyear Publishing, 1977.

Lewis, J.A. & Lewis, M.D. *Management of human service programs*. Monterey, CA: Brooks/Cole, 1983.

March, J.C. & Simon, H.A. *Organizations*. New York: The Free Press, 1958.

Maluccio, A.N. *Learning from clients*. New York: The Free Press, 1979.

Maluccio, A.N. (Ed.) *Promoting competence in clients: A new/old approach to social work practice*. New York: The Free Press, 1981.

Milkovich, G.T. & Glueck, W.F. *Personnel/human resource management: A diagnostic approach*. 4th edition. Plano, TX: Business Publications, 1985.

Nadler, D.A. & Tushman, M.L. A general diagnostic model for organizational behavior: Ap-

160   MANAGING FOR SERVICE EFFECTIVENESS

plying a congruence perspective. In J.R. Hackman, E.E. Lawler, III & L.W. Porter (Eds.). *Perspectives on behavior in organizations*. New York: McGraw-Hill, 1983.

Naylor, J.C., Pritchard, R.D. & Iigen, D.R. *A theory of behavior in organizations*. New York: Academic Press, 1980.

Patti, R.J. In search of purpose for social welfare administration. *Administration in Social Work*, 1985, 9(3), 1-14.

Porter, L.W., Lawler, E.E., III & Hackman, J.R. *Behavior in organizations*. New York: McGraw-Hill, 1975.

Queisser, R.L. Management of mental health in outpatient settings. *HMO Newsletter*, November 1985.

Sarason, Seymour B. *The creation of settings and the future societies*. San Francisco: Jossey-Bass, 1972.

Simon, H. *Administrative behavior*. New York: Macmillan, 1957.

Thompson, J.D. *Organizations in action*. New York: McGraw, 1967.

Weiner, M.E. *Human services management: Analysis and applications*. Homewood, IL: Dorsey Press, 1982.

The Application of Quality
of Work Life Research
to Human Service Management

Elizabeth A. Gowdy, MSW

For human service organizations, the issue of poor quality of work-ing life (QWL) raises an ethical dilemma: To what degree do human services attempt to produce quality outcomes for clients at the expense of their own workers? As Taber (1986) points out, quality benefits for clients result directly from the human interaction between clients and workers. More than public support, funding, policies, or facilities, clients and workers are the critical resources for human service organi-zations. From this perspective, the issue of inadequate QWL becomes a major concern for administrators, as its costs—to individuals, to organizational effectiveness, to society—are significant.

Major shifts have occurred in the composition of the work force and workers' values, to which human service administrators are chal-lenged to respond. In the face of increasing worker-expectations for more humane and participative workplaces, advancing technology, and pressures to improve service effectiveness without increasing costs, human service administrators must embrace a new vision of organizations in which workplaces become learning environments for client-worker interaction, and workers are viewed and treated as as-sets.

This paper provides human service administrators with an overview of current QWL knowledge. The first section outlines the costs of inadequate QWL on individual, organizational and societal levels, ex-amining factors contributing to its prevalence. The concept of QWL is then defined, as is the philosophy on which it is based. The remainder of the paper articulates specific change strategies for administrators to

Ms. Gowdy is Research Assistant, School of Social Welfare, University of Kansas, Law-rence, KS 66045.

161

use in transforming organizations into more humane workplaces, thereby enhancing both the quality of workers' lives and the quality of client outcomes.

COSTS OF INADEQUATE QUALITY OF WORK LIFE

"Is it reasonable to expect that social workers, as members of a profession that subscribes to high ideals, are treated with dignity and respect?" (Maypole 1986, p. 29).

The costs of poor QWL for individuals are immense, affecting their personal and professional lives, and their psychological and physical well being.

A review of the literature reveals evidence of psychological deprivation through "grossly wasted or unused abilities and skills," growing worker dissatisfaction, boredom, fatigue, illness, insecurity, "stunted development, poor social adaptation to leisure," alcoholism, and ineffective interpersonal relations (Wilson et al., 1975, p. 351-52). Additionally, studies regarding work stress indicate its negative effects on job performance, and is associated with anxiety, depression, irritability, and psychosomatic illness (Jayaratne, Chess & Kunkel 1986). Sexual harassment, exposure to health hazards, pay disparities, inequity in status, psychological disturbances, and stress-related disorders such as ulcers, hypertension, and migraines are major costs of poor QWL for many women workers (Gettman & Pena, 1986).

Poor QWL affects organizational performance as well, indicated by increasing absenteeism, worker turnover and withdrawal from work, sabotage, and high administrative cost (Wilson et al., 1975). Growing worker dissatisfaction is also seen in poor management-worker relations, strikes, and increasing demands for workplace innovations (Herrick & Maccol y 1975). Perhaps the most critical cost of poor QWL to organizations is the loss of workers' potential contributions to enhancing organizational performance. For human services in particular, wherein workers comprise the major resource for achieving organizational goals, the price paid in lost ideas, reduced effectiveness, and lack of commitment "when people are never given the chance to think beyond the limits of their job, to see it in a larger context, to contribute what they know from doing it to the search for even better ways" (Kanter, 1983, pp. 180-81) is immeasurable.

The impact of poor QWL upon social institutions is also severe, and of critical importance to human service professions. Treatment for the psychological problems and physical illnesses workers experience due to inadequate QWL is a major cost to human services, as is treatment for substance abuse, marital conflicts, divorce, and child neglect. The increasing costs of unemployment and problems experienced by the unskilled and socially deprived in obtaining work (Wilson et al., 1975) are additional costs borne by society associated with poor QWL. In a political context,

. . . studies suggest that dissatisfied workers on the whole have lower participation rates in local and national elections, lower participation rates in voluntary associations, and greater feelings of powerlessness and lack of trust in the face of political and social forces. (Wilson et al., 1975, pp. 351-52)

The individual, organizational, and social costs of inadequate QWL are alarming, and serve as a "red flag" to human services. When the norm is accepted that smooth organizational functioning is valued over human need,

. . . workers with debilitating social problems are counseled and monitored back into productive work behavior. This implies acceptance of managerial emphasis on productivity and casts aside the negative effects of such organizational criteria. A major problem with this normative orientation resides in the fact that the effect of managerial policies regarding productivity has been to produce many of the problems that social workers aim to ameliorate. (Gettman & Pena, 1986, p. 9)

Factors contributing to inadequate QWL are rooted in socioeconomic values that dichotomize productivity and human need. From this perspective, workers have been objectified and viewed as "unwilling cogs in the machine" whose tasks need not be meaningful and who lack interest in improving performance. Also, this viewpoint assumes a distinct division between workers' personal and work lives. Organizations managed from such a perspective are comprised of rigid hierarchical structures with power centralized in "top management." Jobs are characterized by segmentation, repetitiveness and lack of autonomy or challenge. Also, physical work environments tend to be poor, work schedules inflexible, and pay and benefits inequitable. Lastly, worker-management relationships based on this perspective are typified by excessive control and mistrust.

Major trends in the social, economic and political fabric of our culture have also contributed to a re-examination of QWL. Buback and Grant (1985) identify five trends affecting the business sector that are paralleled in the human service field: increasing operational costs, high technology development, increasing competition, collective bargaining, and increasing pressures to improve quality and productivity. The shift to a postindustrial, service, and information-producing society has resulted in increasing the rapidity of changing environmental demands on organizations, leading to the need for increased worker commitment to respond to such change (Camman, 1984).

Additionally, a "silent earthquake" has occurred in the composition of the work force over the last several decades, resulting in workers' expectations directly challenging outmoded organizational values regarding QWL. These trends include: more highly educated and trained workers with expectations for humane workplaces; more women in the work force with demands for similar job challenge and satisfaction formerly reserved for men; and later entry and earlier exit of workers from the work force (Wilson et al., 1975). The double role of women as full-time workers and "homemakers" negatively affects organizations wherein inadequate QWL forces women into choosing between job and home responsibilities due to inflexible work schedules, lack of child care, and inadequate benefits such as maternity and family sick leave. Also, many "younger generation" professionals, female and male, are no longer willing to accept alienation as a cost of having jobs, and they expect humane organizations and jobs for themselves and their clients (Cherns & Davis 1975).

THE CHALLENGE TO SOCIAL WORK

The concept of QWL originated over the last two decades in the private business sectors of Europe and the United States. Abundant research literature exists concerning efforts to humanize workplaces through implementing QWL values and strategies in a variety of business and corporate settings. In contrast to the hundreds of QWL studies done in the private sector, the author located only one book concerning QWL efforts in human services. It seems ironic that such a broad-based movement toward humanizing work, founded on values central to those of social work, has so far been fundamentally ignored by human service professions.

Organizational change strategies based on QWL concepts and values are a logical response for human service administrators to make in seeking solutions to this problem analysis. The remainder of this paper is devoted to providing administrators with a summary of the knowledge and strategies needed to humanize the workplace while enhancing service effectiveness.

DEFINING QUALITY OF WORK LIFE

In defining QWL conceptually, a review of that literature reveals general consensus that managerial values play a key role. Kanter (1983) cautions against the temptation to segment the idea into "a special 'quality-of-work-life program' to 'be nice to workers'" without including it in broader change strategies (p. 181). Cherns and Davis (1975) emphasize also the importance of viewing QWL efforts as a major factor in organizational design innovations, underscoring the need to define QWL as a process as well as an end to greater organizational performance.

In the United States, QWL definitions contain a dual focus on improving outcomes for both workers and organizations. Similiar to Nadler and Lawler's QWL definition in which concern for the impact of work on people and organizational effectiveness is a key element, Camman (1984) defines QWL as a type of organizational change program whose prime objective is to create organizations that more effectively deliver services and products valued by society while simultaneously being rewarding, stimulating places for employees to work.

Nadler and Lawler (1983) offer a working definition of QWL as a way of thinking about people, work, and organizations. The key elements of this definition are: (1) concern about the impact of work on people and organizational effectiveness, and (2) the idea of participation in organizational problem-solving and decision-making. By defining QWL as a way of thinking, the focus for administrators becomes a combined concern for how people can work better and how work can cause people to be better.

On a conceptual level, then, it is crucial to the effectiveness of QWL efforts to go beyond a simplistic, mechanistic definition to one that recognizes and values the interrelationships among the values, needs, and goals of workers and organizations. Paying attention to each dynamic of this process as it unfolds over time in system-wide change strategies is of paramount concern in defining QWL effectively.

Quality of Work Life Values

Values articulated by the QWL philosophy directly challenge more traditional views of the workplace, wherein workers are perceived and treated as components of the production system whose knowledge and endurance may essentially be exploited for the goal of organizational productivity (Gardell, 1975). Viewing workers as objects is based on assumptions that people don't want responsibility, only work because they must (Gardell, 1975), and thus must be controlled within closed, centralized hierarchical structures in which administrators remain aloof from worker emotions and passive to a changing environment (Clark, 1975). In contrast to this traditional, mechanistic view, QWL values perceive workers as whole persons with basic needs to be met within open, organic structures in which administrators relate to workers as equals and take an active stance to changing environmental conditions (Clark, 1975).

Central to the QWL philosophy is a view of workers as capable of learning (Camman, 1984) and of organizations as learning environments (Cherns & Davis, 1975). Learning organizations are those that make continuous efforts to improve service effectiveness and productivity, staff morale, and resource acquisition (Rapp & Poertner, 1983). This view emphasizes that workers are assets, with abilities and ideas that, if given opportunity to develop, will result in enhanced personal growth as well as enhancing the quality of interaction between workers and clients from which service effectiveness results.

Grant (1985) identifies four beliefs about work underlying a QWL philosophy congruent with social work values: work is vital to a person's self-worth and self-identity; most people want to do a good job; most people want to exercise some power and control over their work life; and synergy (combined, cooperative action) is a real, desirable goal of the workplace.

These values translate into principles on which QWL efforts may be founded (Allen & Kraft, 1982):

1. Involve people in the problems and programs affecting them.
2. Use win-win, non-blame placing strategies.
3. Have clear goals, objectives, purposes, and tasks.
4. Focus on results, both short- and long-range.
5. Work from a sound information base.
6. Be systematic and use multilevel change strategies.
7. Integrate concern for people and achievement.
8. Emphasize sustained cultural change. (p. 28)

Perhaps the feature of QWL philosophy most critical to human service administrators is the sharing of power (Grant, 1985). Historically, the social work profession has recognized that empowering others so they may realize their full potential enriches the quality of people's lives. In the context of human service organizations, in which service effectiveness depends upon the quality of human interaction between clients and workers, it seems apparent that empowering workers is key. It seems apparent to this author that when organizations are designed to assist workers in meeting their own needs for self-determination, equality, security, learning, and meaning through cooperative efforts in the workplace, their ability to do the same with clients is enhanced.

From this analysis it becomes apparent that real differences exist between current organizational values and QWL values. In human service administrators' efforts to transform organizations into humane work environments, it is critical that change efforts address these philosophical conflicts.

QWL STRATEGIES

Comprehensiveness of vision is the key for successful QWL, as the focus becomes that of translating the concept of QWL into concrete strategies for designing humane organizations. While a review of the literature indicates scant empirical research attributing specific QWL strategies to specific performance outcomes, it does reveal that it is often the sheer number of QWL interventions per se that result in creating innovative and supportive organizational climates (Gadon, 1984).

Based on a review of 550 studies regarding job satisfaction, industrial organization, and productivity, Cummings, Molloy and Glen (1975) identified nine "action levers" (independent variables) that could be manipulated to result in enhanced performance. They also categorized these action levers into four primary change orientations (distinguishable patterns of strategies) to provide organizations with reliable and effective interventions. Kanter and Stein (1985) similarly identified ten interventions for enhancing productivity and QWL. For purposes of simplification, these two models have been combined (see Figure 1).

Sociotechnical/Autonomous Work Groups

This strategy is based on the theory that no innate conflict exists between organizational goals and group goals. Sociotechnical/Autonomous Work Groups are effective for workers whose tasks are interdependent, where jobs can be designed to form distinct "wholes," and where technology or work methods can be adapted to allow for greater worker discretion.

For example, in a human service agency providing services in an 18-county region (such as an area agency on aging), workers' auton-

168

Figure 1

"ACTION LEVERS" (INDEPENDENT VARIABLES)	CHANGE ORIENTATIONS	POSITIVE OUTCOMES (DEPENDENT VARIABLES)
1. Broader pay/reward/recognition systems, and flexible policies to provide balance between home and work life.	1. Sociotechnical/Autonomous work groups.	1. Costs (Efficiency)
2. Increased autonomy/discretion with visible and relevant work teams.	2. Job restructuring	2. Productivity
3. Increased support services providing career path data, counseling, and technical assistance upon demand.	3. Participative management	3. Quality (Effectiveness)
4. Training, education, and formal "mentor sponsorship" systems.	4. Structural change	4. Withdrawal Behavior (Absenteeism and turnover)
5. Simplified organizational structure cross-functional, cross-hierarchy project teams.		5. Attitudes (Job Satisfaction)
6. Technical and physical environment adapted to human needs.		(Cummings, Molloy and Glen)
7. Job "stretching" by adding responsibility and task variety, and "bridging" positions out of traditionally "stuck" jobs.		6. Commitment/Motivation
8. Increased information and feedback to increase communication about all workers' job content and to provide data on performance to workers.		7. Self-esteem
9. Increased interpersonal and group process among work teams and hierarchical layers.		8. Aspiration/Innovation
		(Kanter and Stein)

(Cummings, Molloy and Glen, 1975, and Kanter and Stein, 1985) omy and discretion could be increased by forming three teams to over-see all agency programs in three 6-county areas. Each team would have discretion, within broad guidelines mutually established with agency administrators, to implement, monitor and evaluate programs in their counties. This would increase workers' task variety and inter-personal and group process, as well as resulting in pay and reward systems based on team versus individual performance. While each team would have a great deal of autonomy in determining methods and goals specific to its region, interactive systems of shared information and feedback among teams and administrators would insure program coordination to meet overall agency standards.

Job Restructuring

This strategy is based on the theory that motivation results from workers having opportunities for achievement, recognition, advance-ment, growth and responsibility. Job Restructuring is recommended for workers whose jobs are usually routine and monotonous, and whose work is performed relatively independently of each other.

This strategy is effective for enriching a variety of job types. On a professional staff level, for example, public health nurses could be trained in preventive health and administrative skills, provided with technical assistance, and assume additional responsibilities in organiz-ing and managing community health programs (Greenburg, 1970).

Regarding positions such as bookkeeping, receptionists, and secre-taries, jobs can be restructured into "horizontal careers" (Cherns & Davis, 1975). Examples within support staff include: increasing au-tonomy and discretion by having workers determine their own work schedules; instituting multiple skills acquisition and increasing task variety by training support staff to rotate job tasks (such as sharing bookkeeping responsibilities), and assuming responsibility for produc-ing agency newsletters and publicity materials; and "stretching" jobs by having workers perform a meaningful portion of the service pro-cess, such as receptionists carrying out "comprehensive relations" with clients (Agassi, 1975).

Participative Management

This change orientation is based on the theory that a democratic leadership process results in enhanced productivity, higher morale, less resistance to change, and less conflict with management. Partici-pative Management is recommended where the knowledge and skill levels of workers are advanced, and where direct supervision is either difficult to perform or inappropriate to the setting. As these criteria are true for most human service organizations, QWL strategies that increase participation in decision-making and problem-solving demand particular attention by administrators.

In implementing participative strategies, it is helpful to conceptualize a "continuum of democracy" delineating varying kinds of participation (Wilson et al., 1975). Decisions can be made by workers themselves; by workers with consultation from advisory staff; by workers and managers as equal partners; by managers after consulting with workers; by managers, with workers having veto power. Wilson also identifies three levels of participation: workers participate in general management matters; workers participate in decisions only in areas directly affecting their spheres of responsibility; and workers participate in deciding matters of the actual context, nature, and tasks of their jobs. Finally, Wilson recommends that the scope of participative management be widened to include an organization's multiple constituencies. For human services, this would include participation of varying kinds and levels by clients, volunteers, consumer advocacy groups, community organizations, and funders.

Examples of instituting each of the five kinds of participative management are as follows:

1. *By workers themselves*: A human service agency that oversees grant monies for community projects could give its workers authority to set funding priorities for the grants; decide on grant application and allocation methods; and determine their own work schedule regarding meeting with grantees for purposes of monitoring and evaluation.

2. *By workers with advisory staff*: Workers could be delegated the project of reviewing and redefining an agency's mission statement. After devising their own recommendations, workers would meet with an advisory committee to finalize decisions.

3. *By workers and managers as equal partners*: A work team with representatives from all organizational levels could be formed to address the problem of client accessibility to agency services, resulting in a proposal to the board of directors to open a satellite office in a downtown location.

4. *By managers after consulting with workers*: A management team, assigned to revise the worker benefit package, could use a written survey method to gather input regarding workers' recommendations for innovations in benefits. This information would

then be reviewed, fed back to workers for additional comments, and used to make final decisions by agency management.

5. *By managers, with workers having veto power:* A management team could be given the responsibility to investigate implementing a new program (i.e., a battered women's shelter adding transitional living facilities). The team would submit its proposal to shelter staff, who then have the opportunity to revise and/or veto the idea, based on the proposal's impact on existing agency goals and resources.

Structural Change

The fourth change strategy is based on the theory that organizations are fluid, interactive with the internal and external environment, and exist for people in order to meet their needs. Structural Change is recommended for organizations needing innovations in their technology or work methods, their policies or internal environment. Alterations of structure are usually in response to demands for change due to major alterations in goals, procedures, or its external environment.

Innovations in organizational structure usually fall into three categories:

1. *Reducing the number of hierarchical layers:* An example of this intervention is that of a human service agency providing services from four office locations, with each office managed by its own supervisor. By redesigning the structure to disperse management responsibilities to the staff of each office, a layer of supervision is removed, decreasing the distance (perceived and real) between workers and agency administrators.

2. *Broadening the span of control:* For instance, in a crisis center providing anonymous counseling on a call-in, walk-in basis, those workers staffing each day/night shift could be organized and trained to assume responsibility for performing its own recordkeeping and statistics, thus eliminating an administrative assistant level positioned between staff and director.

3. *Simplifying role relationships:* In a residential treatment facility, for instance, roles may be simplified by changing supervisors' responsibilities. Formerly, each 24-hour work shift for social work supervisors is divided into two 12-hour sections, each with its own supervisor. To eliminate confusion regarding which shift supervisor is responsible for assigning residential staff to their eight-hour shifts and holding staff meetings, one supervisor can

be given responsibility for the entire 24-hour period on a rotating basis, thus reducing two layers of supervision to one.

It is important to note that these four change orientations identify the primary action levers to use in their implementation, and that additional action levers exist to enhance each strategy. For instance, the literature concerning QWL implementation stresses the importance of three of the action levers in all QWL efforts, i.e., rewards, support services, and training. While Cummings, Molloy and Glen (1975) not specifically delineate these in each of their four change orientations, the literature consistently recommends their inclusion in any QWL effort to insure effective outcomes. Moreover, these change strategies are not mutually exclusive, and may be implemented in tandem with each other according to the specific needs of an organization's various departments, programs, and job types.

CONCLUSION AND PRACTICE IMPLICATIONS

The purpose of this paper has been to develop the outlines of an approach for human service administrators to become leaders in the movement toward transforming organizations into humane, empowering environments for workers and clients while enhancing service effectiveness. The paper is a preliminary contribution in a neglected area of administrative practice, and it provides administrators with the conceptual framework and concrete strategies needed to integrate QWL in human services.

Several practice implications emerge from this review. First, empirically based research and application of QWL in human services is needed. While sufficient evidence exists in the private sector that QWL values and strategies effectively enhance both workers' lives and organizational performance, only through similar experimentation in the public sector will the particular contributions of QWL to the unique needs of human services be identified.

Secondly, human service administrators and staff are called to begin learning and applying QWL concepts in their daily practice. As elucidated by this paper, the goals and values of QWL are synonymous with those of the social work profession; to ignore this movement toward humanizing workplaces raises an ethical dilemma of considerable proportion.

Thirdly, those involved in training and educating current and future social work practitioners need to include QWL knowledge, values and skills in their practice. Reframing courses and workshops concerning personnel management, program design, and management skills using a QWL framework will result in providing administrators with the vision and skill needed to respond to the dual challenge of achieving both service effectiveness and humane organizations. The response by human service administrators to the issue of poor QWL, in the final analysis, depends on perception. Rather than viewing poor QWL as a "problem to be solved," increasing demands for humanizing the workplace may be seen as an opportunity for administrators to review and expand their ethical commitments to workers and clients alike.

REFERENCES

Agassi, J.B. The quality of women's working life. In L.E. Davis & A.B. Cherns (Eds.). *Quality of working life*, Vol. I. New York: The Free Press, 1975.
Allen, R.F. & Kraft, C. *The organizational unconscious*. Englewood Cliffs, NJ: Prentice-Hall, Inc., 1982.
Buback, K.A. & Grant, M.K. *Quality of work life: Health care applications*. St. Louis: The Catholic Health Association of the United States, 1985.
Camman, C. Productivity of management through QWL programs. In Frombun (Ed.), *Strategic human resource management*. New York: Wiley, 1984.
Cherns, A.B. & Davis, L.E. Assessment of the state of the art. In L.E. Davis & A.B. Cherns (Ed.), *Quality of working life*, Vol. I. New York: The Free Press, 1975.
Cherns, A.B. & Davis, L.E. Goals for enhancing the quality of working life. In L.E. Davis & A.B. Cherns (Eds), *Quality of working life*, Vol. I. New York: The Free Press, 1975.
Clark, A.W. The client-practitioner relationship as an intersystem engagement. In L.E. Davis & A.B. Cherns (Eds.), *Quality of working life*, Vol. I. New York: The Free Press, 1975.
Cummings, T.G, Molloy, E.S. & Glen, R.H. Intervention strategies for improving productivity and the quality of work life. *Organizational Dynamics*, 1975, *4*, 52-68.
Gadon, H. Making sense of quality of work life programs. *Business Horizons*, 1984, *27*, 42-46.
Gardell, B. Compatibility-incompatibility between organization and individual values: A Swedish point of view. In L.E. Davis & A.B. Cherns (Eds.), *Quality of working life*, Vol. I. New York: The Free Press, 1975.
Gettman, D. & Pena, D.G. Women, mental health, and the workplace in a transitional setting. *Social Work*, 1986, *31*, 5-11.
Grant, M.K. Organizational values and QWL in health care facilities. In K.A. Buback & M.K. Grant (Eds.), *Quality of work life: Health care applications*. St. Louis: The Catholic Health Association of the United States, 1985.
Greenburg, S.B. Curriculum development and training for community health workers. *Comprehensive Health Services, Career Development, Technical Assistance Bulletin*, 1970, *1*, 1-8.
Herrick, N.Q. & Maccoby, M. Humanizing work: A priority goal of the 1970s. In L.E. Davis & A.B. Cherns (Eds.). *Quality of working life*, Vol. I. New York: The Free Press, 1975.
Jayaratne, S., Chess, W.A. & Kunkel, D.A. Burnout: Its impact on child welfare workers and their spouses. *Social Work*, 1986, *31*, 53-59.
Kanter, R.M. *The changemasters: Innovation for productivity in the american corporation*. New York: Simon and Schuster Inc, 1983.
Kanter, R.M. & Stein, B.A. Improving productivity and QWL together: The role of opportunity and power. In K.A. Buback & M.K. Grant (Eds.), *Quality of work life: Health care applications*. St. Louis: The Catholic Health Association of the United States, 1985.

Maypole, D.E. Sexual harassment of social workers at work: Injustice within? *Social Work*, 1986, *31*, 29-34.

Nadler, D.A. & Lawler, E.E. Quality of work life: Perspectives and directions. *Organizational Dynamics*, 1983, *11*, 20-30.

Rapp, C.A. & Poertner, J. Organizational learning and problem finding. In M. Dinerman (Ed.). *Social work in a turbulent world*. Silver Spring, MD: National Association of Social Workers, 1983.

Taber, M. A theory of accountability for the human services and the implications for social program design. *Administration in Social Work*, this issue.

Wilson, A.T.M. et al. Report on the task force on assessment of substantive knowledge. *Quality of working life*, Vol. II. New York: The Free Press, 1975.

SECTION FIVE:
MANAGING INFORMATION

Introduction

Peter Drucker has characterized modern organizations as knowledge organizations, and those within these organizations, at all levels, as knowledge workers. This is particularly true of social service agencies. In modern social service organizations, large amounts of resources are devoted to the collection, storage, and retrieval of data whose purpose is to inform on the performance of program and personnel.

Feedback on individual behavior has long been recognized as essential for learning and motivation. The skillful management of information can have significant impact on agency performance, while misused information can lead to reduced staff morale and decreased program performance. Each of us can identify colleagues who are adept at managing people and skillful at manipulating budgets and other resources. There are few examples of managers who are proficient in using information to enhance performance. The skillful use of information includes determining what information is required, formatting the information for maximum impact, recognizing the effect of organizational culture on the use of information, and determining the actions to be taken based on data based reports.

The first paper by John Poertner and Charles A. Rapp, describes a performance monitoring model for management information systems which enhance performance and positive outcomes for people. Design tasks are identified which begin with determining the desired client

175

outcome and include creating measures and formatting reports. A specific design process is described and illustrated with an example from a large public agency.

M. Susan Taylor contributes recommendations for managers' use of feedback. Drawing upon feedback research, she describes the effect of feedback on individual behavior. She also makes recommendations to managers for improving the effectiveness of feedback systems.

Harold H. Weissman considers implementing a client feedback system. Assumptions about such systems are described as are ways to overcome client and agency resistance. Finally, the institutionalization of such systems is described.

Designing Social Work Management Information Systems: The Case for Performance Guidance Systems

John Poertner, DSW
Charles A. Rapp, PhD

Information systems have been heralded as indispensable tools for enhancing the performance of human services and producing positive outcomes for people. Technological advances have occurred at such a rate that computerized management information systems are frequently seen as "the answer" to nearly any organization or management problem. These sweeping technological changes which hold such promise for the management of human service organizations have resulted in a proliferation of uses and meanings for management information systems. This has led some to observe that "Management Information System (MIS) is a prime example of a 'content free' expression. It means different things to different people and there is no generally accepted definition recognized by those working in the field" (Keen & Morton, 1978, p. 33).

This paper compares three major types of management information systems — housekeeping, decision support, and performance guidance systems. It is argued that the performance of human service organizations is more likely to be enhanced by developing and using guidance systems. A model for designing and implementing a performance guidance system is described and illustrated by the development of one such system in a large state human service agency.

BACKGROUND

Perhaps the largest payoff from computer and information systems has come from the replacement of clerical operations or the use of

Dr. Poertner is Associate Professor, and Dr. Rapp is Associate Professor and Associate Dean, School of Social Welfare, University of Kansas, Lawrence, KS 66045.

computers for "housekeeping" (Keen & Morton, 1978; Rapp, 1984). Word processing has become ubiquitous. Payroll systems and variations of these systems increase the efficiency and accuracy of getting checks to staff and clients. Fiscal accounting systems maintain budget records and increase a manager's ability to monitor and control budgets. These systems, when applied to purchase of service, enhance fiscal accountability of contractors. Most medium to large human service organizations devote considerable resources to the use of computers for housekeeping. These uses are well-developed and undoubtedly increase the efficiency of human services.

A second line of development views management information systems as ways for data and computers to help managers make better decisions (Ackoff, 1967; Mintzberg, 1975; Vogel, 1985). In its current form, Decision Support System (DSS) involves analysis of decisions and the decision maker, developing mathematical and psychological models, and presenting these models to managers for their use. Yet one DSS advocate states:

> The literature on the application of computers in government and business indicate very little use of DSS. . . . In general, the main problem seems to be a mismatch between DSS design or performance and the requirements of decision makers or decision making. . . . Because of the mismatch, many systems which are developed cease to be used or are used for routine report generation rather than for direct support of decision makers. (Bennett, 1983)

Thirty years of research and development have not produced systems which managers use to make decisions and enhance organizational performance. Feldman and March (1981) include an insight into this dilemma.

> Organizations, as well as individuals, collect gossip. They gather information that has no apparent immediate decision consequence. As a result, the information seems substantially worthless within a decision-theory perspective. The perspective is misleading. Instead of seeing an organization as seeking information in order to choose among given alternatives in terms of prior preference, we can see an organization as monitoring its environment for surprises. . . . The surveillance metaphor suggests either a prior calculation of needed information or a kind of thermostatic linkage between observations and actions. (p. 176)

This suggests that the emphasis on developing MIS to help managers make decisions or solve problems has been based on a primarily false premise. While managers need information for problem solving, MIS may be most effective in meeting managers' guidance or problem finding requirements. Some have in fact suggested that problem finding skills are a more reliable basis for distinguishing adequate and inadequate managers than do problem solving skills (Mackworth, 1969; Livingston, 1971). Rapp and Poertner (1983) view MIS in a similar vein, suggesting that management information systems should assist organizational learning. "A learning organization is one that takes periodic readings on its performance and makes adjustments so that performance is improved" (p. 77). It is as a tool for the learning organization that this new type of management information system, the performance guidance system, is directed.

COMPARING SYSTEMS

Guidance, decision support, and housekeeping systems can be compared along several dimensions. First, the goal of a housekeeping system is to improve the efficiency and accuracy of a routine clerical operation. Housekeeping systems may be thought of as labor saving and problem preventing systems. By automating a routine process, they reduce errors and the number of staff required to maintain the process. The goal of a decision support system is to help solve problems or make decisions. Once a decision is made, action steps need to be formulated, assignments made, and follow-up monitoring agreed to. Implementation of the decision follows and a series of meetings and memos initiated before anything gets done. The goal of a guidance system is to instigate action. The data produced by the system lead directly to action. The guidance system monitors performance, senses problems, and informs staff where to act.

Second, the design of each of the three systems is very different. Housekeeping systems are designed by identifying a well-structured operation, routinizing the process, and writing computer programs and procedures for operation of the system. Decision support systems are designed by identifying the decision, identifying the decision maker, modeling the decision making process, and implementing the model. The design of the performance guidance system begins at the heart of the human service enterprise. It begins with a clear definition of organizational purpose from which performance measures are developed. There is nothing amorphous about the relationship between guidance systems and organizational performance.

Third, the level of complexity of both housekeeping and guidance systems is low while decision support systems tend to be complex. Decision making is a complex psychological phenomenon which is not well-understood. The decision models developed are often mathematical and intricate. Consequently decision support systems are frequently dismissed as not including the correct data or sufficient data or are too complex to understand fully. This complexity makes implementation of decision support systems difficult. Performance guidance systems filter and condense information rather than requiring more. The relative simplicity of housekeeping and guidance systems enhances implementation.

A fourth characteristic of information systems is the level of involvement of direct service staff. Housekeeping systems frequently seek to free front line staff from routine clerical functions so they can spend more time in direct service. Management information systems, when designed as decision support systems, serve the manager and consequently do not involve front line staff until after the decision is made. Guidance systems systematically and automatically involve all relevant staff. The clear focus on performance and involvement of all levels of the organization can unify the organizational agenda with a performance focus. This is one of the guidance system's greatest strengths.

DESIGNING PERFORMANCE GUIDANCE SYSTEMS

The design of a guidance system involves four tasks, and a specific process which has been developed to enhance implementation of the system. Knowledge of the four tasks is necessary before the process can be understood. The four tasks are: (1) defining organizational purpose; (2) defining organizational productivity; (3) creating measures of purpose and productivity; and (4) formatting the surveillance reports and setting standards.

Defining Organizational Purpose

The design of the performance guidance system must focus on organizational performance, and therefore the process must be guided by a clear conception of what the agency or program intends to accomplish for its clients. Defining information requirements without this guide frequently results in an information system with too much data. The statement of intended program effects acts as a filter against which proposed information can be judged as to its relevance or importance. A few examples could be:

—a battered woman's program seeks to have women live in non-battering situations;
—a public child welfare program seeks to protect children who are identified as abused or neglected and to provide them permanent homes;
—a program for the chronically mentally ill seeks to maintain people in the community with the highest possible quality of life.

These examples tend to camouflage the difficulty of this first task. Most organizations do not possess a clear statement of purpose that helps define the agency's desired performance. Purpose is often described in terms of lofty ideals, broad mandates, and vague descriptions. As Peter Drucker (1973) has suggested, there is no more important management function than deciding what is the business of the organization.

Defining Organizational Productivity

All human service organizations monitor productivity in terms of client counts, service episodes, service events, and/or elapsed time (Taber & Finnegan, 1979; Rapp & Poertner, 1983). These measures are designed to capture overall organizational effort: How much service was delivered? A guidance system, however, requires not only a summary measure of productivity but careful delineation of the critical programmatic efforts or behaviors which contribute directly to the attainment of organizational purpose. In other words, what are those service events that result in attainment of organizational purpose?

The answer to this question is derived from the relevant research, practice wisdom, and the underlying program theory. In some fields, the practice research is capable of providing strong relationships between behavior and outcomes. For example, there is an increasing body of research suggesting that to maintain chronically mentally ill people in the community (prevent hospitalization) and to enhance their quality of life, the following program behaviors are influential:

1. client attending regular medication clinic appointments (Hogarty, 1979; Linn, Coffey, Klett, Hogarty & Lamb, 1979);
2. early appointment with mental health clinic following discharge from the hospital (Nuehring & Ladner, 1980: Altman, 1982);
3. linkage of client to community resources (Test & Stein, 1980; Rapp & Chamberlain, 1985);
4. support to the family (Anderson, Hogarty & Reiss, 1980; Hat-

field, 1978; Boyd, McGill & Falloon, 1981; Shenoy, Shires & White, 1980);

5. outreach mode of service delivery (Test & Stein, 1980; Rapp & Chamberlain, 1985).

The list can be extended or altered based on the practice wisdom of agency personnel. Their experience often contains implicit or explicit linkages between their behavior and successful client outcomes. In addition, every program is built on an underlying theory which states if we do this then this benefit will accrue to the client. Interviews with a variety of organizational personnel will often uncover these implicit connections.

From these three sources, the manager or guidance system designer creates a list of "key" service events which, if increased in frequency or quality, would increase the percentage of successful client outcomes and therefore improved attainment of the organization's purpose.

Creating Effectiveness and Productivity Measures

A third task is translating the organizational purpose into a set of effectiveness measures and the list of key service events into a set of productivity measures. It is these performance measures which get communicated to the manager and throughout the organization. The importance of this task is underscored by the research of Nadler (1971), who found that information energizes and directs behavior to what is measured. When data are made available, people respond.

Effectiveness measures in the human services can be reflective of three forms of client outcome: client behavior change, client status change or maintenance, and client satisfaction (Rapp & Poertner, 1983). The preferred outcome for the human service manager is for clients to have their problems solved, their statuses become more desirable, and to be satisfied with the services received. In many ways this is the "bottom line" for social programs, yet few management information systems systematically report client satisfaction, behavior change or status change.

In developing performance measures, six criteria which guide the selection of what information will be reported are: (1) validity (2) observable, replicable, uniform (3) understandable (4) susceptible to change (5) as few measures as possible, and (6) extracted from existing information. It simply does no good if the measures miss the mark, are not understood, or are so difficult to obtain that the information is not collected. Issues of measurement are important considerations in the design of a management surveillance system.

Formatting and Standard Setting

The next component of the performance guidance system is feedback of the data to relevant audiences. Social workers are well-versed on the effects of feedback on individual behavior. The format of the performance report is the feedback mechanism. Unfortunately, the dominant report format in most current systems is the row by column table. These two dimensional tables frequently contain so much data that the feedback has little chance to affect behavior. In a study of the reports of a statewide agency, report formats were almost exclusively two dimensional tables with up to 684 separate data items (Rapp, 1982). For a management report to act as a feedback mechanism and affect individual behavior, the report should "speak" for itself. Principles for designing management reports and innovative display formats have been developed by Wainer (1984), Taber and Poertner (1981), and Rapp (1982).

The most important principle for a surveillance report to help improve performance is the need for standards. Numbers reflecting performance are meaningless and useless if there is not something to which they can be compared. What does the figure 4,442 children receiving day care services in February 1981 mean? Is it adequate performance? inadequate? outstanding? The selection of a standard (the actual number reflecting desired performance and the type of standard) is based on (1) achievability (but not too easy), and (2) importance.

Achievability involves setting a standard that can be attained for the vast majority (75-100%) of people or organizational units. This is not to say that all will attain it nor that it will be equally easy for all the parties. An exaggerated example might be to increase the number of cases closed within 12 months from 48% to 90%. There is no way a team could do this without hurting some children, parents, and staff in the process. On the other hand, the standard cannot be too easy to attain. More specifically, if the person or unit need not do anything more to achieve the norm, there is little satisfaction in getting it done.

Importance relates to how necessary a given level of performance is. Indicators which reflect statutorily based policy often require a higher standard than other indicators. Reviewing cases within six months is a policy which probably requires a high standard (e.g., 90-95%). Similarly, some outcome indicators may be judged more reflective of organizational mission than others. Perhaps the number of children returning home vs. number of children adopted may be seen as more central. The importance of process (or productivity) measures often leaves room for discretion. For example, the research indicates that the frequency of caseworker contact with the families of children in placement, frequency of parental visiting, and timely service planning are all critical to returning a child home. Which is most critical is not known. It would be nice if all three could be high, but over one year this is unrealistic. The manager can make some judgments, however, of which one should receive primary attention this year and reinforce that priority by setting a higher standard on that dimension.

Design Process

The design process may be the most critical element in the success or failure of a performance guidance system. The process outlined here is a refinement of that suggested by King and Clelland (1974) and has been found to be useful in a variety of contexts. The process used for designing a performance guidance system has two explicit goals: (1) the system produces the most worthwhile and important information in a usable form; and (2) to enhance implementation of the system once developed.

The first goal is achieved by blending organizational knowledge and concerns with the best information from the professional literature. This is done with each of the four guidance system design tasks. For example, the first task is focused on defining the agency's purpose or mission and desired client outcomes. This is often difficult for agency people. Vague descriptions may eventually give way to lists of purposes or outcomes. The professional practice literature normally suggests desired client outcomes. Agreement on one or at most two statements may entail interorganizational discussions of a protracted nature. Agreement may never be reached. In this case, a guidance system to enhance performance cannot be designed (Carter, 1986).

The second goal of enhancing implementation is achieved by keeping the process incremental and developmental. When agreement is reached on agency purpose and desired client outcome the next task is undertaken. Designers do not ask the agency to review and approve the completed system but participation and approval are required for each design increment. This assures personnel more fully understanding the system, thus enhancing the likelihood of implementation.

PUBLIC CHILD WELFARE: A PERFORMANCE GUIDANCE SYSTEM APPLICATION

The authors designed a performance guidance system with a large state child welfare agency which at any one time has responsibility for 24,000 children. This agency provides or contracts for a full range of child welfare services with a division of responsibility between protective services and follow-up child welfare service. It is the child welfare unit which has responsibility for permanency planning. This agency operates more than six separate computerized information systems, each of which provides reports for central office and regional personnel. The authors were brought in to help managers use the products of the system to increase performance.

Stage I: Defining Purpose

This step, which is often difficult and consumes a great deal of time, was not a problem in this situation. It was clear from the outset that permanency planning performance was the desired area. More specifically, the project team wanted to increase the number of children and the speed with which these children were moved to permanent arrangements (e.g., adoption, returned home, independent living). It was decided that this collaborative effort would be viewed as a permanency planning performance enhancing project, not a management information system project, and that the focus throughout was to be performance with MIS as a means to the end.

Stage II: Measuring Purpose

While permanency planning is rather precise, there remain myriad ways to measure it. This stage is critical since together these effectiveness or outcome measures become the operational statement of permanency planning performance. Four measures were selected and developed: (1) goal achievement index; (2) number of terminations of parental rights; (3) number of adoptions consummated; (4) child movement table and index.

The first outcome dimension is permanency goal achievement. To standardize the measure across workers, teams, regions, etc., this was expressed as a rate — that is, as a number of goals attained per 100 cases. The initial testing of this measure indicated that the validity measurement criteria was being injured by agency's current data system. That system included as permanency planning goals, goals which were not permanency planning goals (e.g., long-term foster care) and were not seen as desirable outcomes by the agency. To focus on permanency, the goals would need to be restricted to remaining at home and closing the case, returning home, and adoption. While this would drastically reduce the number of goals attained, and therefore the apparent success, the result would be a valid permanency goal achievement measure against which all units could be compared. Changes in the current system were accordingly recommended.

The responsibility for adoptions and the intermediate step of terminating parental rights is assigned differently across the state. Some areas assign responsibility for both to a special adoption unit; others divide the two between an adoption team and the regular child welfare team; others place both under the child welfare team. A separate outcome measure for adoption is probably warranted, especially in the case when a special adoption team is in place. These measures in such cases become the outcome measures for these special units. Because of the organizational variations, two measures were proposed: (1) the number of adoptions consummated, and (2) the number of terminations of parental rights.

The third dimension reflects the movement of children through various placement statuses, the ultimate status being a permanent home. In lieu of a permanent plan being achieved, the child welfare manager needs to know how wards are moving through the statuses which compose the system — institutional care, group home care, foster care, and permanent placement.

Movement tables are a relatively new innovation designed to capture client status change (Taber & Poertner, 1981). While the idea of movement tables is new, the notion of client transitions between statuses over time as a central property of social systems is well-established. Deinstitutionalization in mental health and child welfare, recidivism in corrections, in home care for the elderly, and the movement in child welfare for permanency are all focused on the movement of clients through the service system.

Movement tables, if designed properly, can provide extensive information in an economical fashion. The levels of service are in hierarchical order in terms of intensity of service, restrictiveness of service, cost of service and desirability. For example, providing services to maintain a child at home is usually the least intense, least restrictive for the child, least costly, and viewed as most desirable. Therefore, a movement table not only captures movement but can also be used to tell the manager something about cost, service intensity, etc. Another feature of the movement table is that a monthly index of movement can be easily computed (Rapp & Poertner, 1985).

Stage III: Defining Organization Productivity

Based on the rather extensive literature on permanency planning, and the practice wisdom of the agency project team, the authors listed a variety of factors which influence permanency planning outcomes (effectiveness). The factors included:

1. the length of time in foster care;
2. the frequency of caseworker contact with parents;
3. the frequency of parental visiting with the child in foster care;
4. regular and systematic case reviews;
5. amount and quality of services provided to parents;
6. age of the child (particularly important in adoption);
7. worker's ability to assess parental adequacy;
8. setting permanency planning goals in a timely fashion;
9. explicit service contracts between the family and agency.

These factors, with the exception of the child's age, can be influenced by agency behavior. The factors were viewed as the key elements of productivity which in turn influence agency effectiveness — permanency planning goal attainment.

Stage IV: Measuring Organizational Productivity

Decisions needed to be made concerning which productivity dimensions were going to be included. Based on the criteria for measurement development, three dimensions were selected: frequency of caseworker contact with parents, regular and systematic case reviews, and setting permanency goals in a timely fashion. These three were selected because each one was based on an explicit agency policy which made accurate reporting likely, were deemed critical to any permanency effort, were measurable, were already included in the data base, and were susceptible to change. Selecting only three productivity measures helps organizational personnel focus their efforts, and made the reading and digesting of the reported data more likely.

The other six were eliminated for a variety of reasons based on the criteria described earlier. The worker's ability to assess parental adequacy, explicit service contracts between family and agency, and the amount and quality of services provided to the parents are critical factors but are not easily amenable to data based descriptions and were judged to be the province of the casework supervisor. In other words, these three dimensions should be the subject of review and discussion in every case between the worker and supervisor and systematically included in case planning and case review.

The most troublesome omission was the frequency of parental visiting with the child in foster homes. Child welfare research indicates that one of the most powerful determinants of returning children from foster care to their homes is the frequency of parental visiting. However, no current agency automated system systematically collects this information. The ideal permanency planning information system would include this, yet when developing the permanency planning report package, we did not include this vital piece of information. This decision was based on the criteria of efficiency. At the present time the resource costs to develop or change an information system to include tracking of parental visiting is just too great.

There are important lessons from this example. First, no information system will ever be able to do it all. Particularly in large complex organizations, information systems are vital but not a panacea. Second, there is no substitute for good casework. The training and expertise of front line workers is critical to permanency planning success and this needs to be supported and enhanced whenever possible. Third, the first line supervisor through regular systematic case review is the primary location for tracking important elements of permanency planning performance which are not efficiently tracked by the information system. The point is simply that all permanency outcomes and behavior which contribute to permanency outcome must be systematically monitored and attended to, but the formal information system cannot be expected to always be the vehicle for this monitoring.

Stage V: Formatting Reports and Setting Standards

The agreed upon performance measures were formatted according to the principles of performance reports. Each report contained only a few measures. Whenever possible, graphs of various types were developed. The intended audience was carefully considered when determining the degree of data aggregation. Labels and wording of each report were carefully considered.

The project team quickly adopted the new reports. The reports were perceived as being able to stand alone with little or no interpretation required. The information management division was charged with producing the reports on a routine basis.

CONCLUSION

The promise of management information systems as performance enhancers has yet to be realized. In part, this is due to a misguided preoccupation with designing systems which are complex to develop, cumbersome to implement, and fail to link explicitly the system to organizational performance. In contrast, performance guidance systems are easier to design and implement, and explicitly relate information to organizational performance.

The incremental design process described in this paper was evaluated positively by agency personnel involved in the project as was the final design product. The process uncovered a host of organizational issues (e.g., definition of permanency planning performance, definition of legitimate permanency goals which were previously thought to be clear throughout the organization but which in fact were ambiguous or not consensually agreed to). The process therefore helped the organization to further define "what its business is." As a result, it began to unify the agenda of multiple levels of organizational personnel based on permanency planning performance.

REFERENCES

Ackoff, R. Management misinformation systems. *Management Science*, 1967, *14*(4), B-147-B-156.
Altman, H. Collaborative discharge planning for the deinstitutionalized. *Social Work*, 1982, *27*(5), 422-427.
Anderson, C.M., Hogarty, G.E. & Reiss, D.J. Family treatment of adult schizophrenic patients: A psychoeducational approach. *Schizophrenia Bulletin*, 1980, *6*(3), 490-505.
Bennett, J.L. (Ed.). *Building decision support systems*. Reading, MA: Addison-Wesley, 1983.
Boland, R. Control, causality and information system requirements. *Accounting, organizations and society*, 1979, *4*(4), 259-272.
Boyd, J.L., McGill, C.W. & Falloon, J.R.H. Family participation in the community rehabilitation of schizophrenics. *Hospital and Community Psychiatry*, 1981, *32*(9), 629-632.
Carter, R. Measuring client outcomes: The experience of the states. *Administration in Social Work* (this issue).
Drucker, P. Managing the public service institution. *The Public Interest*, 1973, No. 33, 43-60.
Feldman, M.S. & March, J.G. Information in organizations as signal and symbol. *Administrative Science Quarterly*, 1981, *26*, 171-186.
Hatfield, A.B. Psychological costs of schizophrenia to the family. *Social Work*, 1978, *23*(5), 355-359.
Hogarty, G.E. Aftercare treatment of schizophrenia: Current status and future direction. In H.M. Von Praag (Ed.). *Management of schizophrenia*. The Netherlands: Van Garcum, Assen, 1979.
Keen, P.G. & Morton, M.S. *Decision support systems: An organizational approach*. Reading, MA: Addison-Wesley, 1978.
King, W.R. & Clelland, D. The design of management information systems: An information analysis approach. *Management Science*, 1979, *22*(3). 286-297.

Linn, M.W. et al. Day treatment and psychotropic drugs in the aftercare of schizophrenic patients. *Archives of General Psychiatry*, 1978, *36*(10). 1055-1066.

Livingston, J.S. Myth of the well educated manager. *Harvard Business Review*, 1971, *49*, 96-108.

Mackworth, N.H. Originality. In Dael Wolfe (Ed.). *The discovery of talent*. Cambridge, MA: Harvard University Press, 1969.

Mintzberg, H. *Impediments to the use of management information*. New York: National Association of Accountants, 1975.

Nadler, D.A. *Feedback and organizational development*. Reading, MA: Addison-Wesley, 1971.

Nuchring, E.M. & Ladner, R.A. Use of aftercare programs in community mental health clinics. *Social Work Research and Abstracts*, 1980, *16*, 34-40.

Rapp, C. Principles of performance report design. In *The evaluation and use of information service to area offices*. Lawrence, KS: University of Kansas, 1982.

Rapp, C.A. & Chamberlain, R. Case management services for the chronically mentally ill. *Social Work*, 1985, *30*(5), 417-422.

Rapp, C. & Poertner, J. Organizational learning and problem finding. In Miriam Dinerman (Ed.), *Social work in a turbulent world*. Silver Spring, MD: NASW, 1983.

Shenoy, R.S. Shires, B.W. & White, M.S. Using a schiz-anon group in the treatment of chronic ambulatory schizophrenics. *Hospital and Community Psychiatry*, 1980, *31*(6), 421-422.

Taber, M. & Finnegan, D. Social service productivity: Measuring units of service. Manuscript, School of Social Work, University of Illinois, 1979.

Taber, M. & Poertner, J. Modeling service delivery as a system of transitions. *Evaluation Review*, 1981, *5*(4). 549-566.

Test, M.A. & Stein, L.I. Alternatives to mental hospital treatment. *Archives of General Psychiatry*, 1980, *37*, 409-412.

Vogel, L.H. Decision support systems in the human services: Discovering limits to a promising technology. *Computers in Human Services*, 1985, *1*, 67-80.

The Effects of Feedback on the Behavior of Organizational Personnel

M. Susan Taylor, PhD

INTRODUCTION

Work organizations have long been recognized as complex information environments that place heavy cognitive demands upon individual members (Duncan, 1979; Weick, 1979). Members' ability to deal with such complexity is often further taxed by the equivocality of the information itself, since available data is often noisy, that is, subject to multiple interpretations (Daft, 1986). Thus, organizations may be viewed as massive and noisy fields of information where data is sometimes redundant, sometimes biased, and sometimes conflicting.

In order to survive and function effectively with such environments, employees must be able to sort through complex information environments, determine what is relevant and what is irrelevant data, and make sense of it (Katz, 1980; Louis, 1980). As an example, consider the awesome learning task faced by organizational newcomers. They must determine the norms and values that are most important within the organizational culture, identify specific requirements associated with their particular work roles, determine the availability of organizational rewards, identify relationships between these rewards and particular work results, and learn how to achieve these results. Furthermore, established employees also may face significant learning tasks when their environmental demands change due to job transitions, mergers or acquisitions, organizational restructurings, etc.

Feedback or information about the effectiveness of one's work behavior (Ilgen, Fisher & Taylor, 1979), is a necessary component of the individual learning process in organizations. It is also extremely valuable as a corrective mechanism for maintaining a consistent, goal-directed course of action (Ashford & Cummings, 1983; Carver &

Dr. Taylor is Associate Professor, College of Business and Management, University of Maryland, College Park, MD 20742.

191

Scheier, 1982). Thus, feedback is important in helping individuals learn how to become effective performers in an organizational setting, and for maintaining high levels of performance over time. In addition to performance effects feedback may influence employees' attitudes towards their work and towards others in the organization, as well as their beliefs about personal competence and their performance standards (Taylor, Fisher & Ilgen, 1984). Unfortunately, the complexity and noise that describe the general information environment in organizations, also characterize their feedback systems. As a result, feedback often has unintended and undesirable effects on individual members, causing them to dislike and distrust organizational leaders and lower the levels of effort devoted to work tasks and smooth performance. These results are quite undesirable from both an individual and an organizational perspective.

Although the body of knowledge concerning feedback effects is far from complete (Taylor et al., 1984), previous research findings can be used to develop a body of recommendations for improving the effectiveness of organizational feedback systems. Organizational administrators play major roles in any attempts to improve the feedback system, since they generally possess both the formal and informal power needed to implement change in feedback policies and procedures, and the visibility needed to increase organizational acceptance of such changes through use of the modeling process. Therefore, the primary objective of this paper is to develop a body of recommendations that might be used by organizational administrators to develop feedback systems that result in favorable work attitudes and high levels of individual performance. The paper selectively reviews existent knowledge about the feedback process and individual performance. The paper selectively reviews existent knowledge about the feedback process and individual responses to feedback. It then identifies several obstacles to the operation of effective organizational feedback systems and develops a series of recommendations for overcoming such obstacles. Finally, it uses the performance model of human service agencies developed by Rapp and Poertner (1986) to predict the impact of feedback systems upon organization effectiveness.

THE FEEDBACK PROCESS:
A CONTROL SYSTEM PERSPECTIVE

Control Theory Applications and Features

Recent writings and research have taken a control or cybernetic system perspective in explaining individuals' responses to performance feedback (Campion & Lord, 1982; Taylor et al., 1984). Although control theory has been used in the design of electrical and mechanical systems for many years (e.g., Dransfield, 1968), its application to the understanding of self-regulation in human systems has evolved much more slowly (Carver & Scheier, 1981).

Feedback applications of control theory have focused fairly exclusively on a single system characteristic, the feedback loop that supplies information to the system about the nature of its products or outputs. Undoubtedly the most popular presentation of this feedback loop is that of Miller, Galanter, and Pribram (1960) who described a test-operate-test-exit sequence often referred to by the acronym TOTE. The feedback sequence begins when a system receives information about how it is currently functioning and compares or tests the information with some standard or desired state of operation (sometimes termed a comparator). If there is a match between current functioning and the standard, no further action is taken and the system exits from further regulation for the time being. However, assuming there is a discrepancy between standard and current functioning, the system initiates action operates intended to bring its functions more in line with the comparator. At this point, another test (comparison of current state with standard) is made and operations continue until the discrepancy is resolved. The system then exits from further regulation for the present time.

The classic illustration of the TOTE model is that of a room thermostat which receives information about the current room temperature and compares this information to some temperature setting. If there is a significant discrepancy between current temperature and temperature setting, the thermostat operates via the heating or air conditioning system to resolve this discrepancy, repeatedly tests the temperature against the setting until the discrepancy is resolved and then shuts down the heating or cooling system.

Essential Features of Human Feedback Systems

The thermostat example describes the basic TOTE process in a mechanical system; it also offers a number of insights about essential features of the feedback process in humans. First, the example suggests that in order for organizational feedback systems to operate effectively, individuals must have a well-developed set of performance standards that guide behavior and serve as a basis of comparison for current performance information. These standards are hierarchical in nature and more complex than might be initially obvious. At the highest level, standards are essentially moral principles that individuals acquire throughout life, e.g., the "do unto others" principle, "a full day's work for a full day's pay," etc. (Carver & Scheier, 1981; Powers, 1973). Lower level standards are really programs of behaviors that specify the strategies needed in order to attain a particular goal state (e.g., being a high performer) and a set of contingencies or situational conditions that specify when different strategies are likely to be more effective. Thus, an example of a lower level standard might be "if one wishes to be a high performing caseworker employed by a human service agency with severe budgetary constraints, then strategies specifying the efficient provision of quality service to clients must be emphasized over those specifying high quality and long term client service (effectiveness) alone." At the lowest level, standards specify a set of smaller support behaviors needed to carry out a particular activity so that once behavioral control is relinquished to a particular standard, these support behaviors can be implemented almost automatically. For example, the hospital nurse who attempts to increase treatment efficiency by explaining to a group how mediation should be taken at home is likely to have a standard for this behavior specifying when to hold the presentation, when to blend in patient specific references, how to end to presentation on a motivational note, and test for patient comprehension.

The complexity of the standards that guide individual behavior suggests that considerable developmental time is required in order to specify strategies and contingency factors as well as the small support behaviors which result in strategy implementation. Furthermore, individual standards for work behavior must be fairly consistent with those of the organization or feedback will have unintended and undesirable effects (Taylor et al., 1984).

As a second requirement, organizational feedback systems must provide individuals with accurate and clear information about current performance and state this information in a manner that can be compared with existing standards. Feedback is available from a number of different sources in the organizational environment, e.g., from the task or job itself, from one's supervisor, coworker, clients, the formal organization (Hanser & Muchinsky, 1978). However, these sources often focus on different dimensions of work behavior, e.g., coworkers may emphasize one's willingness to cooperate and share resources, while supervisors focus on total sales and customer complaints. Furthermore, different sources may vary considerably in the feedback dimensions used and thus, in their overall evaluations of performance. Therefore, individuals are often forced to combine different dimensions and different metrics, in order to arrive at an overall assessment of their current performance.

A third requirement of organizational feedback systems is that they stimulate recognition of discrepancies between current performance and standards. This recognition is often obstructed by individuals' tendencies to avoid negative feedback that generally poses some threat to the self-esteem and to assume that discrepancies are unlikely after acquiring a certain level of job tenure (Swann & Read, 1981; Taylor et al., 1984). Each of these factors may reduce the speed with which individuals recognize performance-standard discrepancies.

A final requirement of human feedback systems is that they guide in the selection of responses that will reduce performance-standard discrepancies, individual display affective, and cognitive responses to feedback as well as behavioral ones (Taylor et al., 1984). Thus, an understanding of each response is valuable for the development of feedback systems.

INDIVIDUAL RESPONSES TO FEEDBACK

Affective Responses

Affective reactions to feedback are greatly affected by the nature of the feedback itself. When inconsistent feedback is received, either from the same source or from different sources, or when feedback is widely discrepant from that expected, it is likely to be judged as inaccurate by the recipient and discounted so that it has little effect upon behavior. Equally as important, however, is the fact that such feedback ends to lower the esteem and credibility of the feedback source (coworker, supervisor, etc.) in the eyes of the recipient. Not surprisingly, individuals' reactions to feedback are also influenced by whether it has a positive (favorable) or negative (unfavorable) sign. However, reactions to the favorability of feedback are tempered by the way individuals explain the causes of their behavior. When feedback is attributed to personal causes (e.g., I got a good (bad) evaluation because I am very competent (incompetent) in this area), it tends to evoke more intense affective reactions (whether favorable or unfavorable) from individuals than when it is attributed to external causes (e.g., my supervisor was in a bad mood, the task was impossibly difficult, etc.).

Cognitive Responses

Feedback also influences individuals' beliefs about their probability of success on a task. These beliefs, termed expectancies, play a critical role in the feedback process because they affect individuals' work motivation. The impact of feedback on expectancies is also determined by individuals' explanations for the causes of their behavior. However, the key component in this case is whether or not the feedback is attributed to stable (relatively permanent) or unstable (more transient) causes. When feedback is attributed to stable causes, e.g., ability, task difficulty, etc., individuals tend to adjust their expectancies to approximate the feedback received. Thus, when unfavorable feedback is attributed to ability, expectancies for high job performance tend to decrease causing individuals to exert less effort on the job, give up more easily, etc. However, when feedback is attributed to unstable causes (e.g., I used the wrong technique, I didn't try hard enough, etc.) feedback will have little effect on expectancies (Carver & Scheier, 1981; Weiner, Nierenberg & Goldstein, 1976) and subsequent motivation. Ideally, then, feedback systems should provide cues that enable individuals to make accurate attributions about the causes of their behavior.

Behavioral Responses

Finally, feedback also influences individuals' behavioral responses, including job performance, participation behaviors, and behaviors toward the feedback system (Taylor et al., 1984). The impact of feedback on performance and participation behavior is greatly determined by individuals' expectancies for success. If negative feedback lowers expectancies via the attribution process mentioned earlier, individuals are likely to lower the intensity and effort of their attempts to meet performance standards and may even lower their standards, if this option is personally and organizationally acceptable. Furthermore, if expectancies remain quite low, individuals may decide to leave the organization and turnover. However, if expectancies remain high and the attainment of performance standards is important, individuals are likely to struggle persistently to resolve performance-standard discrepancies even in the face of extremely unfavorable feedback. Favorable feedback also can affect performance by increasing or reinforcing expectancies. However, favorable feedback also may decrease performance if repeated success decreases the value of meeting performance standards (Janz, 1982).

Regardless of its favorability, feedback may have a dysfunctional effect on performance if it causes individuals to believe that they have lost the freedom to perform the job as they wish and are being overly controlled by others in the work environment. This effect, termed "reactance" in the psychological literature (Brehm, 1966; Brehm & Brehm, 1981) occurs when changes in the feedback system lead individuals to believe that they have lost a valuable freedom. Thus, the adoption of a new feedback system that regularly reports back data on client satisfaction to organizational supervisors, instead of allowing coworkers to assess the information themselves, might cause a reactance response. "Reactance" stimulates individual attempts to restore lost freedoms. Such attempts may include performing in the same way despite negative feedback, behaving exactly opposite to the manner expected, or encouraging other employees to violate organizational standards.

In addition to affecting performance, feedback may cause individuals to respond against the organizational feedback system.

When systems are viewed as unfair because standards are applied inconsistently, or they were never communicated, etc., employees may retaliate in a variety of ways, sometimes falsifying data, sometimes withholding information, and sometimes by evaluating organizational supervisors poorly on attitude surveys, etc. (Dornbusch & Scott, 1975; DeNisi, Randolph & Blencoe, 1980)

In summary, feedback influences individuals' affective cognitive and behavioral responses in multiple ways and through fairly complex processes. Not surprisingly, then, there are many obstacles to the development of effective organizational feedback systems and attempts to improve feedback systems must be undertaken in consideration of these obstacles.

IMPROVING THE EFFECTIVENESS
OF HUMAN FEEDBACK SYSTEMS
IN WORK ORGANIZATION

There are many obstacles to the effectiveness of organizational feedback systems but perhaps one of the most crippling is the absence of clear standards for individual behavior. As the TOTE model indicates, in the absence of behavioral standards, feedback about current performance is uninterpretable. Yet Katz and Kahn (1978) have reviewed several studies suggesting that even long tenured employees often experience significant uncertainty about the job behaviors expected of them by the organization. Presumably, this ambiguity results because performance standards are never defined at the organizational level, because broad organizational goals are never translated into behavioral requirements at the individual level, and/or because employees are not explicitly informed of the relative importance or priority of standards.

In the absence of fairly explicit information about organizational standards of behavior, employees will quickly begin to rely upon their own. However, successful organizational performance is dependent upon administrators' ability to coordinate the efforts of members possessing different knowledge, skills and values and such coordination is unlikely to occur spontaneously. Employees need assistance if they are to reach a common or shared interpretation of the organization's expectations. Thus, administrators must facilitate the sense-making process by developing long term goals (three to five year time frames) or standards for the organization as a whole, along with relative priorities between goals. These organizational standards should be explicitly communicated via written and verbal exchanges with employees, e.g., in letters and notices, in newsletters and annual reports, in training programs, etc. Furthermore, the administration's commitment to the standards should be demonstrated behaviorally with high level administrators modeling behaviors that contribute to agency effectiveness, efficiency, productivity, etc., and publicly recognizing others who make important contributions in this area.

In addition, organizational goals must be translated into subunit contributions and subunit managers charged with the responsibility of working with their employees to develop standards at the individual level. Managers should be encouraged to negotiate with individuals concerning the strategies and time frames used to attain standards in order to make organization standards as consistent as possible with those held by individuals in order to give employees a sense of ownership. Thus, the caseworker who wishes to increase productivity by scheduling similar client services at particular periods during one or two week intervals might be allowed to use this method as long as it has the intended effect on productivity and does not significantly compromise the quality of service. Negotiations between managers and employees serve to reduce the possibility that standards will be ambiguous or that conflicts between individual and organizational standards will go unrecognized.

A second obstacle to the effectiveness of organizational feedback concerns the availability of data about current effectiveness. As noted earlier, individuals naturally avoid assessing discrepancies between performance and standards because of threats to the self-esteem and the assumption that with long job tenure, high performance is maintained over time. This tendency is exacerbated when current performance is difficult to assess because data relevant to productivity, effectiveness, etc., is unavailable or unequivocal. As a result, wide discrepancies may go unnoticed for long periods of time. Administrators should encourage employees to "test" for performance-standard discrepancies by first demonstrating in a nonthreatening way that such discrepancies exist. Often simply publicizing discrepancies for typical subunits, as opposed to individuals (e.g., the productivity or effectiveness figures for the pediatric, coronary, and oncology units), is sufficient to convince many employees to check for similar discrepancies on the individual level. The message accompanying such a communication should be that the organization's goals are shared goals and that they can be achieved only through the attainment of individual standards. Individuals are expected to monitor their own performance, not just to assume that it is high, and to make the behavioral adjustments necessary to insure that standards will be met.

However, administrators must also make certain that the information needed to judge individual effectiveness is collected and made accessible to employees in a manner that is unlikely to evoke reactance. In general, this information will be more effective when provided by impersonal sources in dimensions and metrics consistent with performance standards. For example, data on service episodes, client status changes, etc., might be collected monthly by a staff group in the human service agency and quickly reported back by that group (as opposed to the subunit manager) directly to individual employees without any personalized reference or evaluation. Although this same data accumulated across a six or twelve month period will ultimately provide input into individuals' formal performance appraisals, when regularly distributed directly to individuals in an impersonal manner, the feedback can stimulate employees to monitor their performance while avoiding the sensation that one's behavior is constantly being closely watched by others. Thus, employees are given the information needed to monitor their current performance and the expectation that it is their responsibility to notice performance-standard discrepancies and to resolve them during the interim between formal performance evaluations.

A third obstacle to the effectiveness of organizational feedback systems is that they fail to provide specific information about the reduction of performance-standards discrepancies. Administrators should encourage subunit managers to hold staff meetings where the primary goal is improved unit performance. Individuals should be asked to discuss performance difficulties and the relative utility of various performance strategies under different situational conditions. High performing staff members might be encouraged to allocate a portion of their work time to assisting other staff members on an individual basis, resolving performance-standard discrepancies. Emphasis should be placed upon helping employees make attributions for the causes of unfavorable feedback, e.g., whether discrepancies are caused by using inappropriate strategies, not devoting enough effort to particular tasks, a lack of ability in certain areas, etc. Performance attributions are more likely to be accurate when feedback sources are careful to give consistent feedback over time and when feedback is made specific enough to identify what the source perceives is the major cause of performance. In this manner, the elimination of discrepancies becomes less of a time consuming trial and error procedure conducted secretly by the individual.

A final weakness of organizational feedback systems is a failure to evaluate system effectiveness. As noted previously, individuals respond to feedback with affective and cognitive reactions as well as with behavioral responses. Therefore, it is possible to monitor several aspects of system effectiveness by measuring individuals' attitudes toward the system, the attributions made to explain the causes of performance, and the expectancies held for successful performance. All of this information could be obtained when the organization collects regular attitude survey data. Feedback systems which provoke extremely negative employee attitudes, yield predominantly external performance attributions, and/or result in low expectancies, are likely to have undesirable effects on employee performance. They should be examined closely to determine the cause of these reactions and modified in order to enhance work related attitudes, cognitions, and behaviors. Such results are often caused by the inconsistent application of performance standards, a failure to communicate standards clearly, the provision of very general feedback providing little information about the causes of performance, the requirement that employees be responsible for performance results not really under their control.

In summary, recommendations for improving performance feedback systems center around the need to set explicit standards for behavior, to provide clear data on individual performance in an impersonal rather than a controlling manner, to encourage employees to test for performance-standard discrepancies through specific but nonthreatening assistance in resolving discrepancies, and to use employees' attitudes and beliefs about the feedback system to monitor its effectiveness. These kinds of changes should contribute significantly to organizational effectiveness.

THE IMPACT OF FEEDBACK SYSTEMS UPON ORGANIZATIONAL EFFECTIVENESS

In a recent paper on human service agency performance, Rapp and Poertner (1986) proposed client service as the major outcome variable by which the value of these agencies should be assessed, and specified five primary dimensions of agency performance: (1) effectiveness of quality of service; (2) productivity or quantity of service; (3) resource acquisition or the ability to obtain needed resources from the environment; (4) efficiency or the ratio of inputs to service products; and (5) staff morale or the job satisfaction of agency employees. The authors also hypothesized that these five performance dimensions are influenced by four clusters of management activity program design and evaluation, and the managing of people, information, and resources. In terms of Rapp and Poertner's (1986) model, human feedback systems typically aid individuals by providing relevant and specific performance information about the results of organizational programs. Thus the development and maintenance of effective organizational feedback systems is an activity falling under at least three of Rapp and Poertner's management clusters—program design and evaluation, as well as the managing of information and people.

As a component of the three management clusters, organizational feedback systems are expected to affect at least four of the performance dimensions proposed by Rapp and Poertner (1986). First, systems designed according to the recommendations developed earlier within this paper are expected to have positive effects on employee morale because they reduce individuals' anxiety about the organization's evaluation of their contribution and contribute to the reduction of performance-standard discrepancies. Thus, employees are more likely to attain valued rewards in the work setting when feedback is available to them. In addition, productivity and effectiveness standards cue employees concerning the relative value of different behaviors and direct efforts toward these objectives. Thus, as long as performance standards are developed around productivity and effectiveness objectives, organizational feedback systems should also facilitate individuals performance along these two dimensions. Finally feedback systems should also increase the organizational effectiveness through their impact on individuals' performance. Effective feedback systems stimulate individuals to recognize and reduce performance-standard discrepancies by encouraging employees to routinely monitor their behavior, providing relevant feedback, and by placing primary responsibility for performance improvement upon the individual. Employees are able to achieve and maintain high performance levels more efficiently when working in an environment that encourages openness about performance deficiencies and stresses self-control, rather than organizational control, of behavior. Therefore, the Rapp and Poertner (1986) model suggests that organizational feedback systems play a major role in the organizational effectiveness of human service agencies.

REFERENCES

Ashford, S.J. & Cummings, L.L. Feedback as an individual resource: Personnel strategies of creating information. *Organizational Behavior and Human Performance*, 1983, *32*, 370-398.

Brehm, J.W. *A theory of psychological reactance*. New York: Academic Press, 1966.

Brehm, S.S. & Brehm, J.W. *Psychological reactance: A theory of freedom and control*. New York: Academic Press, 1981.

Campion, M.A. & Lord, R.G. A control-system conceptualization of the goalsetting and changing process. *Organizational Behavior and Human Performance*, 1982, *30*, 265-287.

Carver, C.S. & Scheier, M.F. *Attention and self-regulation: A control theory approach to human behavior*. New York: Springer-Verlag, 1981.

Daft, R. Organizational information requirements, media richness and structural design. *Management Science*, 1986, *32*, 554-571.

DeNisi, A.S., Randolph, W.A. & Blencoe, A. Peer evaluations: Causes and consequences. Proceedings of the 12th Annual Meeting of the American Institute for Decision Sciences, Las Vegas, November 1980.

Dornbusch, S.M. & Scott, W.R. *Evaluation and the exercise of authority*. San Francisco: Jossey-Bass Publishers, 1975.

Dransfield, P. *Engineering systems and control*. Englewood Cliffs, NJ: Prentice-Hall, Inc., 1968.

Duncan, R. What is the right organizational structure? Decision tree analysis provides the answer. *Organizational Dynamics*, 1979, *7*, 59-80.

Hanser, L.W. & Muchinsky, P.M. Work as an information environment. *Organizational Behavior and Human Performance*, 1978, *21*, 47-60.

Ilgen, D.R., Fisher, C.D. & Taylor, M.S. Consequences of individual feedback on behavior in organizations. *Journal of Applied Psychology*, 1979, *64*, 349-371.

Janz, T. Manipulating subjective expectancy through feedback: A laboratory study of the expectancy-performance relationship. *Journal of Applied Psychology*, 1982, *67*, 480-485.

Katz, D. & Kahn, R.I. *The social psychology of organizations*. 2nd edition New York: Wiley, 1978.

Katz, R. Time and work: Toward an integrative perspective. In B. Staw & L.L. Cummings (Eds.), *Research in organizational behavior*, Vol. 2. Greenwich, CT: JAI Press, 1980.

Louis, M.R. Surprise and sense making: What newcomers experience in entering unfamiliar organizational settings. *Administrative Science Quarterly*, 1980, *23* 226-251.

Miller, G.A., Galanter, E. & Pribman, K.H. *Plans and the structure of behavior*. New York: Holt, Rinehart & Winston, 1960.

Powers, W.T. *Behavior: The control of perception*. Chicago: Aldine, 1973.

Rapp, C.A. & Poertner, J. A performance model for human service management. Working paper, School of Social Welfare, University of Kansas, 1986.

Swann, W.B. & Read, S.J. Self-verification processes: How we sustain our self-conceptions. *Journal of Experimental Social Psychology*, 1981, *17*, 351-372.

Taylor, M.S., Fisher, C.D. & Ilgen, D.R. Individuals' reactions to performance feedback in organizations: A control theory perspective. In K.N. Rowland & G.R. Ferris (Eds.). *Research in personnel and human resource management*, Vol. 2. Greenwich, CT: JAI Press, 1984.

Weick, K.E. Cognitive processes in organizations. In B. Staw (Ed.), *Research in organizational behavior*, Vol. 1. Greenwich, CT: JAI Press, 1979.

Weiner, B., Nierenberg, R. & Goldstein M. Social learning (locus of control) versus attributional (causal stability) interpretations of expectancy of success. *Journal of Personality*, 1976, *44*, 52-68.

Planning for Client Feedback:
Content and Context

Harold H. Weissman, DSW

For the last two years I have been involved in a feedback project with my soon-to-be two-year old son. This project involves my telling him that I love him. Since he is just beginning to speak, I am yet to hear the words in return, "I love you."

It is my contention that this parent-child metaphor in feedback corresponds basically to what occurs between agencies and clients. The agency pictures itself as constantly saying, "I love you, I love you." It appears eager to get the same response back from the clients. Yet, compared to what the parent does with the child, it tends to expend little effort in helping the client to talk. This notwithstanding, parents and agencies share a predilection for one way communication to their charges. Both have well worked out means of avoiding listening from labeling, such as "he's spoiled," "she's resistant to the use of authority"; the meanings are "shut up," or "close the case."

If the analogy between parent and agency holds, then one reason for reluctance of the agency to allow the client to speak is quite understandable. Parents hear many things from their children besides "I love you."

If the child says "I don't love you," the parent can ignore the child, lecture it on how ungrateful it is, tell the child it is no matter, he is still loved, among many other possible responses. Similarly, agencies can engage in a range of responses to feedback. Yet, while parents are generally unable to avoid getting some feedback from their children, or responding to it in some fashion, agencies by their very nature as a secondary construct, have a much easier time avoiding feedback.

I will contend in this paper that they are generally wise in not getting it. This wisdom, though, is not the earned variety. It is simply based on the fact that client feedback can be the most disruptive and unsettling activity an agency can institute.

Dr. Weissman is Professor, Hunter College School of Social Work, The City University of New York, 129 East 79th Street, New York, NY 10021.

To prevent it from becoming an organizational Pandora's box, agencies will have to be clear about the goals they hope to achieve through its use, how to operationalize feedback systems to achieve these goals, what to anticipate in the way of problems, and what concepts to draw upon to deal with both the expected as well as the unanticipated problems that emerge.

It is my view that in the long run it is disastrous for organizations not to get feedback from their clients, but in the short run feedback can be quite dysfunctional. The intent of this paper is to describe these dysfunctions and provide a means for agencies to overcome them so that feedback projects can achieve their goals.

GOALS

Feedback from clients generally refers to a systematic attempt by agencies to get reliable and valid data from clients regarding their perception of both how services were given, and the benefits they derived from it. Client feedback in this paper refers to a wider range of processes and projects including, e.g., ad hoc efforts to garner information about a particular problem, assess risks in changing procedures, develop marketing strategies; to broader and long-term purposes such as staff development and motivation; as well as to institutionalized efforts to evaluate and understand program success and failure.

The consumerism movement of the 1970s and 1980s spurred a great deal of interest in client feedback. Unfortunately, the goal was simply assumed to be the provision of better service. As such, not much attention was given to thinking through how feedback could promote a variety of ends as noted above, or thinking about the manner in which the organizational context affects an agency's ability to use feedback.

In some ways a simplified set of assumptions existed that assumed a linear relationship between client feedback and service effectiveness.

One assumption in this set is that organizations share common values about ends. In fact, there is considerable disagreement in organizations over the priorities that should be given to equally good ends. Thus there is not necessarily an acceptance of the need to change in a particular program or a particular organization.

Another assumption is that rationality is the single factor that determines the structure of programs in organizations. Status and power are not determining factors. Further, there is no limit on rationality. There is an unlimited capacity to discriminate among and between a plethora of data.

A third unwarranted assumption is that the organizational risks of responding to criticisms are not great, that the rewards will always outweigh the costs of changing. Organizations or programs can and will tolerate, as well as adjust easily to, attacks on themselves and their survival. They can transcend negative feedback.

Fourth, the structure and reward system of an organization or program supports change and adjustment, innovations and alteration. This view does not grasp the ambivalence toward change that inevitably exists and is imbedded in programmatic structures and reward systems (Wildavsky, 1972).

Lastly, the assumption exists that there is a willingness on the part of organizations to accept limitations on their autonomy. Inevitably, client feedback, when taken seriously, will provide power to the less powerful and limit the autonomy of those who have it.

The consumer movement has a view of organizations as mechanisms designed to achieve service ends and goals. They do not see that organizations lead a life of their own, dictated by the needs of their members, for security on the job and by the needs of the organization for survival. They do not accept the view of organizations as coalitions of various interests who use the organization to achieve their particular purposes (Pfeffer & Salancik, 1977).

Even when organizations are clear about the complexities of organizational life, they have a further problem in determining just what type of change they are aiming at by instituting client feedback. For example, a father asks an adolescent about her allowance. Is it sufficient? Is she handling it wisely? Depending on what is said, some training on money handling may be called for or the allowance may have to be raised.

Nelsen (1980) calls this first order change. "This term connotes fluctuations in the behavior of system members while the system itself remains unchanged. That is, as long as the operating rules which govern system functioning persist, no real change within the system will take place" (p. 39). As such in the example given above the parent doesn't change his basic approach to his child — the allowance is merely fine-tuned. Similarly with first order change, an agency would not change its basic approach to helping clients — it would try to improve on it with the help of feedback.

Even though this type of feedback is not easy to operationalize in an agency, Nelsen (1980) suggests that there is a second order of change whose intent is much broader and deeper. "Systems change or second order change occurs by definition when there is change in the system operating rules . . . the information which stimulates second order change conflicts in its implications with the system's basic operating rules" (p. 39).

Consider the example above of the teenager and her parent discussing her allowance. The parent is anxious to get feedback about how the teenager is handling the allowance. Instead of simply providing this information the teenager goes on to say, "You'd be a lot better father if you weren't right so often." This feedback is what Nelsen describes as conflicting in its implications with a system's basic operating rules. The competence and confidence of the adult has to have been jolted, at least momentarily.

Such feedback from clients can threaten the stability of agencies. Yet, these threats of system upset are usually countered by homeostatic mechanisms in agencies — values, norms, decision-making premises, communication patterns, and the like — which enforce existing operating rules.

Argyris (1982) calls for double-loop learning as a way of dealing with homeostasis, where an organization and its leadership question their reasoning processes and raise questions about organizational norms and decision premises that limit their capacity to process new information such as might come from client feedback.

While it is beyond the scope of this paper to discuss the methodology of double-loop learning, it is clear that simply hoping that client feedback will rid the organization of actions that escalate errors, lead to self-fulfilling prophecies, and enforce taboos on discussions of core values and beliefs, is an underestimation of the power of homeostasis in organizations.

Most feedback projects do not distinguish between first and second order change and as such are not prepared for the problems that accompany either of these purposes. While the distinction between the two may not be as sharp as the words "first" and "second" imply and one may trail into the other, at some point there is a qualitative difference. As such, the issue for organizations is to know that point on the continuum of change they are shooting for when they set up a client feedback system, so that problems can be anticipated.

INITIATING CLIENT FEEDBACK

Client feedback programs are best viewed as attempts at organizational change. A simple model for understanding such change refers to three stages: initiation, implementation, and institutionalization of change (Gross, Giaquinta, & Bernstein, 1971).

The initiation of a change refers to those activities related to getting an organization to define problems, decide on solutions, and commit resources for implementation. Thus, a crucial issue is: What is the problem with which the client feedback system is designed to deal? There are, for example, more limited ends for which client feedback can be designed than simply program improvement and evaluation of client satisfaction. Does the agency need information about a problem, does it need to surface alternative solutions to problems, does it need help in assessing risks related to certain decisions, or help in setting priorities or assessing reactions to program changes or estimating resource needs? Depending on the purpose there are varying degrees of detail and complexity that can be anticipated.

Thus, the first step in instituting a client feedback project relates to getting acceptance of the problem definition, and of feedback as the solution, or part of the solution. One can expect that there will be those at the top, middle, and bottom of the organization who will not be enthusiastic about feedback, and who can withhold their sanction or the allocation of resources to the project. A client feedback project at the initiation stage must rest on a plan of how to handle the need for sanction and the need for resources.

Similarly, those who suggest feedback as a cure for a problem must be sure that the side effects are not greater or worse than the original disease. Social *iatrogenesis* is not an unknown factor. If top administration in an agency are the ones promoting client feedback, are they aware of the problems that feedback can make for staff? Are they aware of the problems that feedback make for clients? Without awareness they will generally reap very little for their efforts. The same can be said for staff if they see feedback as a panacea for their problems and are unaware of why the administration might have difficulty with it, or why the clients might have difficulty with it.

Reasons Clients Resist Providing Feedback

Many of the clients of social agencies are unsophisticated about formal organizations and quite suspicious of them. Many are convinced, for example, that if they criticize, they may be punished by having service denied. Many have a fear of any formal record, so they do not want anything written down with their name on it. Many clients have a sense of helplessness and dependency. They feel they must please, and their feedback is colored by this feeling. Taking their feedback at face value can give a false view of what is going on in an agency or program.

Other clients are very cynical, they don't believe anything will come of it. The kinds of data obtained from these clients can be quite biased. And lastly, some clients are very protective. They sense that perhaps the agency would like to fire somebody, maybe their worker, and they do not want to the be the cause, or they are afraid of retaliation from that person. They simply do not tell the truth. So a feedback system designed with the idea of improving service for the client is not at all necessarily perceived that way by the clients themselves (Shaw, 1976; Lebow, 1974).

Staff Attitudes to Feedback

There are a number of attitudes that have to be surfaced and dealt with if staff cooperation is to be enlisted in feedback projects. There is first of all, the obvious fear of exposure and threats attached to it. ''I may be pointed out as not competent.''

On the more sophisticated level there is the possibility of reinforcement of self-doubt. ''Am I really a competent social worker?'' There is also resistance to change. It is threatening to change, and it is threatening to be put into a situation where you may be forced to change.

Staff, on the other hand, often present some rather compelling and positive reasons why it makes good sense for them not to get involved with client feedback. First of all, they often say that the feedback is directed toward the workers, and what the workers did, but the feedback is not directed toward the agency or the system which may be at fault for the bad service. The wrong questions are being asked of the wrong people about the wrong thing.

Workers are also quick to point out, often with some justification, that they already have so much to do that they would be overwhelmed by a feedback system which requires a considerable amount of work on their part. And lastly, they point out that feedback systems are often geared to finding out what is wrong and not what is right. They never get praised, and they see the feedback system as another critical gun aimed at them (Weissman, 1977).

Problems the Agency Has With Client Feedback

Some of the problems that agencies exhibit are defensive. Others make a certain amount of sense. Many administrators are concerned, for example, that feedback from clients often has a result of raising expectations. If clients are asked how services can be improved, they will expect that something will be done; and it may be that the agency, because of resource or other constraints, cannot meet these expectations. Similarly, agencies often are somewhat dubious about the feedback they get because they are unsure of its reliability. To act precipitously can create many problems. Likewise the agency has many goals, not all of which can be dealt with simultaneously. If feedback focuses on a certain set of priorities, it may not be prudent for the organization to readjust its resources to these ends, certainly not an immediate basis. Executives are highly sensitive to such issues.

Likewise administrators are highly sensitive to anything which threatens the stability of the agency. The feedback may be accurate, but in a turbulent environment it can be used in a very detrimental way. Even if the administrator would like to do something, in crisis situations all resources and energy have to be put into surviving. The outside environment isn't always benign and administrators are aware of this.

On a more negative level, some administrators do in fact feel that the clients are not their crucial constituents so they don't have to pay them great mind. Other administrators have the feeling they know what is right for the client and that the client is really incapable of providing information that is really usable for program planning. After all, are they not mentally ill, or children, or criminals?

Overcoming Client Resistance

In terms of dealing with the concerns of clients, a number of potential solutions have emerged. First, clients should be assured of anonymity. There is really no need in most cases for using the client's name on feedback forms. Timing, when feedback is secured, is also important. When the client is about to leave the agency is a better time than when the client is receiving service in terms of allaying the client's fear of retaliation. Who the interviewer is who asks for the feedback is important. Where the interview takes place could have an effect.

Making sure that one has a representative group of clients could help to insure reliability. Also helpful is feeding information back to clients to deal with the issue of their feeling that nothing will come of feedback. Hearing about what others may have said indicates that the agency is serious about what clients have to say.

There are also some data to show that by asking clients and involving them in formulating the questions to be asked of other clients, they may ask different types of questions than staff or administrators would ask. For example, clients have been known to ask such questions as "Did the worker visit me in my home?" Such a question was not deemed important in at least one study that was carried out by professionals (Prager & Tanaka, 1980).

Overcoming Staff Resistance

Clearly, feedback from clients can be made more palatable to staff in anonymity is respected. Probably the worst thing that can be done to a client feedback system is to use it to pick out problem staff. Other more normal means of supervision should be used for this purpose. What a client feedback system should be doing is picking up problems that cut across an agency's way of dealing with clients rather than with problem workers. Another useful way of diffusing staff resistance is to involve them in developing the procedures that will be utilized in securing feedback. This is not merely a ploy, but is an important factor to consider as staff have quite good ideas about the amount of time, and about where and when and how programs should be carried out.

Similarly, it would be very important to involve the staff in an evaluation of agency practices and programs prior to instituting a client feedback system. In a certain sense, the feedback is only as useful as those who receive it are willing to make it. If staff feel interested in finding out what clients are saying and not threatened by this, they are more likely to utilize the information. Similarly, if the agency administration has been involved in evaluating the organization, thinking about the total organization, then client feedback can be seen in this context, rather than simply in the context of what staff do or don't do.

Ways of Overcoming Agency Resistance

Certainly a feedback system should best be piloted on a small basis, to understand the consequences for the total operations of the agency. Generally pilot projects engender less resistance. Likewise, client feedback projects initially should focus on ad hoc issues such as assessing reactions to program change, rather than total agency effectiveness, as a way of defusing organizational resistance.

There is nothing that makes an organization more defensive than threats to its adaptive system, the system that provides the resources it needs. An agency should develop a climate of support among its input system for critical evaluation before engaging in client evaluation of services. There is nothing more likely to cause evasiveness and defensiveness than the feeling that criticism is going to be used in a hostile and negative manner.

Perhaps the key to helping administration to move forward with client feedback is a clear step-by-step plan of how such projects will be implemented. Confidence in judging consequences and problems is heightened by planning.

For example, there are a number of questions, the answers to which can either gain the support or alienate an agency administration. These include: (a) under what organizational conditions are staff and agency able to make maximum use of client feedback; (b) what is the relationship of client feedback to staff training and other forms of research; (c) how much time, money and effort are required for staff to mount a client feedback project; (d) what are the effects of disparate auspices in carrying out the feedback? Should it be under a particular department, such as the training department, or at a particular organizational level, etc.?

What often happens to a plan is that compromise is inevitably called for to get the needed sanction and resources to implement it. The question is: Will the compromise the administration insists upon doom the project, or will it promote the ends of the project? The more one can project forward around issues of implementation, the more likely it is that one will not compromise the essence of what the project is intended to be nor lose the support of an administration.

IMPLEMENTING CLIENT FEEDBACK PROJECTS

The key issue of the implementation phase of any change project is getting an organization to change its procedures and to change the behavior of its members to fit the new mold. This requires getting an appropriate fit between the social and technical systems of the organization.

The problems of implementation have generally been attributed to insufficient or inadequate planning, or if the plan is well laid out, to not having enough political power actually to implement it. Graham Allison (1971) suggests a third factor. He makes a case for the fact that organizations have standard operating procedures (SOPs) for implementing various programs. If one is proposing something like a client feedback system that requires a different SOP, than, say, the agency's regular intake procedures, there is a risk of implementation proceeding as always, using the regular procedure with little or no notice being taken of the new manner in which is should be done if it is to be successful.

Planning

As noted, problems can emerge because the plan has not been well thought out or, for a variety of reasons problems can emerge because the plan is poorly executed. Poor planning is generally related to not asking sufficient questions and therefore not being able to anticipate inevitable problems.

For example, are people being asked to change their behavior radically? What are the rewards for doing so? How can organizational commitment to feedback be maintained when other projects or goals require shifts in agency priorities? How much control is required of whom to implement the plan successfully? When and how can a feedback project be delayed and what contingency plans exist to handle this delay?

Perhaps the most important part of the implementation phase is to have the feedback on the feedback system in place, so that problems can be surfaced quickly. Often, for example, what occurs is a drop in staff morale. What is hoped for does not materialize. Clients are not so happy. Problems are surfaced for which there is not an easy solution. Unless these issues are surfaced quickly and unless management can deal with them quickly, the emergent problems will destroy the feedback system. Thus the development of a plan for operationalizing client feedback requires a clear understanding of what happens when feedback is given. Von Glinow and Sethia (1983) suggest that feedback is a three-phase process: the acceptance phase, the action planning phase which related to usability, and the utilization phase which actually relates to the outcomes. Acceptance relates to factors that influence the agency or staff person to pay attention to the feedback and regard it as a basis for future action.

Acceptance refers to staff's belief that feedback is an accurate portrayal of their performance. Whether or not this belief is correct is inconsequential for its acceptance. It is staff's inclination to pay attention to feedback and consider it as the basis for modifying particular task-related behavior that is important.

Studies have shown that source credibility, the expertise and trustworthiness of the source, is a major factor influencing acceptance of feedback. In addition to credibility, the basic source characteristic is power, power based on expertise, or power that derives form actual authority to administer punishments (Giardin, 1977).

Clients are not thought to have considerable expertise, perhaps not viewed as particularly trustworthy, and certainly have very little power in most agencies. so if these are the factors which influence the acceptance of feedback, one can see that it is difficult indeed to set up a client feedback system and have it utilized.

On the other hand, the values of social workers strongly support the clients' right to determine what happens to them, so there may be some off-setting factors operating in an attempt to gain acceptance of feedback processes. Nevertheless, if staff don't believe that they are really capable of doing anything about client concerns nor are able to acquire the skills or authority to respond to clients then this perceived reality is going to affect their ability to accept as well as use the feedback (Warfel, Maloney & Blase, 1981).

There are also some studies which show that different personality types have different needs and expectations about performance, and that they would differ in their receptivity to any given type of feedback (Rilgin, Fisher, & Taylor, 1979). While it would seem hard to tailor feedback to individuals re their personality types, one at least should anticipate that there will be differential responses to the feedback.

There are also data to show that the characteristics of the feedback message itself have an effect on staff acceptance. The salient factor according to Nadler and colleagues (1976) is that the feedback system should increase the type and quality of information available to employees. Probably another would defeat a client feedback system more than trivial information where staff felt they were learning nothing new.

The action planning phase of the feedback begins once the feedback has been accepted by the recipient. Then a decision has to be taken on a specific plan of action in response to the feedback. The key issue here, according to Von Glinow and Sethia (1983), is the usability of the feedback for the recipients, which determines the likelihood as well as the promptness of the response.

Other factors also make it easier or harder for staff to develop a specific plan of action in response to client feedback. Four emerge from the literature (Von Glinow & Sethia, 1983). These include: validity, specificity, consistency, and timeliness of feedback information. In a certain sense, these are fairly self-evident. How specific is the information, and how valid is it? How reliable is it? Are we getting consistent information? Is it really true? How timely is it? Can we do anything about what we are hearing?

Power and Leadership

The plan of action for using feedback hinges on the ends to which feedback is to be put. So does the utilization phase which refers to what the staff and agency actually do with the feedback. For example, if second order change is the intent, management will have to deal with the homeostatic controls that enforce adherence to the status quo.

Feedback can have: (a) a directing function through goal adjustment, error correction and role clarification; (b) a motivating function by giving staff a sense of their performance and also by providing them with a sense of competence; (c) a development function by enabling staff to learn new things, ask different questions, and develop a new self-awareness; and (d) an attitude sharing function by giving staff a sense that they are involved in a serious endeavor and thereby increasing organizational commitment (Von Glinow & Sethia, 1983).

As such, a feedback system will inevitably involve some shift in the power balance. Some formal authority will be eroded, as questions about agency practice which formerly were not considered legitimate become very legitimate. There will be status threats.

Similarly, a client feedback system often increases the level of dissent in an organization. Unless the organization has institutionalized mechanisms for dealing with dissent, it is going to be tossed and turned and perhaps ripped apart by the feedback system. In essence a client feedback system will reveal the tension and lack of congruence between the survival needs of an organization and its need to be effective.

Organizational ignorance is often functional in that it limits tension and limits dissent. A generalized client feedback system is anathema for organizational ignorance. The implementation phase thus hangs on the ability of those who have instituted it to maintain the sanction and support, as well as have sufficient power to overcome emerging problems. It is at this implementation phase that those who have had doubts or been opposed, suddenly find ammunition to stop the project (Rosentahl & Weiss, 1966).

Perhaps the most crucial issue is whether management has both the skill and style of leadership commensurate with the problems. A client feedback system instituted across the agency is a system that has to have the absolute attention of the executive director; it initially cannot be delegated, because the issues will be large and complex. If, for example, the client feedback system begins to surface problems in service delivery, one can anticipate that staff in a variety of levels will be insecure about suddenly being exposed. Leadership will be required that makes it known that in fact it wants and will reward staff for openness about problems. Problems are opportunities rather than problems are demerits (Schein, 1985).

In this vein, Williams (1975) notes that:

> Subordinates may be unable, or find it difficult, to make changes in their role performance unless management conforms to a set of expectations that subordinates "have a right" to hold: for its performance. More specifically, subordinates have a right to expect management (1) to take the steps necessary to provide them with a clear picture of their new role requirements; (2) to adjust organizational arrangements to make them compatible with the innovation; (3) to provide subordinates with necessary retraining experiences, required if the capability for coping with the difficulties of implementing the innovation are to develop; (4) to provide the resources necessary to carry out the innovation; and (5) to provide the appropriate supports and rewards to maintain subordinates' willingness to make implementation efforts. (p. 23)

Structure and SOPs

The key issue for leadership is to utilize the client feedback system so that there are shared tensions. This really requires a communication system that surfaces problems that staff and clients feel: (1) tension generated in clients deriving from discrepancies between what clients expect and what they receive; (2) tension generated by the staff resulting from the differences between what they are asked to do and what they think they should do; and (3) tensions generated in management between what they perceive they want to do and what they perceive they can do. In other words, a client feedback system without a staff and agency feedback system is probably dangerous. And one without the other probably won't work. Shared tensions, or mutual understanding of the pressures that various parties operate under will not singlehandedly lead to actions that will satisfy everyone or even to good problems solutions, but they are a necessary condition for successful execution of feedback projects (Weissman, 1983).

INSTITUTIONALIZING CLIENT FEEDBACK

No matter how well-implemented, another danger awaits client feedback projects, when the attempt is made to institutionalize them as an ongoing part of an agency's operation. One problem related to institutionalizing a project is that there is often no plan for securing the resources needed on an ongoing basis.

Likewise, there is no plan for getting the enlarged sanction that such a system requires, nor is there a plan for handling recalcitrants. Moving to the institutionalization phase without having a sense of how to handle these three issues is dangerous and perilous.

Feedback does not usually have a linear relationship to productivity. It will, as noted, create conflict, especially in a turbulent environment where resources are scarce and agencies may be threatened. There is ample opportunity for a counter-revolution. A plan for handling the opposition has to be in place.

For example, board support is crucial. If the agency operates in a political atmosphere, crucial actors outside of the agency should be brought along, and their support should be generated. Internally, if one has started with a pilot project, at the implementation phase a plan should have been developed to keep people in the agency abreast of the problems and successes, thereby generating their commitment for the institutionalization phase.

Institutionalization of feedback is primarily involved in monitoring a project and routinizing it. This involves clarity over tasks and building in a set of rewards for all concerned. It also involves setting up an accountability system for determining that its procedures are working well and that it is achieving what it intended to achieve.

A client feedback system should provide the kind of data that will help workers do a better job, that will surface problems, and surface potential solutions. Such intentions will be defeated if, as noted, it is used in the supervisory process to find out which workers are not doing well. This will usually generate sufficient hostility and fear to cause the system ultimately to break down.

A client feedback system that aims at evaluation of services usually involves the retraining of staff when it is institutionalized. It will inevitably result in a redistribution of internal power and authority, and to a certain extent re-orient the agency's external relations as changes in different directions are suggested.

Ultimately, a feedback system is one of the most profound changes that can be introduced into a social agency. Workers somehow must come to own the change. They must see it as a self-rewarding mechanism which involves the provision of a new cognitive structure. For this to occur, they must have some opportunity to influence how it operates and to improvise with it. Similarly, there must be verification that the system is really doing something good, not only for the workers but for the agency itself. Otherwise, it will probably collapse.

CONCLUSION

Client feedback is not a panacea. It is one thing to be aware of a problem and another thing to be able to do something about it. Skill and knowledge are clearly important variables.

Nevertheless, it is a panacea in one sense, because it provides a counterforce to the one-sided provider perspective that is prevalent in many social agencies. It is also an important issue if agencies are serious about helping clients help themselves.

Sidel (1976) points out that the responsibility for quality service rests with professionals because of their greater knowledge. Yet he notes that "professional responsibility for the quality of . . . care should be to help those who receive . . . services increasingly to take over the responsibility and authority for maintaining and improving the quality of their own care." While this may be a utopian view, nevertheless it is unlikely that a passive client is really a learning client.

While this paper has emphasized the problems related to developing client feedback projects, these are not insurmountable. Agencies require clarity about the purposes for which they intend to use feedback, a plan and a strategy for implementation, and a capacity to utilize the feedback effectively once they get it.

The potential gains are enormous. To return to the parent-child metaphor. Parents who are concerned about feedback from their children are more likely to see their children develop into healthy adults. An agency which pays attention to client feedback can improve its decision-making, increase mutual understanding among its participants, create an atmosphere for trial and error learning, and heighten commitment to its ends, as well as more effectively deliver services to clients (Maluccio, 1979).

REFERENCES

Allison, G. *Essence of decision.* Boston: Little Brown, 1971.
Argyris, C. *Reasoning, learning and action.* San Francisco: Jossey-Bass, 1982.
Giardino. P. The clients' perspective in agency evaluation. *Social Work,* 1977, *22,* 35-36.
Gross, N., Giaquinta, J. & Bernstein, M. *Implementing organizational innovations.* New York: Basic Books, 1971.

Lebow, J. L. Consumer assessments of the quality of medical care. *Medical Care,* 1974, *12,* 328-337.

Maluccio, A. *Learning from clients: Interpersonal helping as viewed by clients and social workers.* New York: The Free Press, 1979.

Nadler, D., Mervis, P. & Cammann, C. The ongoing feedback system. *Organizational Dynamics,* 1976, *4,* 63-68.

Nelsen, J. *Communication theory and social work practice.* Chicago: University of Chicago Press, 1980.

Pfeffer, J. & Salancik, G. The case for a coalitional model of organizations. *Organizational Dynamics,* 1977, *6,* 15-29.

Prager, E. & Tanaka, H. Self-Assessment: The clients' perspective. *Social Work,* 1980, *25,* 32-36.

Rilgin, D., Fisher, C. & Taylor M. Consequences of individual feedback on behavior in organizations. *Journal of Applied Psychology,* 1979, *64,* 349-371.

Rosenthal, R. & Weiss, R. Problems of organizational feedback processes. In Bauer (Ed.) *Social indicators.* Cambridge: M.I.T. Press, 1966.

Schein, E. *Organizational culture and leadership.* San Francisco: Jossey- Bass, 1985.

Shaw, I. Consumer opinion and social policy. *Journal of Social Policy* 1976, *5,* 19-32.

Sidel, V. Quality for Whom? Effects of professional responsibility for quality of health care on equity. *Bulletin of the New York Academy of Medicine,* 1976, *52,* 175.

Von Glinow, M. & Sethia, N. The role of feedback in the creation of useful knowledge. In Kilmann et al. (Eds.) *Producing useful knowledge for organization.* New York: Praeger, 1983.

Warfel, D., Maloney, L. & Blase, K. Consumer feedback in human service programs. *Social Work,* 1981, *26,* 151-155.

Weissman, J. Accountability and pseudo-accountability: A non-linear approach. *Social Service Review,* 1983, *57,* 326-328.

Weissman, H. Clients, staff and researchers. *Administration in Social Work,* 1977, *1,* 56-48.

Wildavsky, A. The self-evaluating organization. *Public Administration Review,* 1972, 509-520.

Williams, W. Implementation, analysis and assessment. *Policy Analysis,* 1975, *1,* 548.

SECTION SIX: MANAGING ENVIRONMENTAL RELATIONS

Introduction

The acquisition, allocation, and use of resources in ways that enhance organizational performance are critical managerial tasks. The ability to effect positive differences in the lives of those served by social work programs depends a great deal on how administrators manage the funds, clients, community influence, professional knowledge, staff, facilities, the organizational base, and public goodwill of human service organizations.

These myriad human and material resources on which human service organizations depend in order to produce client benefits must be obtained and managed within a complex socio-political environment. In the face of a broad and often conflictual array of environmental values, human service administrators often feel trapped between meeting multiple constituents' demands and meeting clients' needs. Patricia Yancey Martin analyzed this dilemma well in her work, "Multiple Constituencies, Dominant Societal Values, and the Human Service Administrator: Implications for Service Delivery" (*Administration in Social Work*, 1980, *4*(2), 15-27). Her work is a significant contribution to understanding the apparent dilemmas administrators face in the realm of managing resources, and explains why administrators often shunt client centered practice to the "back burner" in their attempts to ease this dilemma.

The multiple constituent dilemma makes the management of influence with external and internal constituents a critical skill, as it is often through the persistent and thoughtful use of influence that administrators obtain the funds, staff, material goods, and community goodwill which programs require to meet clients' needs.

In the first article, Martin builds on her previous work, cited above, by articulating ten action strategies for administrators to apply in bringing service effectiveness to the forefront of program operation. These strategies are based on the concept of proactive leadership, in which administrators' daily practice is guided more by values, action, and vision, and less by rationality, control, or analysis. The author argues that much opportunity exists within social welfare organizations' environment of competing and conflicting values to champion service effectiveness. Administrators committed to quality client outcomes can use these action strategies to promote and inspire similar commitment among their programs' various constituents.

In the second article in this section, Ronald L. Simons focuses on one aspect of managing influence, the use of persuasion. The author identifies specific principles for administrators to apply in using persuasion, illustrated with examples from social work management practice. Building on previous research in this area, Simons argues that developing and using influence is one of the key skills comprising generic social work practice.

Multiple Constituencies and Performance in Social Welfare Organizations: Action Strategies for Directors

Patricia Yancey Martin, PhD

Organizational performance has been an issue in the human services for over a decade (Glisson & Martin, 1980; Austin & Hasenfeld, 1985). In social welfare organizations (SWOs), performance encompasses a multitude of activities and criteria, some of which involve service effectiveness (Patti, 1985), and identifying good versus poor performance is a difficult task. The multiple constituencies nature of welfare organizations (Martin, 1980a; 1980b) means that performance must be defined broadly enough to include the competing interests, activities, and goals of individuals and groups both inside and outside the organization's boundary. Additionally, it must include organizational well-being as well as service effectiveness (Meyer & Rowan, 1977).

This paper concerns performance of social welfare organizations in a multiple constituencies milieu. Multiple constituencies are the many individuals and interest groups, internal and external to the SWO, who have expectations of it, a stake in its fate, and/or control over valued resources (Scott, 1977; Martin, 1980a, 1980b; Connolly, Conlon, & Deutsch, 1980; Cameron, 1984). Particularly important in a multiple constituencies conception of SWO performance is the organization's director. An SWO director, or chief executive officer, is the titular head of the organization or, in large state agencies, the head of categorical programs. A director has greater internal authority (official power) than any other organizational member and is the premiere representative of the SWO to the external world. Effective daily operations are greatly affected by the director's knowledge, skills, and behaviors relative to constituents inside and outside of the SWO and

Dr. Martin is Professor, School of Social Work, and Affiliated Professor, Department of Sociology, Florida State University, Tallahassee, FL 32306.

223

successful organization change projects require a director's full-fledged involvement and support (Boss & Boss, 1985). Lack of vision and proactive leadership on the director's part can lead to passive, ineffectual organizations whose primary achievement is avoidance of repudiation or penalty. In a resource-scarce environment where competition for funds is intense while the need for social services and benefits remains great, welfare organizations cannot afford to be passive or ineffectual. One aim of this paper is to identify Action Strategies for use by SWO directors. Action Strategies are prescriptive tactics which directors can use with internal and external constituents to promote service effectiveness and organizational well-being.

PERFORMANCE AS SERVICE EFFECTIVENESS AND ORGANIZATIONAL WELL-BEING

Performance in social welfare organizations includes two broad forms of activity: (a) core work activity engaged in by SWO members in accord with the organization's official mission, and (b) legitimacy activity engaged in by SWO member's (or others on its behalf) to foster organizational well-being. The former concerns service, control or public interest activities whereas the latter consists of conformity to standards and practices which are valued by the organization's primary constituents, especially in the environment (Meyer & Rowan, 1977). Discussions of core work activities focus on effectiveness of work performed or the quality of service delivered (Cameron, 1986b; Cameron & Whetten, 1983; Martin & Segal, 1977),whereas discussions of legitimacy focus on compliance of the organization with valued themes in the organization's institutional, task, and resource environments (Meyer, Scott & Deal, 1981). In the Action Strategies section, tactics are identified for use by SWO directors to maximize both service effectiveness and organizational well-being.

Core work activities (CWAs) can be one of two types: (1) actions which assist or control clients, and (2) actions which foster the public interest or collective good. Core work activities in a juvenile detention center consist of monitoring and restricting the whereabouts and activities of young people who are under the aegis of the juvenile court, whereas core work activities in Ralph Nader's consumer advocacy organization involve lobbying legislators, exposing manufacturers who violate safety standards, and so forth. From an open-systems perspective, core work activities transform or process raw materials (clients, information, etc.) for exchange with the environment (Hasenfeld, 1983).

Performance as service effectiveness concerns the quality and content of core work activities performed by SWO staff. This conception of performance reflects a Goal Achievement Model of organizational effectiveness (Cameron, 1984). SWO directors are responsible for the quality, quantity, and appropriateness of core work activities performed by agency staff (Kaufman, 1981; Carter, 1983). They must assure also that aspects of core work activities which are important to powerful constituents are conducted in ways that are consistent with their expectations. These include proper record-keeping, documentation, due process actions and so forth. The latter are internal legitimacy activities which, if violated, threaten organizational well-being.

Legitimacy activities. Practices which demonstrate compliance with legal statutes, regulations, and valued themes in the SWO's institutional environment are legitimacy activities. Some activities are mandated by the environment as when legislatures or courts require investigation of reported child abuse cases within 24 hours or mandatory reporting to law enforcement of incest cases. Other legitimacy activities are optional such as "celebrating rationality in organizational operations" (Meyer & Scott, 1983, p. 212) to gain support from a business-minded public for the SWO's approach to management. Both types affect organizational well-being because SWO outputs are as much symbolic as concrete in nature (Scott, 1983).

Legitimacy activities which involve external constituents are: showing compliance with local, state, and federal government laws, rules and regulations, maintaining good relations in and with the community, participation in a "web of service network" (Czarniawska, 1985), developing positive relations with the media, facilitating the work of other SWOs (Molnar & Rogers, 1976), and providing jobs for citizens (Martin, 1986). These activities affect the SWO's ability to acquire financial resources and community goodwill, attract and retain qualified and respected staff, and attract appropriate and sufficient clients. Readers acquainted with the organizational effectiveness literature will note that these activities reflect the System Resource, Legitimacy and Multiple Constituencies Models of effectiveness (Cameron, 1984).

Internal legitimacy issues include the manner in which core work activities are performed relative to legal statutes (timeliness, documentation, etc.), requirements for proper expenditure of funds, appropriate conduct of staff (competent, ethical), staff's motivation to be helpful (Prottas, 1979), prompt, fair, courteous, and friendly treatment of core activity recipients (Lipsky, 1980), and staff initiative, enthusiasm, and cooperation in performing core work activities (Whiddon & Martin, 1986). All these activities are organizational performance and all affect, directly or indirectly, the effectiveness of work performed by staff. If an SWO loses financial resources or the public's goodwill, core work activities may be reduced both quantitatively and qualitatively, staff morale may suffer, and so forth. In a test of the multiple constituencies model of organizational effectiveness, Cameron (1986b) found that the most effective organizations were "those that satisfied the most separate constituency group expectations, even when different constituencies held contradictory expectations. Highly effective organizations were paradoxical. They performed in contradictory ways to satisfy contradictory expectations" (p. 550). The effective use of paradox is a theme of Peters and Waterman's (1982) bestseller, *In Search of Excellence*. Successful directors of social welfare organizations can benefit from this skill as well.

LEADERSHIP AND THE SWO DIRECTOR

Directors of social welfare organizations spend an inordinate amount of time (over 50 percent) dealing with external constituents (Files, 1981). Compared to managers in the private, for-profit sector:

Public sector managers are under more stress, under the public eye constantly, have so many demands for appearances they cannot refuse. Also, they're always on a tight rope of balancing time for internal management and external contacts and appearances. There is no consensus for them to do only internal. (Czarniawska, 1985, p. 102)

Consistent with this, SWO directors spend far more time in interorganizational relations (negotiating, bargaining) than do business managers whereas the latter spend more time supervising and motivating staff (Files, 1981). SWO staff often complain about directors who are "never at the agency," failing to appreciate that the job requires extensive and continual dealings with a multiple constituencies environment.

Effective SWO directors exhibit proactive leadership both inside and outside the organization. Leadership is defined as unleashing energy, building, and freeing (Peters & Austin, 1985) and as interpreting changes on the outside for inside needs and focusing on the environment as opportunity rather than obstacle (Czarniawska, 1985). It also includes the management of meaning for organizational members and the creation of an organizational culture—a positive work climate characterized by enthusiasm, proactivity, and commitment to high quality (Lemke & Moos, 1986). There are no obvious effectiveness criteria in social welfare organizations, thus directors who show leadership must be innovative, willing to buck the tide, and capable of "selling" their conception of the excellent agency (or program) to a variety of publics and interest groups (Martin, 1980b; Carter, 1983).

ACTION STRATEGIES FOR LEADERSHIP BY SWO DIRECTORS

Action Strategies for SWO leadership reflect three conclusions from the foregoing analysis. (1) External and internal constituents must be nurtured if service effectiveness and organizational well-being are to be maximized; (2) legitimacy concerns must be addressed in both internal and external realms; and (3) a proactive vision of the SWO's service mission and goals must be articulated, enacted and promoted by the director if core work activities are to be effective. Patti (1985) describes the latter as an "effectiveness driven" model of social welfare administration.

The Action Strategies which follow make three assumptions about the SWO director. They assume the director: (1) possesses a vision of purpose regarding the SWO's service mission and goals (e.g., has an effectiveness driven conception of social welfare organizations); (2) is committed to seeing it implemented; and (3) has the skills to implement it. Although each of these assumptions is problematic and deserves extensive treatment, this paper addresses the first and third only: the vision of purpose around which organizational members and constituents can be rallied and strategies for implementation. Commitment to implement is, we hope, instilled in graduate social work programs where values regarding the public interest and the alleviation of human want are emphasized (Patti, 1985). Skills for implementation are perhaps the most problematic of the three assumptions. The present analysis suggests that legitimacy skills (associated with negotiation, dealing with constituents, monitoring internal regulations and processes) and leadership skills (associated with culture-building and directing and inspiring staff) are both essential. Social work Master's degree curricula tend to concentrate on skills associated with a rational-technical conception of management where internal administrative tasks (budgeting, staffing, organizing) are primary. Curriculum changes may be called for if present conclusions are correct.

A Vision of Purpose

This concerns what to value and why. To promote service effectiveness, an SWO director must have a vision of purpose for the organization including understanding of its mission and a conception of how to fulfill it (Patti, 1985). This includes culture-building activities to foster a sense of purpose, mission, and meaning in organizational members and external constituents. The aim is to maximize service effectiveness by providing inspiration, direction and support for excellent core activity work which emphasizes service, control, and/or the public interest as the premiere organizational value. The premise that SWO directors desire a high quality of core activity presumes a conception of what that is. A frequent problem with directors who are uneducated in the social services is the lack of such a concept. Unfortunately, many social work trained directors also lack a clear and viable vision of purpose. Social welfare administration curricula must address the contributions of social welfare organizations to the common good and explore the pivotal role of the director in their success.

Commitment to the Vision

It is not enough to believe that SWOs have a service mission nor is it enough to be "a good manager." The effective SWO director has a personal belief in and commitment to the SWO's mission and promotes it as the primary organizational value to both internal and external constituents. Without commitment to a service effectiveness vision, SWOs tend to drift, to succumb to powerful constituents, and to live by the letter of the law (and regulations) rather than by a vision of purpose.

Skills to Implement

Skills to implement are concrete actions by directors which produce results in accord with the vision of purpose. Many SWO administrators say "the right things" but have little notion of how to produce desired results. For example, the practice of "management by wandering around" (MBWA), a hands-on management style identified by Peters and Waterman (1982) as characteristic of outstanding companies, is endorsed by SWO directors who have no idea of how to practice it. Directors who claim to practice it, but do not, are frequently the butt of staff jokes and derision (Kanter, 1983; Peters & Austin, 1985). Mastery of leadership skills which are consistent with one's vision of purpose and which promote a proactive, service-oriented culture is important. Also, legitimation skills to gain the support of multiple constituents are necessary. The former promotes service effectiveness, the latter organizational well-being.

What to value and how to achieve one's goals are problematic in the multiple constituencies context of social welfare organizations (Gornick, Burt & Pittman, 1985). The Action Strategies which follow contain elements of both what and how. Although they reflect a concept of proactive leadership, translating them into concrete action is not easy. The SWO director who fosters excellence will leave the secure realms of "management" and "administration" and venture into the less well defined world of vision, experimentation, and commitment (Peters & Austin, 1985). Leadership in the social welfare arena is not well conceptualized or defined and may not be rewarded by important constituents (Carter, 1983; Kaufman, 1981). If legitimacy claims can be made to engender meaning and give a sense of pride and satisfaction to those who have a stake in the SWO, however, benefits can emerge. The Action Strategies which follow reflect both legitimacy and effectiveness concerns.

Action Strategy I

Tie organizational mission to environmental values. To enhance legitimacy, SWO leaders should articulate organizational goals which are consistent with valued environmental themes. In US society, efficient, well managed organizations are admired; thus, assurance that the SWO is well managed can enhance legitimacy and respect. Standards of efficiency and "good management" in the social welfare arena are nebulous but awareness of the importance of such criteria can reassure powerful constituents that the SWO director knows what s/he is about (Wiewel & Hunt, 1985). Since SWOs in the governmental and not-for-profit sectors are supported with public funds, claims of efficient use of resources assure constituents (including the media) that the public trust is deserved. Statements by directors to external constituents promote legitimacy when they claim that rational, technical, and scientific approaches have been taken to the matter at hand (Czarniawska, 1985). A "bit of pathos" can be employed if not overdone. My research suggests that pathos is particularly effective with certain audiences. If the audience is the local Kiwanis Club, mostly middle class males, emphasis on efficiency and rational management may be the key. If, however, the audience is Junior League women, dramatization of a wife/mother and her children who were physically abused by their stock broker husband/father may be most effective.

Legitimacy theme utility varies by constituency, including gender and social class. Multiple values should be called upon (Wiewel & Hunt, 1985). The proper mix of message and audience can do much to create goodwill, support, and a sense of pride in the social welfare organization. Audiences want to feel good and accountings which provide this opportunity produce positive benefits. Finally, in an individualistic society such as ours, SWO leaders who persuasively promote the common good can stimulate support for their organizations and for overall societal welfare. In a society which has little use for collective humanitarian goals unless personal self-interest is involved, SWO directors have a unique opportunity to translate the self-interest of various constituency groups into values and strategies which promote the common good.

Action Strategy II

Action over analysis. Effective organizational directors are those who engage in "action rationality" not "decision-making rationality" (Brunsson, 1985). Action rationality consists of choosing a course of organizational action or change based on values, preferences, and beliefs and building support for that option, from the ground up. The decision-making model urges consideration of all alternatives, full analysis of each one, and a "rational" decision on the basis of all the facts of the single best choice. In his research on for-profit and public sector organizations, Brunsson (1985) found that this approach undermines the ability of organizations to get things done. Action requires certainty not uncertainty and consideration of all possible alternatives tends to generate uncertainty; many possibilities make commitment to a single one difficult. If organizational members need to be convinced of a course of action, directors should select a reference alternative which is clearly less attractive than the chosen one (Brunsson, 1985). Build a case by choosing the alternative which is believed to be best, which has the best chance of being adopted, and for which real support can be developed. Brunsson's finding of the utility of action over analysis (rational decision-making) is consistent with Peters and Waterman (1982) who found that America's best-run companies spend relatively little time in analysis and much effort in "getting on with it."

Action Strategy III

Maintain good (positive, cooperative, honest, frequent) relations within one's "web of influence." Web of influence is Czarniawska's (1985) term for all constituents and organizations with which a SWO relates directly and indirectly. Communication and active contact with all groups in an organization's web of influence are necessary, particularly with organizations similar to one's own (Wiewel & Hunter, 1985). Whetten's research (1978) found that community leaders believe a social welfare organization is effective if they are familiar with it and ineffective if not. Visibility is interpreted as effectiveness. Opportunity to establish legitimacy claims is limited if the director remains aloof from the environment. Dealing with the conflicting interests associated with scarcity of resources requires a track record of courteous, good faith relationships over time. One of Czarniawska's (1985) public directors describes this as follows.

> Now, good relations do not mean that you always have the same opinion as everybody else but you can have good relations by always appearing, by always taking part in the dialogue, by always answering questions, by not hiding yourself in some kind of an isolated room. (p. 66)

Action Strategy IV

Use power to help others. Ironically, power is used by those who understand it to help, not control, others. Kanter (1977, 1983) defines power as clout or the ability to make things happen. People who successfully innovate in work organizations are those who use their clout, to make things happen, in a positive, productive way. Molnar and Rogers (1976) found that organizations with more resources (larger budgets, more staff, more programs) give more assistance to other organizations than they receive. They had assumed that larger, more resourceful organizations would be more successful at exploiting their environment of resources yet found they give more resources to their environments. The facilitative or giving organization realizes that assisting other organizations (and the community) builds bridges of support, goodwill, and commitment. Assistance also obligates the recipient to the provider. Assisting others in the community pays off in many ways.

This principle applies internally as well as externally. Kanter's research (1977) found that "powerlessness," not power, was the key to organizational turfguarding, rigidity, and lack of cooperativeness. People who have opportunities to make things happen develop a sense of efficacy and pride and are far more likely to in turn help others. The right to act autonomously is an important requisite for an effective and productive staff (Whiddon & Martin, 1986).

Action Strategy V

Continually educate your constituents. Organizational phenomena have a short half-life; they are, that is, quickly forgotten. SWO staff turn over frequently, particularly on the front-line in stressful work contexts such as county welfare agencies (Prottas, 1979). Legislatures and local elected bodies change not only due to election of new members but rotation of chairpersons and associated authority. Clubs and organizations such as neighborhood associations, garden clubs, civic clubs such as Pilot, Altrusa, Kiwanis, Rotary, and churches have turnover in voluntary leaders who serve a term and relinquish their positions to others. As a result, the SWO leader can never assume the field has been covered. Support from a given constituency may disappear with a change in leadership. Of course, leadership changes in the SWO as well. An urgent task of the new SWO leader (new to the position) is to meet and educate important others in the organization's web of influence. Constituents inside the SWO have to be educated also. Articulation of the organization's mission, basic values, and fundamental direction must be repeatedly told — and sold — to staff inside the SWO (Scott, 1977; Martin, 1980a).

Action Strategy VI

Demonstrate good service delivery and the support of clients (or constituents). Legitimacy claims around service — to individuals, the community, and the common good — are important to both internal and external constituents. Claims by core activity recipients that services are effective are especially impressive. A director of a large public library in central Florida introduced a Books-by-Mail service for library patrons who were elderly, disabled, or shut-in. They were encouraged to telephone the library to requests books. If available, the books were mailed to them along with a return envelope. With each book, a one-page questionnaire asked about the service: Is it helpful? If so, why? Would you like it to continue? Would you be willing to pay postage both ways? Etc. Most who returned the questionnaire praised the program. This gave the director support for continuing it, going to the press, impressing county commissioners (who fund the library), and so on. An innovative service to a select target population on a trial basis turned into a permanent program funded by county general revenue. Citizens who used the service said they benefitted and services which satisfy citizens impress resource controllers. In a limited but concrete way, the two interests become one.

Action Strategy VII

Translate symbols into action; action into symbols. The SWO leader is responsible for translating policy decisions of boards, legislators, state agencies, county commissions, and so forth into concrete actions for SWO staff and clients. Translation of symbol into action (Brunsson, 1985) requires directors to plan and implement programs (along with staff and possibly other organizations) and to use the action over analysis approach noted earlier. In addition, SWO directors are responsible for translating the concrete actions of their organizations back into symbols so resource controllers and other constituents can make use of them. When the library director described earlier took his questionnaire results to the County Commission, he praised them for assisting the elderly, disabled, and shut-ins and for adding to the quality of life in the community. Commissioners see votes in programs such as this, feel good about doing good, and become more committed to the library. Because the librarian translated "action into symbols," commissioners could justify their support for the program. Local citizens take pride in such programs and feel good about their government and its responsiveness to their needs.

Action Strategy VIII

Vision and inspiration over supervision and control. This primarily internal strategy concerns the culture-building and meaning development tasks of SWO directors. A director's conception of the fundamental values, service mission, and ultimate purpose of the organization is of great significance. If the director's primary concern is to pacify important external constituents, this will be communicated to organizational members through emphasis on the organization's authority hierarchy, concern with record-keeping, due process, and other mandated procedures, and little discussion and attention to the quality of core work activity. State and county welfare departments are often like this (Prottas, 1979; Lipsky, 1980); avoiding pink slips, memorizing rules in the manual (or manuals), and so forth become primary goals. SWOs in which staff receive work performance feedback only when they make errors are headed by directors who lack a vision of purpose. Constant supervision and checking of workers communicate a lack of trust (Peters & Waterman, 1982), prompting workers to invest as little as possible in their work.

SWO leaders with a vision of purpose will not necessarily be popular with either staff or clients. A proactive vision of core work activity is more demanding than a minimal, care-taking approach and staff, particularly early on, may be resistant (Martin, 1984). The vision and its articulation and enactment by key organizational members are nevertheless important. Comments and action which value quality legitimate organizational members who agree. This legitimation provides normative sanction to promote their views about quality and urge others, in the name of getting along with administration, to behave in "right ways." The absence of a quality of service concept or vision (with attendant examples, practices, behaviors, etc.) fosters a hydra-headed approach where each organizational unit, sometimes each worker, goes in his or her own direction with minimal collective direction or effort. Prottas (1979) and Peters and Waterman (1982) note that organizations which try to "do everything," which have no priorities, basically do nothing. They become maintenance organizations, survivors but not innovators. District Administrators in Florida's Department of Health and Rehabilitative Services (HRS) view the department's lack of priorities as a problem (Imershein et al., 1982). HRS tries to appease all constituencies, particularly the legislature, but there is no consensus on, or conception of, service quality. When asked about service quality, staff say this concept "really doesn't apply here." Quality control (read: program monitoring for legitimacy purposes, accurate and complete records and proper due process), Yes; quality of service, No (Imershein et al., 1982, 1986).

With a clear vision of purpose, battles must still be fought to convince the staff. Different conceptions of organizational mission, professional rivalries, and competing theoretical perspectives (behaviorism, psychotherapy, community organization, etc.) divide staff and make widespread commitment to the SWO's service vision problematic. Normative standards about priorities and the importance of excellent service (responsiveness, respect, etc.) can be established, however, and research by Kanter (1983), Peters and Waterman (1982), and Peters and Austin (1985) is helpful in this regard. Without a conception of effort, people lack a collective sense of direction or mission. They do their job, take their paychecks, and live for five o'clock, weekends, and retirement. This is unfortunately the case in many SWOs. Burnout is an organizational problem, not an individual worker problem (Kanter, 1983). High stress and hard work can be fulfilling and invigorating as well as depleting and demoralizing. The SWO work context, not (only) individual attitudes or experiences, makes the difference.

Action Strategy IX

Highlight basic values and stand by them. Excellent organizations make basic values clear: Certain things must be done, others should never be done (Peters & Waterman, 1982; Sipel, 1984; Gold, 1982). IBM values customer service, and failure to respond promptly to a customer's request is not acceptable. "Break this rule and you're gone." As ideological organizations, social welfare agencies have many, albeit contradictory, values such as: "Be polite to applicants but don't let any cheaters get by you" or "Release patients when they stabilize but keep the bed census up." The challenge to SWO directors is to formulate, and stand behind, certain values which are not negotiable and will not be compromised. This is difficult in public agencies with career service systems but by no means impossible. The means to reprimand, even terminate, uncooperative (rude, offensive, incompetent) staff are available although substantial commitment and effort are required. Usually, however, one successful action is enough to spread the word that "performance matters here."

Both SWO director and service staff have a stake in this strategy. SWOs have difficulty demonstrating "objective" change in clients' conditions or statuses but requirements for courteous, friendly, caring attention from workers should be an absolute standard. If constituents are impressed with sincerity of effort, genuine interest, and respectful treatment — and Prottas (1979) finds clients appreciate these very much — SWOs which tolerate anything else are fundamentally at fault (Schneider, Parkington & Buxton, 1980; Smith, Organ & Near, 1983). Minor actions on the part of organizational members often have major consequences (Staw, Bell & Clausen, 1986). A receptionist who answers the telephone promptly and is informative and responsive is a good SWO representative. One who acts otherwise gives a message of "We don't care about you" from the organization. The telephone caller may be the Governor, a Board Member, or a favored benefactor, as well as a needy client. Directors should remember that SWO legitimacy is affected by manner as much as content and a worker's rude, discourteous behavior is not only morally reprehensible but may threaten organizational well-being.

Action Strategy X

Control essential accountability practices tightly; protect worker discretion in core work activities. The paradoxical "loose-tight" characteristic of excellent companies studied by Peters and Waterman

(1982) is useful for SWO leaders. This strategy concerns assurance of both internal legitimacy and service quality, two seemingly incompatible goals (Camero, 1986a). Record-keeping and paperwork are often blamed for poor or inefficient service in SWOs, particularly public ones (Martin, 1986). Precious time is wasted with paperwork while important service goes unprovided by staff who are professionally trained, able, and willing, or so the argument goes. How can demands for paperwork, due process, and accountability be reconciled with professional social workers' desires to spend time in interesting work rather than completing forms, documenting, or meeting mandatory quotas or deadlines?

When paperwork is required, SWO directors must assure the organizational mechanisms to comply. At the same time, social workers value discretion in the discharge of their jobs and view it as necessary for high quality performance (Olmstead & Christensen, 1972; Whiddon & Martin, 1986). Internal procedures of importance to external regulators must be rationalized, bureaucratized, and controlled in social welfare organizations. Disregard or violation of legally prescribed processes is grave and consequences to individual directors, if not the organization, per se, are substantial. However, if this only is emphasized, if no vision of purpose associated with quality of caring (as defined by mission) is valued, maintenance activities and orientations which emphasize "getting by" become the organizational norm (Prottas, 1979).

Directors should devise innovative, efficient systems for paperwork which meet legitimacy demands and minimize intrusion on staff time. They can lobby powerful regulators against redundant and pointless record-keeping and documentation demands. Legislators and their staffs often have little understanding of the data gathering demands which they impose. Paperwork stifles SWOs and its reduction may be necessary to assure a high quality of work SWO leaders must become: activists on behalf of their programs, workers, and agencies to reduce the burden which nonessential paperwork and regulatory processes impose.

FINAL CONSIDERATIONS

The popular view of social welfare organizations, particularly public ones, is generally negative. Critics on the political Left urge they be allowed to grind to a halt on their own inertia (Rose & Rose, 1982) while those on the Right advocate closing them by transferring funds to the private, for-profit, sphere (Salas, 1982). The rest of us, those who perhaps know and care more, know that Leftist hopes for a collapse and Rightist claims of market superiority are unlikely and perhaps untrue (Offe, 1984). Social welfare organizations are, to some degree, ideological, value-ridden, conflictual, and politicized pawns of their environments (Meyer & Scott, 1983). Although rationalized in some respects, much of what they do is myth and ceremony entailing ritual compliance with dominant themes and rules in their environments. SWOs do not only react and comply however. Although shaped by their dependent (often public) status, success at influencing the world around them, and within, is a reality not a dream.

Social welfare organizations are rife with opportunity. Innovative directors can capitalize on the very characteristics which many view as weaknesses. The pervasiveness of competing and conflicting values means that some values, those promoted by directors, can be championed and celebrated. SWO directors committed to standards of high quality in core work activities can, so long as they assure compliance with important rules in the environment, promote them both outside and inside the organization. Through promotion of the collective good externally (Bellah et al., 1985), SWO directors can win support from, and inspire confidence in, resource and opinion leaders. Through promotion of commitment to high quality standards and involvement. in a collaborative workplace, staff can be inspired to invest personally in their work. Neither is easy but each can be, and is, done every day.

REFERENCES

Austin, D.M. & Hasenfeld, Y. A prefatory essay on the future administration of human services. *Journal of Applied Behavioral Science*, 1985, *21*, 351-354.

Bellah, R.N., Madsen, R., Sullivan, W.M. Swidler, A. & Tipton, S.M. *Habits of the heart*. Berkeley: University of California Press, 1985.

Boss, R.W. & Boss, L.S. The chief executive officer and successful OD efforts. *Group and Organization Studies*, 1985, *10*, 365-382.

Brunsson, N. *The irrational organization: Irrationality as a basis for organizational action and change*. Chichester and New York: Wiley, 1985.

Cameron, K.S. The effectiveness of ineffectiveness. In B.M. Staw & L.L. Cummings (Eds.) *Research in Organizational Behavior*, Vol. 6. Greenwich, CT: JAI Press, 1984.

Cameron, K.S. Effectiveness as paradox: Consensus and conflict in conceptions of organizational effectiveness. *Management Science*, 1986a, *32*, 539-553.

Cameron, K.S. A study of organizational effectiveness and its predictors. *Management Science*, 1986b, *32*, 86-112.

Cameron, K.S. & Whetten, D.A. *Organizational effectiveness: A comparison of multiple models*. New York: Academic Press, 1983.

Carter, R. *The accountable agency*. Beverly Hills: Sage, 1983.

Connolly, T., Conlon, E.J. & Deutsch, S.J. Organizational effectiveness: A multiple-constituency approach. *Academy of Management Review*, 1980, *5*, 211-217.

Czarniawska, B. *Public sector executives: Managers or politicians?* Stockholm: Stockholm School of Economics, 1985.

Files, L. The human services management task: A time allocation study. *Public Administration Review*, 1981, *41*, 686-92.

Glisson, C.A. & Martin, P.Y. Productivity and efficiency in human service organizations as related to structure, size, and age. *Academy of Management Journal*, 1980, *23*, 21-37.

Gold, K.A. Managing for success: A comparison of the private and public sectors. *Public Administration Review*, 1982, *42*, 568-575.

Gornick, J., Burt, M.R. & Pittman, K.J. Structure and activities of rape crisis centers in the early 1980s. *Crime and Delinquency*, 1984, *31*, 247-68.

Hasenfeld, Y. *Human service organizations*. Englewood Cliffs: Prentice-Hall, Inc., 1983.

Imershein, A.W., Polivka, L., Gordon-Girvin, S., Chackerian, R. & Martin, P. Service networks in Florida: Administrative decentralization and its effects on service delivery. *Public Administration Review*, 1986, *46*, 161-69.

Imershein, A.W., Martin, P.Y., Chackerian, R. & Frumkin, M. The integration of health and human services in state human resource agencies. Technical report. The Florida State University, Tallahassee, 1982.

Kanter, R.M. *Men and women of the corporation*. New York: Basic Books, 1977.

Kanter, R.M. *The change masters*. New York: Simon and Schuster, 1983.

Kaufman, H. *Administrative behavior of federal bureau chiefs*. Washington, DC: Brookings Institution, 1981.

Lemke, S. & Moos, R.H. Quality of residential settings for elderly adults. *Journal of Gerontology*, 1986, *41*, 268-276.

Lipsky, M. *Street-level bureaucracy: Dilemmas of the individual in public services*. New York: Russell-Sage, 1980.

Martin, P.Y. Multiple constituencies, dominant societal values, and the human service administrator: Implications for service delivery. *Administration in Social Work*, 1980a, *4*, 15-27.

Martin, P.Y. Multiple constituencies, differential power, and the question of effectiveness in human service organizations. *Journal of Sociology and Social Welfare*, 1980b, *6*, 801-816.

Martin, P.Y. Trade unions, conflicts, and the nature of work in residential service organizations. *Organization Studies*, 1984, *5*, 169-185.

Martin, P.Y. Dilemmas and prospects of state welfare agencies: Florida's Department of Health and Rehabilitative Services as a case example. Manuscript, Florida State University. 1986.

Martin, P.Y. & Segal, B. Bureaucracy, size, and staff expectations for client behavior in halfway houses. *Journal of Health and Social Behavior*, 1977, *18*, 376-390.

Meyer, J.W. & Rowan, B. Institutionalized organizations: Formal structure as myth and ceremony. *American Journal of Sociology*, 1977, *83*, 440-463.

Meyer, J.W. & Scott, W.R. *Organizational environments: Ritual and rationality*. Beverly Hills: Sage, 1983.

Meyer, J.W. Scott, W.R. & Deal, T.E. Institutional and technical sources of organizational structure. In H.D. Stein (Ed.), *Organization and the human services*. Philadelphia: Temple University Press, 1981.

Molnar, J.J. & Rogers, D.L. Organizational effectiveness: An empirical comparison of the goal and system resource approaches. *The Sociological Quarterly*, 1976, *17*, 401-413.

Offe, C. *Contradictions of the welfare state*. London: Hutchinson, 1984.

Olmstead, J. & Christensen, H.E. *Effects of agency work contexts: An intensive field study*. Washington, DC: U.S. Government Printing Office, 1973.

Patti, R. In search of purpose for social welfare administration. *Administration in Social Work*, 1985, *9*, 1-14.

Peters, T.J. & Austin, N. *A passion for excellence: The leadership difference*. New York: Random House, 1985.

Peters, T.J. & Waterman, R.H., Jr., *In search of excellence: Lessons from America's best-run companies*. New York: Harper and Row, 1982.

Prottas, J. *People-processing*. Lexington: D.C. Heath and Company, 1979.

Rose, H. & Rose, S. Moving right out of welfare – and the way back. *Critical Social Policy*, 1982, *2*, 7-18.

Salas, E.S. *Privatizing the public sector: How to shrink government*. Chatham, NJ: Chatham House, 1982.
Schneider, B., Parkington, J.J. & Buxton, V.M. Employee and customer perceptions of service in banks. *Administrative Science Quarterly*, 1980, *25*, 252-267.
Scott, W.R. Effectiveness of organizational effectiveness studies. In P.S. Goodman & J.M. Pennings (Eds.), *New perspectives on organizational effectiveness*. San Francisco: Jossey-Bass, 1977.
Scott, W.R. The organization of environments: Network, cultural, and historical elements. In J.W. Meyer & W.R. Scott, *Organizational Environments*. Beverly Hills: Sage, 1983.
Sipel, G.A. Putting in search of excellence to work in local government. *Public Management*, 1984, *66*, 2-5.
Smith, C.A., Organ, D.W. & Near, J. Organizational citizenship behavior: Its nature and antecedents. *Journal of Applied Psychology*, 1983, *69*, 653-663.
Staw, B.M., Bell, N.E. & Clausen, J.A. The dipositional approach to job attitudes: A lifetime longitudinal test. *Administrative Science Quarterly*, 1986, *31*, 56-77.
Wiewel, W. & Hunter, A. The interorganizational network as a resource: A comparative case study on organizational genesis. *Administrative Science Quarterly*, 1984, *30*, 482-496.
Whetten, D.A. Coping with incompatible expectations: An integrated view of role conflict. *Administrative Science Quarterly*, 1978, *23*, 254-271.
Whiddon, B. & Martin, P.Y. Quality of staff performance, job discretion, and participation in decisions in a state welfare agency. Manuscript, Florida State University, Tallahassee, 1986.

Generic Social Work Skills in Social Administration: The Example of Persuasion

Ronald L. Simons, PhD

Increasingly there is consensus in the literature on social welfare management that social service administration differs in significant ways from general administration and hence requires a particular type of educational preparation (Hasenfeld & English, 1974; Patti, 1983; Steiner, 1977). Having agreed that social service administrators need to be educated in a fashion that differs from that of the general administrator, there is much disagreement concerning the form that education for social welfare management should take (Perlmutter, 1984). Even if a consensus could be reached concerning the ideal curriculum for students interested in social administration, it is not clear that this would have a significant impact upon the way programs are managed as the administrators of most human service organizations are direct service workers who have been promoted into supervisory positions (Patti, 1983).

This paper takes the position that both social welfare administration and direct service social workers require a common set of skills. Of course, both the administrator and direct service worker must also know the proven theories and techniques associated with his or her level of practice. However, these specialized procedures only serve to compliment or build upon generic skills that characterize all social work practice. Hence, the social worker who receives a rigorous education in the generic skills of social work practice would be prepared, with little additional training, to practice as a direct service worker or social administrator.

In an effort to develop this contention, the next section of this paper defines and discusses the concept of generic skills as it relates to the

---

Dr. Simons is Professor, Department of Sociology and Social Work, Iowa State University, Ames, IA 50011.

service effectiveness of human service administration. A set of persuasive strategies is then developed as an example of empirically based generic procedures appropriate to the demands of both administration and direct service work.

GENERIC SKILLS AND SOCIAL ADMINISTRATION

As noted above, most experts in the area recognize social welfare administration to be different from administration in general. One of the major differences is that human service organizations assume a commitment to client welfare or service effectiveness rather than profit or some other outcome (Patti, 1985). In the course of pursuing this performance objective, the social administrator must also be concerned with efficiency, productivity, resource acquisition, and staff morale (Rapp & Poertner, 1985). All of this requires the execution of tasks such as obtaining funds and clients, supervising and motivating personnel, juggling the conflicting demands of multiple constituents, managing information on program performance, and the like. At first glance, this diverse set of activities seems to demand a set of competencies quite different from those assumed in direct service work. However, a closer examination shows that to a large degree these administrative tasks rest upon the ability to carry out the general skills of the problem solving process. Importantly, these problem solving skills are the same ones employed by direct service workers.

As Perlman (1957) noted some years ago, social work is a problem solving activity. This is true whether one is employed as an administrator or a direct service worker. The steps and skills associated with problem solving remain the same regardless of level of practice (Simons & Aigner, 1985). To see how this is so, consider the problem solving process:

First, data must be collected in order to assess the problem. The principles of interviewing, observation, questionnaire construction, and sampling are the same whether one is collecting data on clients, employee morale, or the impact of a management information system. Next, based upon the assessment of the problem, specific goals must be established and a sequence of tasks identified for reaching the goals. The skills associated with goal setting and task planning are the same for direct service and administrative problems. Action systems must often be formulated to carry out the tasks that have been identified, and a common set of skills are required in order to pull together and run a group whether it be a committee or treatment group. Usually some individual or group must be influenced to change if the problem of concern is to be resolved. The target may be a client, a board member, or a funding agency, but the principles for effective persuasion, inducement, or constraint remain the same.

An important component of the problem solving process is the evaluation of the attempted solution. This involves collecting data concerning the impact of the problem solving effort. Thus one schooled in the general skills of problem solving must know quasi experimental research procedures required for evaluation. The canons of quasi-experimental design remain the same whether one is evaluating a direct service intervention or some component of organizational performance.

All this suggests that the human service administrator and the direct service worker employ a similar set of skills. These problem solving skills, which are relevant to any setting or level of practice, should be considered the generic skills of social work. Unfortunately, the term "generic skills" does not have a common meaning among social work educators. Often times it is used to refer to processes such as facilitating, mediating, relationship enhancement, and the like. When defined in this fashion, the skills suggest little in terms of specific practice guidelines and have limited utility for social workers employed in the areas of policy and administration. Stated differently, such formulations are not really informative or generic.

To be generic, a set of skills must be organized around the activities that characterize social work in various settings and level. Thus the skills should relate to the problem solving process endemic to all social work practice (Simons & Aigner, 1985). To be useful, to facilitate effective practice, the skills must indicate specific, empirically bases tasks and activities. The skills should involve clearly identified practice principles based upon empirically proven theories and techniques (Simons & Aigner, 1985).

As an example of a set of principles which meet these criteria, the following section develops a list of practice guidelines with regard to the skill of persuasion. The ability to exercise influence through persuasion is important in human service administration as funding bodies must be persuaded to invest in the program, legislative and policy making groups need to be persuaded to establish priorities and guidelines which facilitate quality programming, community agencies must be persuaded to refer clients, community residents may need to be persuaded to serve as board members or as volunteers, and so on.

The social administrator is constantly attempting to persuade some person or group to contribute the time, energy, or other resources, required for effective service delivery. Hence, the ability to exert influence through persuasion, like the other generic skills, is an essential component of successful human service administration.

Given how often program viability and success hinges upon the manager's ability to influence certain individuals and groups, it is essential that social administrators be schooled in techniques for maximizing the efficacy of the persuasive communications. Recently, the author employed theory and research from the literature on attitude formation and change to deduce various strategies for exercising influence (Simons, 1982, 1984; Simons & Aigner, 1985). These strategies were presented as generic approaches, i.e., as procedures that might be employed to enhance the effectiveness of social workers practicing in any role or setting. Since the publication of these articles, the author has decided that the principles regarding persuasion should be reformulated so as to increase their utility to macro practitioners. It is not that the principles as originally stated are now viewed as incorrect; rather it is a matter of recasting them in a fashion that allows for greater flexibility and ease of use.

The previous statements emphasized the way that role reversal, giving both sides of an issue, stressing consistency, and identifying self-defeating behavior might be utilized to persuade a target system to change. The principles were presented as alternative approaches to constructing a persuasive appeal, or as strategies which might be employed in a serial fashion in the course of dialogue with the target. Although well suited to the needs of the direct service worker, a good bit of ingenuity was required in order to combine the principles into a single persuasive appeal as macro practitioners must do in funding proposals, presentations before boards, media campaigns, etc. In the section to follow, the principles of persuasion are reformulated and integrated with research and theory regarding the adoption and diffusion of new ideas.

PRINCIPLES FOR EFFECTIVE PERSUASION

As noted above, persuasion involves producing change through the provision of new information — that is, the target receives information that influences him or her to think, feel, or act in a new way (Gamson, 1968; Pincus & Minahan, 1973). Or, as Larson (1983) states, "the process of persuasion involves your presenting good reasons to people for a specific choice among probable alternatives" (p. 281). Theory and research on persuasion is concerned with identifying the characteristics of messages which persons find appealing, with discovering the nature of communications which are perceived to contain "good reasons" for adopting the position being advocated. Bases upon the findings of several decades of research, the following factors appear to be important components in effective persuasive appeals.

Emphasize Advantages or Rewards

People are constantly processing the information available to them and making decisions as to how they might best satisfy their needs and achieve their goals. Hence, the probability that individuals will change their behavior in response to a communication is increased when the message provides information indicating that the change will enable them to more effectively satisfy their needs and desires.

Several studies show that a target audience is more apt to adopt a favorable attitude toward a behavior or procedure when they perceive it to have a relative advantage over existing or alternative practices (Coleman, Katz & Menzel, 1966; Rothman, 1974). Rogers (1968) notes that the advantages or rewards associated with an action may not be economic or material. The benefits of adopting the line of action being advocated may be largely psychological, leading to an increase in prestige, status, or satisfaction. People must have sufficient reason for modifying their behavior or for adopting a new procedure. One good reason for doing so is because the new approach yields rewards at a level unavailable through existing practices or alternative actions.

Be Comprehensible

The action being advocated must be presented in a language that is readily understood by the target audience. Technical jargon should be avoided if possible. People will not to adopt a line of action which they do not fully comprehend. Simple, easily understood ideas are more likely to be accepted than arguments which are complex and hard to follow (Glaser, Abeleson & Garrison, 1983; Rogers, 1983; Zaltman, 1973).

Show Compatibility of Values

There is substantial evidence that people are more apt to accept an idea if it is perceived as consistent with their present beliefs, values, and ways of doing things (Rogers, 1983; Rothman, 1974; Zaltman, 1973). For instance, Woolfolk, Woolfolk and Wilson (1977) found that students who were shown identical videotapes of a teacher using reinforcement procedures evaluated the teacher and the technique more favorably when the videotape was described as an illustration of "humanistic education" than when it was labeled behavior modification. And, Saunders and Reppucci (1977) reported that the reaction of school principals and superintendents to a program proposal varied according to whether or not the program was identified as employing a behavior modification approach. Such studies are a clear demonstration of the way that one can destroy an audience's receptivity to an idea by using words or phrases which the group perceives as representing beliefs or practices which are contrary to their value commitments. Indeed, the label or name selected for a program or activity should be chosen with great care (Rogers, 1983).

Various groups, whether human service agencies, funding bodies, or civic organizations, are often committed to a particular sociopolitical, treatment, or practice ideology (Rappaport, 1960; Hasenfeld, 1983). An idea is more apt to be accepted or assimilated by a group if it is perceived to be compatible with the assumptions, principles, and procedures that make up the group's ideological orientation (Glaser, Abelson & Garrison, 1983). Compatibility promises greater security and less risk to the receiver while making the new idea appear more meaningful (Rogers, 1983).

Cite Proven Results

An audience is more apt to accept an idea if its consequences have already been observed. When people can see the positive results of an action or procedure they are more likely to adopt it (Glaser, Abelsen & Garrison, 1983; Rogers, 1983). Given this finding, a stepping stone approach is often the most effective way of selling an idea. First, a small group is persuaded to test the procedure. The positive results obtained in this demonstration project or pilot program are then cited in persuasive communications designed to promote the idea across a broader population (Rothman, 1974; Rothman, Erlich & Teresa, 1981).

Allow for Trialability

The target group will perceive less risk if the new ideal can be tried on a piece meal basis prior to wholesale adoption of the procedure (Rogers, 1983; Rogers & Svenning, 1969). As Glaser, Abelson, and Garrison (1983) observe:

The extent to which a proposed change is known to be reversible if it does not prove desirable may affect its adoption. Not all innovations can be discarded later with impunity; the bridges back to the status quo ante may have been burned. Situations in which the user need not "play for keeps" provide more opportunity for innovation. (p. 61)

People are reluctant to commit themselves to a line of action which does not allow for a later change of mind. An idea is more apt to be adopted if it can be broken into parts which can be tried one step at a time, with the group having the option of discontinuing the new procedure at any time in the process should they decide that it is not producing the anticipated results (Rogers, 1983; Rothman, Erlich & Teresa, 1981).

Link Message to Influential Others

Consistent with the predictions of Balance Theory (Heider, 1958), several studies indicated that people tend to adopt the same attitude toward an object or idea as that held by someone they like, and that they tend to adopt the opposite attitude toward an object or idea as that held by someone they dislike (Tedeschi & Lindshold, 1976). In this way, individuals maintain cognitive balance.

These findings suggest that an idea is more likely to be accepted if it is linked to persons that the target likes. The most direct method for doing this is to have someone the target likes or respects deliver the persuasive appeal. When this is not feasible, reference might be made to influential others as part of the communicated message. For instance, if a city council member is known to be a firm supporter of the state governor, and the governor is known to have the same views on an issue as the social worker who is trying to influence the council member, this information could be presented to the council member. This general tactic can be used whether the favored person is the president, a movie star, a well-known expert on some topic, or the target's colleague, friend, or spouse.

The social worker might cite individuals similar to the target when information about whom the target likes or respects is lacking. This strategy is based on the extensive body of research indicating that people tend to be attracted to people they perceive as similar to themselves. Thus, when attempting to persuade a landlord to make repairs, the worker might name other landlords who have made such repairs; when attempting to persuade a principal to institute a drug education program, the worker might cite principals from other schools in the city who have begun such programs, and so forth.

Avoid High Pressure Tactics

Research based upon Reactance Theory shows that when individuals feel pressured to select a particular course of action, whether through the promise of rewards, the threat of punishment, or intense appeals, they tend to increase their valuation of alternatives to the position being advocated (Brehm, 1966; Wicklund, 1974). High pressure tactics create a boomerang effect. The use of pressure to persuade people to adopt an idea frequently creates resistance and a determination to act in a manner which is contrary to the proposed action. Human beings value their freedom and will resist attempts to circumscribe their choice of self-determination. Therefore, messages should be presented in a manner that minimizes any threat to the target's feeling of freedom. Phrases such as "It's your decision," "But, of course, it's up to you," and "Think about it and see what you want to do," serve this function; whereas words such as "must," "should," and "have to" are likely to arouse resistance (Brehm, 1976).

In addition to using phrases such as those just cited, reactance can be lowered through the use of two-sided messages (Secord & Backman, 1974). Two-sided communications acknowledge the limitations of one's own position and grant some merit to alternative points of view. A two-sided argument is more effective when the opposing view is presented first and the view preferred by the communicator is presented last (Johnson & Matross, 1975). Thus, when attempting to persuade an audience who is committed to another point of view, the social worker should begin by acknowledging the perspective to the group. The worker should assure them that he or she understands and appreciates their point of view. Such a beginning lowers audience defensiveness and makes the worker appear less one-sided and more objective.

Minimize Threats to Security, Status, or Esteem

Change agents often commit the "rationalistic bias" of assuming that people are reasonable beings who, when presented with the logic of a new and better approach, will recognize its merits and embrace it without hesitation (Zaltman & Duncan, 1977). However, events frequently fail to unfold in this fashion. People's logic and reason is often distorted by less rational processes. Sound judgment may be clouded by a defensive emotional response. Emotional defensiveness may be produced because a group fears the new procedure will signal a diminution in their prestige or power (Bright, 1964; Berlin, 1969). Those persons who have benefited the most from existing practices are likely to be threatened by a change in procedures. Other individuals may fear that the new approach will devalue their knowledge and skills and that they will have a difficult time learning the new procedures (Bright, 1964; Glaser, Abelson & Garrison, 1983). In still other instances, persons may be reluctant to adopt a course of action because they feel they will lose face with their friends or some constituency.

The wise change agent will construct his or her communications in a manner that alleviates such threats. Whenever an idea might be interpreted as threatening to the target group's security, esteem, or sense of competence, these fears should be discussed and objectively examined as part of the communication process. By acknowledging and evaluating these concerns through the two-sided approach discussed above, defensiveness may be reduced and reason allowed to prevail.

We began this section by noting that people are persuaded by a message when it provides them with "good reasons" for selecting the advocated course of action over alternatives. Based upon attitude change research and studies of the adoption and diffusion of innovations, eight principles for enhancing the persuasiveness of a communication have been identified. These principles of communication are listed in Table 1. The principles might be summarized as suggesting that people are most apt to perceive that they have good reason to adopt the position being advocated when it has advantages over alternatives, is easily understood, is compatible with existing values and practices, has been shown to have positive results, can be adopted on a trial basis, is endorsed by admired others, may be accepted or rejected, and contains no threats to security or esteem.

EXAMPLES OF THE PRINCIPLES IN USE

As observed earlier, social administrators frequently employ persuasion in an effort to obtain the resources necessary for a viable program, such as funding, clients, personnel, and community goodwill. In this section, two illustrations are provided of the way in which the principles identified above might be combined to maximize an administrator's persuasiveness. The first considers the situation of presenting a funding proposal to a county board while the second concerns the formation of a radio spot designed to solicit local citizens to serve as program volunteers.

Assume that a social worker is interested in persuading the board of

Table I

PRINCIPLES FOR CONSTRUCTING PERSUASIVE COMMUNICATIONS

1.	Emphasize Advantages.
2.	Be Comprehensive.
3.	Show Compatibility of Values.
4.	Cite Proven Results.
5.	Allow for Trialability.
6.	Refer to Influential Others.
7.	Avoid High Pressure Tactics.
8.	Minimize Threats to Security, Status, or Esteem.

supervisors in his or her county to provide funding for a new community corrections halfway house. After reviewing the eight principles of persuasion, the individual might construct a presentation which contains the following: first, the advantages of the program must be noted. Community correctional programs are cheaper and often produce lower recidivism rates than alternative facilities (Advantages Principle). Since the residents of the halfway house would be working during the day and living in the house at night, attention might be drawn to the way in which the program is consistent with community values of work and supporting one's self (Compatibility Principle). Concerns about the dangers posed by convicted criminals living in the community would need to be acknowledged and addressed through a description of the screening procedures to be employed in selecting residents for the house (Threats Principle). The positive results obtained by similar programs in other communities should be cited (Proven Results Principle). Mention might be made of any influential politicians or organizations who support the correctional halfway house concept (Influential Others Principle). The idea could be presented as reversible. At the end of a certain period an evaluation might be planned and a decision made as to whether the results obtained warrant continued support (Trialability Principle). Finally, an effort would be made throughout the presentation to be clear and understandable (Comprehensibility Principle) and to emphasize that it is the board's decision, that they should only adopt the proposal if they perceive that it is a good idea (Minimal Pressure Principle).

Of course, the presentation would need to contain information in addition to the material just mentioned. The board would probably want details regarding where the facility would be located, how it would be staffed, the costs to be incurred, and the like. However, many proposals are largely limited to a consideration of such items. If a proposal is to be persuasive it should also address the issues identified in the eight principles discussed above.

As a second example, assume that a radio spot is to be constructed in an effort to solicit volunteers to work in a psychiatric halfway house. The announcement might begin by describing the problems in living faced by the residents of the facility and the way that volunteers can help solve such difficulties (Advantages Principle). Attention might be drawn to the way in which volunteering is consistent with the American tradition of helping one's neighbor to get back on his feet during hard times (Compatibility Principle). The valuable consequences that have been obtained through the use of volunteers, either in this program or in similar others, could be noted (proven Results Principle). In citing these consequences, the rewards for both the resident and the volunteer should be described (Advantages Principle). The announcement might acknowledge listener concerns regarding the time that may be involved and doubts about being able to function as an effective volunteer (Threat Principle). These issues could be addressed by briefly noting how many hours a week are required and by assuring the listener that volunteer training and supervision is provided. The listener might be informed that the commitment is time limited, say six months or a year, with the option of volunteering again at the end of the period (Trialability Principle). An influential community person might be recruited to read the announcement (Influential Others Principle). Everyday language, rather than psychiatric argot, would need to be used to describe the program and the services provided by the volunteers (Comprehensibility Principle). The appeal should be made in a warm, factual fashion which avoids the appearance of a hard sell campaign (Minimum Pressure Principle).

As these two examples demonstrate, the eight principles of persuasion, so long as they are employed in an honest and forthright manner, do not violate the values of the social work profession. None of the principles involve the use of trickery or hidden agendas. Rather, they merely suggest the types of information that the target will desire prior to committing to the idea being presented. Of course, the principles might be used in an unethical fashion. For instance, a person might claim that a program has been shown to produce certain results when it has not, or that a procedure can be tried on a trial basis when in reality it can only be discontinued through great expense and inconvenience. The principles imply no value dilemmas, however, so long as an individual utilizes them with sincerity and honesty.

CONCLUSIONS AND RECOMMENDATIONS

This paper has exemplified the generic skills approach to social work practice as it relates to the need for administrators to manage their influence with an array of internal and external constituents in order to enhance service effectiveness. The eight principles of Persuasion articulated here may be used by social workers in a variety of administrative and direct service settings. Given the fact that often conflicting demands are placed upon administrators from the political environment in which human service organizations operate, the ability for administrators to use persuasion in their efforts toward improving service effectiveness for clients is a critical skill.

To be truly generic, skill training for administrators and students must be organized around the components of the problem solving process. It is problem solving that characterizes all levels of social work practice. And, if it is to be really useful, this training must focus upon specific techniques and activities which have some empirical basis. In the present paper several principles concerning the skill of persuasion were presented as an example of a set of practice principles meeting these criteria. Elsewhere an effort has been made to identify such practice guidelines with regard to other steps in the problem solving process (Simons & Aigner, 1985).

Given the fundamental nature of generic, problem solving skills for the profession there is a critical need for more social workers to become involved in research concerned with the design and development of such procedures. However, we already know a lot that can be passed along to administrators and students. This material should be taught in a rigorous fashion with a profusion of role plays and exercises directed toward various direct service, planning and administrative problems.

To ensure that students appreciate the general applicability of the skills, instructors in clinical, community, and planning and administration classes should underscore the way in which the material in their courses builds upon and serves to compliment the basic social work skills. Educating students in this fashion would begin to address the problem of most social administrators being promoted direct service workers with little administrative training.

REFERENCES

Berlin, I.N. Resistance to change in mental health professionals. *American Journal of Orthopsychiatry*, 1968, *39*, 109-115.

Brehm, J.W. *A theory of psychological reactance*. New York: Academic, 1966.

Brehm, S.S. *The application of social psychology to clinical practice*. New York: Halsted, 1976.

Bright, J.R. *Research, development, and technological innovation: An introduction*. Homewood, IL: Irwin, 1964.

Coleman, J.S., Katz, E. & Menzel, H. *Medical innovation: A diffusion study*. New York: Bobbs-Merrill, 1966.

Gamson, W.A. *Power and discontent*. Homewood, IL: Dorsey, 1968.

Glaser, E.M., Abelson, H.H. & Garrison, K.N. *Putting knowledge to use*. San Francisco: Jossey-Bass, 1983.

Hasenfeld, Y. *Human service organizations*. Englewood Cliffs, NJ: Prentice-Hall, Inc., 1983.

Hasenfeld, Y. & R.A. English (Eds.) *Human service organizations*. Ann Arbor, MI: University of Michigan Press, 1974.

Johnson, D.W. & Matross, R.P. Attitude modification methods. In F.H. Kanfer & Goldstein, A.P. (Eds.), *Helping people change*. New York: Pergammon, 1975.

Larson, C.U. *Persuasion: Reception and responsibility*. 3rd edition. Delmont, CA. Wadsworth, 1983.

Patti, R.J. *Social welfare administration: Managing social programs in a developmental context*. Englewood Cliffs, NJ: Prentice-Hall, Inc., 1983.

Patti, R.J. In search of purpose for social welfare administration. *Administration in Social Work*, 1985, *9*, 1-14.

Perlman, H.H. *Social casework: A problem-solving process*. Chicago: University of Chicago Press, 1957.

Perlmutter, F.D. Social administration and social work education: A contradiction in terms? *Administration in Social Work*, 1984, *8*, 61-69.

Pincus, A. & Minahan, A. *Social work practice: Model and method*. Itasca, IL: F.E. Peacock, 1973.

Rappoport, R. *Community as doctor*. London: Tavistock Publications, 1960.

Rapp, C.A. & Poertner, J. A performance model for human service management. Manuscript, University of Kansas, 1985.

Rogers, E.M. The communication of innovations in a complex institution. *Educational Record*, 1968, *48*, 67-77.

Rogers, E.M. *Diffusion of innovations*. 3rd edition. New York: Free Press, 1983.

Rogers, E.M. & Svenning, L. *Managing change*. Washington, DC: U.S. Office of Education, 1969.

Rothman, J. *Planning and organizing for social change*. New York: Columbia University Press, 1974.

Rothman, J., Erlich, J.L. & Teresa, J.G. *Changing organizations and community programs*. Beverly Hills: Sage, 1981.

Saunders, J.T. & Reppucci, N.D. Learning networks among administrators of human service institutions. *American Journal of Community Psychology*, 1977, *5*, 269-276.

Secord, P.F. & Backman, C.W. *Social psychology*. New York: McGraw-Hill, 1974.

Simons, R.L. Strategies for exercising influence. *Social Work*, 1982, *27*, 268-274.

Simons, R.L. & Aigner, S.M. *Practice principles: A problem-solving approach to social work*. New York: Macmillan, 1985.

Steiner, R. *Managing the human service organization*. Beverly Hills: Sage, 1977.
Tedeschi, J.T. & Linskold, S. *Social psychology: Interdependence, interaction and influence*. New York: Wiley, 1976.
Wicklund, R.A. *Freedom and reactance*. Hillsdale, NJ: Lawrence Erlbaum and Associates, 1974.
Woolfolk, A.E., Woolfolk, R.L.. & Wilson G.T. A rose by any other name . . . : Labeling bias and attitudes toward behavior modification. *Journal of Consulting and Clinical Psychology*, 1977, *45*, 184-191.
Zaltman, G. *Processes and phenomena of social change*. New York: Wiley, 1973.
Zaltman, G. & Duncan, R. *Strategies for planned change*. New York: Wiley, 1977.

SECTION SEVEN:
CONSTRAINTS AND DILEMMAS

Introduction

The papers in the preceding sections have addressed the management practices and organizational arrangements that appear necessary to the delivery of effective social services. In this section, we turn to the constraints and dilemmas inherent in this approach. Burton Gummer takes a macro view of service effectiveness and suggests that the dominant values in a business oriented society tend to shape the goals of social welfare toward social control and efficiency rather than social change. Moreover, he contends, social work itself is increasingly inclined to adopt a narrow view concept of service which is not well accommodated in publicly supported social care services.

Harold Lewis examines the management effectiveness issue through the lens of the ethicist. After arguing that ethical management is generally possible, he points to some of the ethical dilemmas that may emerge for managers who would make client benefit the primary criterion of agency performance. Lewis argues that even though promoting client benefit is an important ethical standard, there are other values that may be equally compelling for which the administrator may have more immediate ethical responsibility.

255

Competing Perspectives on the Concept of "Effectiveness" in the Analysis of Social Services

Burton Gummer, PhD

The notion of "effectiveness" in a market-oriented society such as ours is, in great part, a rhetorical one used to justify rather than to describe or analyze something. When the economic marketplace is the measure if not of all things, then certainly of most things, the concept of effectiveness, or how well something is done, pales next to its companion idea of efficiency, or how inexpensively it is done. Even in the current business climate of the "pursuit of excellence" and "quality is job one," it would be the naive consumer who thought it safe to abandon the age-old caution of *caveat emptor*. Alfred P. Sloan's dictum that the goal of General Motors is "not to make cars, but to make money" is still, with some important exceptions, the creed of most American enterprises.

Even when effectiveness is used nonrhetorically to refer to the extent to which an activity attains its ends, its meaning is complicated by disagreements over what the "it" is that's to be accomplished. This is especially true when the term is applied to the social services. "Social services" is a rubric encompassing a number of diverse, often incompatible activities. A listing of the problems that social services seek to address would amount to a compendium of difficulties that can befall a person living in the United States today, regardless of age, gender, race, or income. The goals that social services attempt to accomplish are as varied as caring for the distressed, disciplining the deviant, counseling the disturbed, advocating for the downtrodden, and ministering to the discontented. While there have been some noteworthy attempts to identify commonalities among these diverse activities (Gil-

Dr. Gummer is Associate Professor, School of Social Welfare, Nelson A. Rockefeller College of Public Affairs and Policy, State University of New York at Albany, Albany, NY 12222. Dr. Gummer writes "Notes From The Management Literature" for *Administration in Social Work.*

bert, 1983; Austin, 1984; Popple, 1985), the field continues to be a diffuse, broadranging enterprise that escapes easy categorization. Any discussion of service effectiveness must therefore begin by specifying which service one has in mind and what goal it is supposed to achieve. The purpose of the present paper is to contribute to this specification by presenting a framework for disaggregating the broad category of social services into its component parts and identifying the form that effectiveness takes within each component.

SOCIAL SERVICES IN A MARKET ECONOMY

The social services, as part of the larger social welfare system, is one of the major institutions of American society, along with government, the market-economy, and the family. Of these institutions, moreover, one — the market-economy — is generally viewed as central. The control of the economic system by the market, Polanyi (1957) argues,

> . . . is of overwhelming consequence to the whole organization of society: it means no less than the running of society as an adjunct to the market. Instead of economy being embedded in social relations, social relations are embedded in the economic system. (p. 57)

The presence of a dominant institution such as the market means, among other things, that other institutions must decide how they will relate to it. Seeley (1957) suggests four ways in which a secondary institution can relate to a central one: it can be a *poor copy,* a *best defense,* a *contradiction,* or a *complementary system.* This scheme will be used to sort out the components of the social service system and the form that service effectiveness assumes within each of them.

Poor Copy

This approach concentrates neither on the substance nor the goals of social services but on how well they're managed. From this perspective the social agency is like a business, only not as well run. The important thing about social services is that they should be managed in a business-like way. It was this orientation, moreover, that played a major role in the creation of the modern occupation of social work. The first paid social workers in the United States were employed by the Charities Organization Societies toward the end of the last century. Their primary mission, at least initially, was to replace the haphazard and inefficient giving of alms and "friendly visiting" to the burgeoning urban poor with a rationalized system of "scientific philanthropy" (Gettleman, 1963; Lubove, 1969). It is quite likely that the importance placed on proper management of the social services parallels the relative influence of what Reich (1984) calls the "two cultures" of government and business. Americans, he argues,

. . . tend to divide the dimensions of our national life into two broad realms. The first is the realm of government and politics. The second is the realm of business and economics. Our concerns about social justice are restricted to the first realm; our concerns about prosperity, to the second. (p. 4)

Periods of post-Civil War American history can be roughly categorized according to which of these cultures was in the ascendance. The closing quarter of the last century was clearly a time when business interests held sway over both economic and governmental affairs. This was followed by an expansion of the governmental culture during the years preceding the First World War, with the reemergence of business influence during the 1920s. From the mid-1930s until the middle of the last decade, the scope and importance of government, particularly the role of the president and the size of the executive branch, increased significantly. By contrast, the period from the late 1970s to the present has been one in which the influence of the business community has achieved one of its highest levels in modern history.

The notion that efficiency in the management of the social services is associated with the general influence of the business community has certainly been an accurate one for the recent past. The period from 1935 to 1975 was one in which the governmental culture exerted considerable influence in American society. It was also the time when the greatest increase in social spending in the country's history took place. During that period social administration became synonomous with program innovation and development. While resources were by no means unlimited, they were growing from year to year and it was the job of agency and program managers to develop new uses for what appeared to be a permanent upward curve in social spending.

By the late 1970s, however, there were signs that the honeymoon was about to end. The Nixon Administration launched a concerted effort to exclude program professionals (including many social workers) from upper administrative positions, and, for those already in those positions, to reduce or eliminate their influence over program operations (Randall, 1979). This was followed by the cap on open-ended authorizations for social services spending (Derthick, 1975), and emphasis on tighter management control over existing programs (Turem, 1974). The passage of Proposition 13 in 1978 signalled growing disgruntlement on the part of middle-class taxpayers over the costs of social programs. These steps, however, were only harbingers of what was to come. With the election of Ronald Reagan the attack on social spending shifted into high gear. A corollary of that has been the growing influence of business-oriented management practices in the social services, and the effort to redefine program effectiveness to mean fiscal accountability and control (Brodkin & Lipsky, 1983).

It would be a mistake, however, to view the current emphasis on program efficiency solely as a result of the influence of business interests in national politics. Social welfare expenditures as a proportion of gross national product doubled during the period 1960 to 1976. The rate of growth of the welfare system itself has generated a demand for more effective management practices, particularly those related to cost containment. There is a view among conservative economists, as Hirschman (1980) points out, that

. . . in the nature of the capitalist system a fairly rigid limit was set to the ability to divert factor income for purposes of expanding social services and other public expenditures: the system would stop working (that is, capitalists would no longer invest, workers' productivity would fall off, and so on) if that level were exceeded. The inability of the system to stand more than a certain level of transfer payments was declared to be one of its structural properties. (pp. 113-14)

This perspective on the growth of the welfare state carries considerable weight in social policy discussions in both conservative and liberal camps. This is attested by, among other things, Congress' passage of legislation mandating a balanced budget. The desire to contain the expansion of the welfare state is likely to be with us for sometime, regardless of the ideological orientation of the next national administration. Accompanying that will be continued interest in improving program management with efficiency as the major criterion of judging success.

Best Defense

In a market economy it is assumed that people will provide for themselves by participating in the market through work or other profitable activity. It is realized, however, that for a variety of reasons some people will be unable to adjust to this system and will become residual to it (Beck, 1967). Such people are likely to have below standard nutrition, housing, health, education, and job skills, and may, as Shlonsky (1971) suggests,

> . . . create a public menace. Individuals and groups living under such substandard conditions may create economic problems for the community . . . or may become foci for political dissent, for criminal activity, or for other forms of social deviance. (p. 417)

Since the adoption of the Elizabethan Poor Laws a primary purpose of the English and American welfare systems has been to provide for people unable to function in the economic marketplace, but in a manner that does not interfere with the market's operation. Social provisions must be provided in ways that do not undermine the motivations of those who are participating, or seek to participate in the market. With the Poor Law Reform concept of "less eligibility" as a foundation, these societies evolved what Shlonsky (1971) terms the "principle of the minimum," which applies to the

> . . . coverage of welfare programs, to the scope or extent of public investment in such programs, and to the quality or standard of living envisaged for recipients. Welfare . . . attempts to keep the number of recipients at the lowest possible minimum and to provide those few with only the essentials judged necessary for subsistence. . . . [T]he standard considered essential for subsistence is defined in relation to the standard of living that may be attained through profitable work. (pp. 416-17)

From the perspective of the social services as a "best defense" of the marketplace, a major criterion of program effectiveness has been the extent to which the service degrades the recipient. I use that term in Garfinkel's (1956) sense of "status degradation":

> Any communicative work between persons, whereby the public identity of an actor is transformed into something looked on as lower in the local scheme of social types, will be called a "status

degradation ceremony." . . . Degradation ceremonies fall within the scope of the sociology of moral indignation. . . . The paradigm of moral indignation is *public* denunciation. We publicly deliver the curse: "I call upon all men to bear witness that he is not as he appears but is otherwise and *in essence* of a lower species." (pp. 420-21)

Since the beginning of the industrial era, status degradation of those outside the economic marketplace has been one of the major mechanisms for insuring the continued participation and cooperation of the workforce (Matza, 1971). This is particularly true for workers at the lower end of the occupational and income scales whose jobs have little intrinsic satisfactions and whose wages provide only subsistence life styles. Their continued participation is dependent, it is assumed, on their awareness that people who opt to leave or not enter the labor market are considerably worse off than they are, materially, psychologically, and socially.

The operations of those parts of the social service system that directly affect a recipient's economic status do, in fact, conform to this notion of status degradation. This is seen most clearly in the giving and taking of public financial aid (Handler & Hollingsworth, 1969; Lipsky, 1980). The number of people eligible for public assistance but who do not apply is generally estimated at about 50 percent. Refusal to assume the stigma associated with public assistance status is not the only reason for this high underutilization rate, but it is an important one (Bendick, Jr., 1980).

Further support for the notion of status degradation is found in the contrast between social service programs which involve means-tested income transfers with those that seek to improve peoples' physical and mental health and their ability to function in marriages, families, and community life in general. These latter services, Shlonsky (1971) suggests, are free to operate according to the "principle of the optimum":

Guaranteeing individuals . . . a high level of medical care, counseling, access to recreational facilities, or sports activities . . . does not create a readily visible inconsistency with institutionalized mechanisms (i.e., the economic marketplace) for the allocation of rewards. . . . Such services, when provided outside the market with no relationship to the recipient's economic standing, do not seem to upset the social stratification system. (pp. 421-22)

Not surprisingly, most professional social workers have opted out of the income maintenance field and have sought to establish themselves in the less socially opprobrious fields of individual and family counseling. A major factor behind this professional migration is the unwillingness of many social workers to accept the covert mission of income transfer programs—that of supervising and disciplining the nonworking, "able-bodied" poor.

Contradiction

The notion that social services should contradict the principles of the economic marketplace lies at the heart of the philosophical and ideological positions generally associated with social work and social welfare. Historically, social workers have supported the position that social services should provide alternatives to both market mechanisms for the distribution of resources and market-based conceptions of individual worth and importance.

Within a market framework, resources are distributed according to one's relative contribution to the production of society's wealth. In its purest form, this notion holds that there should be no tampering with the equation of individual rewards with individual contributions. The social services, on the other hand,

> . . . politically interfere with the pattern of claims set by the market. They assign claims from one set of people who are said to produce or earn the national product to another set of people who may merit compassion and charity but not economic rewards for productive service. (Titmuss, 1968, pp. 188-89)

The market rewards people on the basis of *what they do* in the productive processes of society, whereas the social services "reward" people (or, at least, provides them with services and benefits) on the basis of who they are, that is, their status as members of families and communities and as citizens of the polity. From this perspective, the criterion of service effectiveness is simple and straightforward: Does the service in question contribute to a more equal distribution of society's resources?

In a corollary fashion, the market defines peoples' worth and importance in terms of the quantity and quality of their contributions to the productive process. In its crudest expression this takes the form of the adage currently popular in some of our finest business schools: "Money is life's report card!" The social services, on the other hand, proceed from the position that every individual is intrinsically worthy and valuable. While first cast in religious terms, the secularization of society has meant that this viewpoint now is presented mostly in humanistic, psychological, or political contexts. The criterion for service effectiveness coming from this perspective, however, is difficult to specify and takes us into the murky area of the "quality of life" and the extent to which social programs contribute to that.

While these approaches to social service reflect long-held values of the social work profession, they have, ironically, become increasingly difficult ones for individual social workers and the profession as a whole to adopt. Social services as a redistributive strategy are only effective in the area of cash transfers, an area that professional social workers have retreated from. Even in fields where social workers are well represented (children and family services, mental health) there is a reluctance on the part of professionals to engage in the political strife that characterizes the arenas in which distribution questions are decided.

The process of professionalization is often associated with a decline in a professional's willingness to engage in activities such as policy advocacy. These activities often require more zeal than skill and rely on bureaucratic and political acumen acquired through experience rather than formal training and which does not carry the mystique of professional expertise. There is, instead, a growing emphasis on a "value-free," apolitical, technical stance (Price, 1965). This process seems as true for social work as it does for other professions. Where trained social workers currently choose to work and the issues given priority by the profession's associations indicate a growing "privatization" of the field, a withdrawal from the combativeness of policymaking arenas and a turning inward toward the perfection of technical skills and the enhancement of professional amenities.

Even in the area of promoting a "quality of life" different from that implicit in the market's definition of individual success and worth, the profession is at a disadvantage. This is due to the proliferation of practice models and ideologies within social work, many with significantly different visions of desirable functioning for individuals, marriages, families, and communities. An important structural feature of the social work profession, Patti (1986) suggests, is a weak "gatekeeper" function. It is a field that is relatively easy to get into, and once in, people with sufficient drive and vision can shape its practices according to their own notions and beliefs. While this makes for considerable autonomy and discretion for individual practitioners, it prevents the profession as a whole from presenting a unified front on most major issues. The current debate over "family policy" is one example of this (Gilbert, 1983).

Complementary System

Finally, we can look at the social services as complementary to the marketplace and measure their effectiveness by their ability to improve peoples' market performance. The appeal of this approach has grown as the country moves to the right politically and business' influence increases. While there is probably something of a "if you can't beat them, join them" mentality behind this, it can also be viewed as a rational response to Emile Durkheim's maxim, "Make yourself usefully fulfill a determinate function."

Much of the current thinking about making the social services more responsive to the needs of the marketplace comes from the literature on "reindustrialization" of the American economy. Reich (1983), in particular, makes a strong case for using the social services as a major strategy for "investing in human capital." Drawing on the experiences of Continental Europe and Japan, he argues that America's place in the evolving world economy will "increasingly depend on its workers' skills, vigor, initiative, and capacity for collaboration and adaptation" (p. 21). If the social services are to play a role in responding to these needs, however, they will have to undergo major changes.

Since around 1970 . . . the ideology of charity and its rigid systems, which "deliver" social services to identifiable "recipients," have been inappropriate to the nation's needs. America's economic future now depends, in large part, on the speed and efficiency with which its labor force can be shifted into flexible-system production. Social programs that prepare Americans to meet the challenges and accept the insecurity of adaptation are central to this transformation. Generous unemployment compensation, well-endowed education and training programs, an adequate supply of housing, and comprehensive health care . . . should promote adjustment within the labor force. They would give people the will and ability to learn new skills, to discover new job opportunities, and to relocate. (p. 219)

While Reich (1983) does not discuss the form these programs should take, they can be expected to follow the patterns of existing employee assistance programs. That is, services would be either under direct corporate control through employment of social workers in company-run employee assistance programs, or under indirect control

266   MANAGING FOR SERVICE EFFECTIVENESS

through contracting out to private practitioners. In 1982 employee benefits represented 28 percent of the total compensation of American workers, compared to 17 percent in 1966. In large corporations, benefits now represent more than 40 percent of total employee compensation (Rainwater & Rein, 1983; Reich, 1983). If social services are to be used on the scale that Reich suggests, current private expenditures will have to be augmented by federal grants to hire the chronically unemployed and to provide a range of social services including day care, health care, counselling, and disability benefits. Under this scheme, Gilbert (1985) suggests,

... a significant portion of the responsibility for delivering social welfare provisions would shift from the public sector . . . to private industries. . . . The scope and functions of government bureauracies that presently administer many social welfare programs would thus be greatly diminished. Joined in this manner to private enterprise, social welfare activities would facilitate economic growth by contributing to productivity and the formation of human capital. (pp. 12-14)

The response of the social work community to emerging opportunities in corporate-based social services is, as could be expected, mixed. While some view it as a largely positive development for social work and the social services, others treat it with considerable suspicion (Stern, 1983). One factor that can be expected to influence responses to industrial social work is the degree to which one subscribes to what Boudling calls "the friendly face" of business organizations. This is a reflection of a "harmony of interest" theme in modern organization theory that "assumes the unity or purpose of the whole and views the parts as they contribute to this unity" (Krupp, 1961, pp. ix-x). Adherents of the "friendly face" orientation focus on integration and functional unity within the business firm. By contrast, those who emphasize the adversarial and conflictual nature of business argue that an interpretation of the business firm through the language of group cooperation "may be analogous to a description of a jungle using a theory of a farm" (Krupp, 1961, p. x).

A second and less controversial way in which the social services can complement the marketplace is through the provision of "social care" for the increasing number of "legitimately" dependent people in our society. Unlike the "best defense" strategy, social care is aimed at those populations whose dependence does not constitute a threat to the operations of the labor market. Advances in the biomedical sciences have lowered infant mortality rates while extending life expectancies, thus increasing the demand for long-term care for both infants (and later, children and adults) with physical and mental disabilities, and for an increasing number of elderly.

These developments have occurred, moreover, at a time when the care-giving capacity of the American family has been greatly reduced. Between 1960 and 1979 the proportion of married women in the labor force with children under six years of age more than doubled. Over nearly the same period, divorce rates rose 112 percent. By 1980, 18 percent of families with children were headed by a single parent, typically a woman, with little or no support from the other parent. Simultaneously, the proportion of the elderly who live with their children declined by approximately 50 percent, while the number of Americans over 65 increased by a similar percentage.

Advocates of the social care strategy argue that this is an area which enjoys considerable societal support and is one in which social workers have extensive experience, recognized expertise, and is consonant with the profession's values and service goals (Austin, 1984; Neugeboren, 1985; Popple, 1986). Moreover, unlike some of the service strategies discussed here, measures of effectiveness in this area are conceptually and operationally clearer (maintenance or enhancement of current levels of functioning, prevention of deterioration). However, for the profession to seriously pursue this strategy, there would have to be significant changes in the preparation of social workers.

IMPLICATIONS FOR SOCIAL WORK: TRANSFORMATION OR INTRANSIGENCE

In addition to external forces pushing and pulling the social work profession along a number of paths, there are factors internal to the profession moving it in yet other directions. Primary among these is the drive for more "professionalism" as social workers seek to increase their status and influence within their profession and the status of the profession in society. An individual's status within a profession and the status of the profession as a whole are determined by different variables. Abbott (1981) suggests that professionals gain status within their profession by doing work with a high degree of "professional purity," defined as the "ability to exclude nonprofession . . . or irrelevent professional issues from practice" (p. 823). By contrast, professionals gain status *outside* their professions through the application of their esoteric knowledge to taming "disorderly" situations (Shils, 1965).

In psychiatry, for example, high status within the profession is accorded to consultants who deal with esoteric therapeutic problems presented by other psychiatrists and from which non-psychiatric "impurities" have been refined out. For the general public, however, the most important psychiatrists are those hospital and clinic line-workers who use their knowledge to bring order to "messy" situations. These situations, moreover, are usually ones in which psychiatric issues are only one component, confounded by complicated social, legal, cultural, and other factors. However, as these and other professionals seek the admiration and recognition of their peers, they gradually withdraw from front-line practice. As a result,

> . . . the whole profession gradually shifts toward purer practice until . . . the original disorder is the shadow of a shade. This withdrawal from . . . disorders, both within individual careers and within professions over time, is a kind of drawing back into purity, a regression. (Abbott, 1981, p. 830)

While the social work profession has not yet retreated from front-line practice to the extent that psychiatry has, there are indications that it is moving in this direction. For social work, the "front-line" means dealing with "the individual in situation," and the situations are usually pretty messy. When professional social workers begin to view themselves as mental health professionals — as recent occupational trends indicate — they also begin to view their clients in individual, clinical terms, removed from their social contexts.

The dynamics of professionalism clash with several of the trends operating outside the profession, particularly the demand for social care services. This is an important opportunity for the social work profession to establish itself as the primary provider in an expanding area for which there is growing public support and which is consonant with the profession's values and traditions. However, the skills needed in the social care area differ from those which receive primary emphasis in current social work education. For example, as Austin (1984) suggest,

> . . . it would be essential that administration be addressed as a major social work function, because administrative authority is important in social care. In addition, the profession and the professional schools need to address the concept of psychosocial assessment in social care in a serious and systematic manner. Direct services in social care — in particular, case management —

would need to be dealt with in professional education as an advanced form of direct service practice. (p. 487)

These changes can be expected to encounter considerable resistance as they contradict much of social work's current definition of its role as a primary professional component in the treatment of acute mental illness. During its nearly 100 year history, the social work profession has successfully gone through a number of transformations as it adjusted to a changing environment. However, many of the past transformations — the shift from volunteer to paid status the search for new roles after the expansion of the public welfare system, the move from agency to university-based training — were complementary to and facilitated the field's quest for professional status. The juncture at which the profession currently finds itself presents a sharper and more difficult choice. If social workers are to play a central role in the field of social care, they must be prepared to work in an area which will be predominantly publicly-funded, bureaucratically-structured, and organized to provide tangible support services. This will require a "reframing" of our notions of professionalism to bring them in line with the essentially public-service profession that we are, rather than the private-sector profession that we would like to be (Howe, 1980).

The decisions that social workers and the social work profession must make reminds me of the oft-quoted statement of the turn-of-the-century Congressman that he would "rather be right than president." Unfortunately, the response made by the Speaker of the House has not received the attention it deserves. The Speaker's reply was, "You, sir, have neither to worry about."

REFERENCES

Abbott, A. Status and status strain in the professions. *American Journal of Sociology*, 1981, *86*(4), 819-35.

Austin, D. M. Observations on the search for an institutional base for social work. *Social Work*, 1984, *29*(5), 485-87.

Beck, B. Welfare as a moral category. *Social Problems*, 1967, *14*(3), 258-77.

Bendick, Jr., M. Failure to enroll in public assistance programs. *Social Work*, 1980, *25*(4), 268-74.

Brodkin, E. & Lipsky, M. Quality control in AFDC as an administrative strategy. Social Service Review, *1983*, 57(*1*), 1-34.

Derthick, M. *Uncontrollable spending for social services grants*. Washington, DC: The Brookings Institution, 1975.

Garfinkel, H. Conditions of successful degradation ceremonies. *American Journal of Sociology*, 1956, 61(*5*), 420)24.

Gettleman, M. E. Charity and social classes in the United States, 1874-1900. *The American Journal of Economics and Sociology*, 1963, *22*, 313-329, 417-426.

Gilbert, N. *Capitalism and the welfare state: Dilemmas of social benevolence.* New Haven: Yale University Press, 1983.

Gilbert, N. The commercialization of social welfare. Paper presented at the NASW Professional Symposium, Chicago, November 1985.

Handler, J. F. & Hollingsworth, E. J. Stigma, privacy, and other attitudes of welfare recipients. *Stanford Law Review*, 1969, *22*(1), 1-19.

Hirschman, A. O. The welfare state in trouble: Systemic crisis or growing pains? *American Economic Review: Papers and Proceedings*, 1980, *70*(2), 113-116.

Howe, E. Public professions and the private model of professionalism. *Social Work*, 1980, *25*(3), 179-191.

Krupp, S. *Pattern in organizational analysis: A critical analysis.* New York: Holt, Rinehart and Winston, Inc., 1961.

Lipsky, M. *Street-level bureaucracy: Dilemmas of the individual in public services.* New York: Russell Sage Foundation, 1980.

Lubove, R. *The professional altruist: The emergence of social work as a career, 1880-1930.* New York: Atheneum, 1969.

Matza, D. Poverty and disrepute. In R. K. Merton & R. Nisbet (Eds.), *Contemporary social problems.* 3rd edition. New York Harcourt Brace Jovanovich, Inc., 1971.

Neugebren, B. *Organization, policy, and practice in the human services.* New York: Longman, 1985.

Patti, R. J. Personal communication to the author. February 1986.

Polanyi, K. *The grate transformation: The political and economic origins of our time.* Boston: Beacon Press, 1957.

Popple, P. R. The social work profession: A reconceptualization. *Social Service Review*, 1985, *59*(4), 560-77.

Price, D. K. *The scientific estate.* Cambridge, MA: The Belknap Press of Harvard University Press, 1965.

Rainwater, L. & Rein, M. The growing complexity of economic claims in welfare societies. In *Evaluating the welfare state: Social and political perspectives.* New York: Academic Press, 1983.

Randall, R. Presidential power and bureaucratic intransigence: The influence of the Nixon Administration on welfare policy. *American Political Science Review*, 1979, *73*(3), 795-810.

Reich, R. B. *The next American frontier.* New York: Penguin Books, 1984.

Seeley, J. R. et al. *Community Chest: A case study in philanthropy.* Toronto: University of Toronto Press, 1957.

Shils, E. Charisma, order and status. *American Sociological Review*, 1965, *30*(1), 199-213.

Shlonsky, H. R. Welfare programs and the social system: A conceptual examination of "social services" and "income maintenance services." *Social Service Review*, 1971, *45*(4), 414-25.

Stern, M. J. Work and social change: A review essay. *Administration in Social Work*, 1983, *7*(2), 111-23.

Titmuss, R. The role of redistribution in social policy. In *Commitment to welfare.* New York: Pantheon, 1968.

Turem, J. S. The call for a management stance. *Social Work*, 1974, *19*(5), 615-23.

Ethics and the Managing
of Service Effectiveness
in Social Welfare

Harold Lewis, DSW

Is ethical management possible, or is this combination of terms an oxymoron? Sufficient doubts have been expressed about the possibility of ethical management, to warrant some response to this question. To attempt an analysis of the influence of ethics on managing for program effectiveness, without first establishing that ethical management is possible, could be an exercise in futility. I would be on uncertain grounds to simply assume that ethical management is possible, and to proceed on such an assumption.

IS ETHICAL MANAGEMENT POSSIBLE?

Herbert Kaufman, retiring as senior fellow at the Brookings Institution after more than 15 years in Washington and a lifetime studying public and private bureaucracies, concluded that the greatest factor in the success of a federal agency or private business organization is sheer, unadulterated luck (*New York Times*, 1986). This observation, if true, has serious ethical implications, not fully explored in Thompson's (1985) recent effort to answer the question: Is ethical administration possible? Thompson concludes that

> . . . administrative ethics is possible — at least the two major theoretical views that oppose its possibility are not compelling. We are forced to accept neither an ethic of neutrality that would suppress independent moral judgment nor an ethic of structure that would ignore individual moral agency in organizations.

Dr. Lewis is Professor and Dean, Hunter College School of Social Work, The City University of New York, 129 East 79th Street, New York, NY 10021.

271

I am more than willing to accept the need to include luck as a critical ingredient in any management evaluation equation. But another question must be answered before such an equation can be used with some assurance by evaluators. As with serendipity in scientific discovery, chance plays a role, but for real and compelling reasons, such chance contributions occur for some people and not for others. When Baker stumbled upon the plastic that carries his name; when Galileo observed the peculiar behaviors of the moons circling Jupiter; when Pasteur was challenged to explain the changing molds in his preparation, and when Archimedes punctuated his insight into flotation with the legendary "Eureka," serendipity appears always to be wedded to highly intelligent and informed observers who were prepared and able to note the unexpected. We have yet to determine if "luck" in management also entails a "lucky" manager, i.e., one on whom good fortune seems to smile. The good manager may be the one prepared to recognize and take advantage of the chance occurrence, and the bad manager is one who misses the opportunities as they arise. If this is so, all our work on theory of administration and our conceptualization of managers, their functions and roles, may prove to be more useful than we now believe. Possibly, by chance, someone will be prepared by these efforts to recognize the unanticipated. Serendipity may lead to a deeper understanding of this difficult, troublesome subject.

The possibility that the largest part of managerial success is a matter of luck, does, however, raise ethical issues that warrants further consideration. Much of any profession's code of ethics is premised on the expectation that the practitioner will confine her interventions to areas in which she has special competence. The sanction to intervene is given by society to those whose skills warrant trust that their practice will fulfill purposes for which such interventions are intended. If, in fact, the effectiveness of the intervention is largely a matter of chance, by what criterion can adherence to this ethical imperative be evaluated? In this area, at least, an ethical management practice may not be possible. A doubt similar to that generated by the "luck" hypothesis concerns the manager's relationship to her clients' interests.

Recall that the Code of Ethics of the social work profession commits the professional worker to the proposition that primacy must be given to clients' interests. Success in the provision of social work service thus hinges on the degree to which clients' interests are satisfied. If we are to develop clarity on our chosen topic, we must start with some agreement as to who is the manager's client. In terms utilized in normative ethics, this exercise is essential in order to determine the reach of the moral obligations and duties incumbent on the professional in her function as manager.

Unhappily, the typical manager is confronted with a plethora of possible clients whose interests she must consider: the service recipient; the staff; other administrators; the board; the funding body; and that vague entity, the wider community. Failure to consider the interests of any of these "clients" can harm the organization's work, detract from its possible successes. Concurrently satisfying the interests of these "clients" is rarely possible. When achieved, it is usually at great cost to the manager's personal well-being. How, then, can the primacy requirement be satisfied?

One option is to deny the possibility of ever meeting the primacy requirement. It can be argued, for example, that the manager cannot be considered a moral agent since she is constrained by having to satisfy all these interests and hence is not free to choose to satisfy any. The requirements of her assignment are such that she lacks the freedom to make decisions based on choices available to her. This image of the manager as a functionary whose actions are totally determined for her by the preferences of those to whom she is obligated was caricatured in the not guilty plea of the Nazi Eichmann; it was rejected in that case, and is not likely to find much support when used to justify the lack of ethics of a social welfare manager.

Assuming the manager to be a moral agent, one can expect that her performance of the tasks associated with his function, will involve her in making moral choices, often in ethically ambiguous situations. One such situation, and one that will influence all others that follow, is choosing who is to be her client in any particular service transaction.

Having rejected the notion that the manager is not a moral agent, we might agree that she is free to make choices, but that in each instance, all possible interests have equal claim on her services. The outcome of this option is no different in its effects than the earlier denial of agent status. By accepting equal obligations to all clients, the manager is, in effect, relinquishing any responsibility for priority choices in particular situations, thus failing to function as a moral agent.

Granted the need to satisfy the interests of a range of clients, there is good reason to believe that every client does not have equal claim on the manager's service, nor does the manager owe each equal obligations. How to calculate the uneven weights to be attached to these varying interests, which would constitute the manager's total obligations, is problematic. One possible approach to this calculus is to utilize the "coupling" framework to evaluate the tightness of fit between management and client involvement in the service transaction (Meyer, Scott & Deal, 1981).

For example, consider the dean as a manager of sorts. She would readily be able to list the range of clients whose interests she would be expected to satisfy and whose interests should be given primacy. At the outset, she would have to recognize that the impact of her interventions would be more immediate and telling in allocating budgeted resources, making faculty assignments, overseeing registration, field work and admissions, than in directly controlling the content and style of classroom teaching and student advising. There is the need to respect academic freedom. It is also impractical to conceive of the dean attending to her necessary concern for students' interests by regularly monitoring teacher behavior. Similarly, the Dean is tightly coupled with the vice-president for academic affairs, somewhat less with the president and other deans, and very loosely linked with the board of the university, the funding body, and the wider community. For the dean, then, it is possible to identify degrees of coupling which can and will change. She can assign greater obligation to the primacy of interests represented by the close, rather than the loose coupling.

It is possible to depict this schemata in the form of a matrix with clients along one dimension, and functional tasks along the other. For each of the cells generated, a rough assignment of degree of coupling can be designated. The resulting distribution could serve as a useful tool in arriving at measures of clients' interests to be given primacy.

Of course, for most situations, the relative obligations owed will have been established by trial and error, precedent, and bureaucratic routinization. The need for conscious calculations would arise in ambiguous situations, often the most troublesome.

Let us now return to the "luck" hypothesis and re-examine it in light of the discussion of the primacy of interest principle. What becomes clear as one examines the proposed matrix for analyzing degrees of interest, is that the coupling framework challenges a global view of chance as a factor in determining program effectiveness. If the closeness of the coupling has merit in relation to choosing the client whose interest is to be primary, it is in large measure because chance plays less of a role in such tightly fitted situations. The closer the coupling, the more likely the control of direction and intensity of influence and the less likely is pure luck to determine outcome. Thus, a differential analysis of the proposed matrix permits a partialization of the "luck" hypothesis. It should be possible to demonstrate sufficient evidence of management competence for the task involved, to warrant a belief in ethical management.

This brief exercise, while serving to explicate some of the complexities hidden in the assumption that ethical management is possible, suggests a series of issues for consideration. Assuming that it is possible to demonstrate ethical management, it would be useful to know:

1. How, if at all, do ethical constraints influence the selection of criterion variables?
2. How significant is the ethical behavior of the manager, in shaping program and product?
3. Do ethical considerations strengthen or weaken other functions necessary to the effective delivery of services?
4. Are there practice principles that managers should follow in order to avoid unprincipled behavior and improve program effectiveness?

I do not intend to answer these questions. Simply stating them and exploring their meaning in a preliminary way should promote discussion and possibly provide an agenda for a future retreat.

CRITERION VARIABLES

Given a matrix of clients' interests and managers' obligations, many successes and failures can concurrently result from their interventions. Outcome measures reflecting interests to be satisfied will differ by client and by categories of clients. For example, the manager may satisfy the funding source's interest in cost-effective and balanced budget criteria, while failing to satisfy staff interest in improved and equitable salaries, or the community's interest in reduced frequency of those problems that generate requests for the agency's services. Thus, the manager conceivably may experience many small successes while failing to attend to the interests of one or more client constituencies. An overall judgment of failure, despite some successes, is often justified when closely coupled clients whose interests are to be given primacy, fail to have their interests realized. Note that this approach to evaluative criteria directly addresses the interests of the manager's clients at all points in a service transaction. It suggests the need to evaluate the effect of the manager's interventions before attempting to evaluate her contributions to the overall program effectiveness.

THE MANAGER'S ETHICS

With the complexity of a calculus that a consequentialist ethical assessment would require, it is no wonder that attention often shifts from a focus on the management process, to the virtues of the manager herself. The manager's attributes become more significant when her calculations involve difficult judgments in ambiguous situations. Trusting the person when the process is prone to error is not an uncommon ploy for resolving the uncertainties of the process. In uncertain situations, the expectation that a principled person will act in a principled way may be the most supportable judgment to make.

Of all the personal attributes one can look for in a manager, the one most relevant for judging ethical behavior is trustworthiness. To trust a manager is to grant her more than the authority of her competence. Because of the position she occupies in the organization, the attribution of trust carries with it the belief in and acceptance of her motives. Devoid of guile, free of cant, not given to manipulative use of relationships, the trusted manager is appreciated for her honesty, candor, courage, commitment and adherence to professional standards in her presentation of self and of the program she manages. Trust can serve to justify acceptance of her choices as meriting support when the consequences that follow may be in doubt. The belief that the manager's intentions are good, when wedded to a belief in her competence, is a persuasive combination on which to rely when ambiguities cloud situations in which choices must be made.

But such absolute trust in a manager is not often encountered in the real world of practice. In part, a lack of trust may stem from the fact that there is confusion as to whose interests the manager is ultimately obligated to serve. A common resolution of this confusion is to assert, without condition, that the recipients of the organization's services, whose needs justify the program, should be persons whose interests must be served. While this resolution is relatively uncomplicated, it is also problematic. Given the loose coupling that characterizes the relationship of the manager to the service recipient, and the closeness of coupling of direct service staff to these recipients, it is reasonable to expect that the manager who hopes to heed the recipients' interests conveys his influences primarily through the actions of line staff, over whom she exercises some control. Exercising such influence on staff will be of little use if staff's interests are not concurrently addressed as well. Thus the closely coupled relationship is the medium through which the loosely coupled relationship will be managed.

Failure to appreciate this pattern of influence results in organizational rigidity. The manager attempts to control, by rules and procedures, the practice of the organization at every level. The outcome of such efforts is the reduction of choices available to line staff, the routinization of actions and the calcification of the crucial worker-recipient service encounter. Inevitably rigor mortis comes to characterize the service transaction, which is reduced to a technical rather than a professional operation. Implicit in such a development is the distrust the manager communicates in her apparent doubt that her intentions will be followed. Such distrust on her part promotes a reciprocal response from those who are its targets. From doubt as to whose interests the manager will favor, and her need to assure adherence to her intentions through control of loosely coupled relationships, the manager generates distrust.

It is useful at this point to distinguish effective management from the larger concern of this issue—i.e., management for service effectiveness. Focusing on the attributes of the manager as moral agent is relevant to the former, but less so for the latter. The assumption that an effective manager, here viewed as one who acts as responsible moral agent, will necessarily contribute to management for service effectiveness may be a logical inference not supported by actual organizational experience. It is conceivable that a ship's captain may do all the right and good things a captain is expected to do, yet not avoid the catastrophe that results when the ship is capsized by a tidal wave. This analogy is not farfetched, given the impact of wider societal forces on social welfare programs. The problem of "too little, too late" more often than one would want to admit, describes the situations in which agency managers are called upon to carry out their managerial functions. Thus, they may meet a standard of effective management in a number of areas yet not contribute significantly to service effectiveness.

The relationship between effective management and management for service effectiveness in some way resembles the relationship of objectives to goals. Management objectives may include cost-effective use of resources; improved staff morale; clarification of territorial domains; linkages with related social service programs, etc. If these objectives are attained, it may erroneously be expected that the consequences will advance the goal of effective service.

Evaluation of managerial interventions, the services the manager provides, calls for more than a measure of objectives and goals achieved. For one thing, it asks that we demonstrate how the manager's interventions contributed to or brought about the changes evident in outcomes. We ought to heed the lessons drawn in this regard by Stephen Jay Gould (1986) in his review of logical fallacies in his discipline. Of lesser importance is the mistaken notion that one can infer a causal link from a correlation alone. This is not an uncommon error in evaluation research in social welfare. But a larger error is the assumption of a false equation between magnitude of difference and the amount of time needed to bring it about. Gould contends that small inputs, channeled through complex systems with meaningful histories, may engender large and unexpected results: that the probability exists in natural phenomena of fast transitions not attributable to miracles or truly instantaneous appearance.

Consciously directed human interventions, while not natural events, are nevertheless complex. They involve complex natural systems — persons and groups of persons. Avoiding the fallacy that relates the magnitude of difference with the amount of time needed to bring it about, is important in evaluating effective management. One ought avoid attributing major changes to chance, even when they are associated with minor inputs by the manager. For example, when the manager intends to allocate resources in a manner that promotes distributive justice, it is possible that the timeliness of the intervention, rather than its frequency and length of duration, deserves major weight in calculating distributive portions.

There is some evidence that the more disadvantaged are less likely to seek services as early in their problem state than the more advantaged, and are more likely not to be able to sustain participation in a service. For those disadvantaged, the timing of the intervention associated with the complexity of their life-space may be a more reasonable measure of intensity of service than frequency or duration of contact. Put differently, failure to impact on the problems of the most disadvantaged may be the result of untimely intervention, not insufficient resource.

Attending to Gould's hypothesis, remarkable changes may result when timely managerial interventions treat equals equally, and unequals unequally; where a small difference in favor of the unequals may be a matter of sustaining a life, rather than sustaining a style of life. In short, quantitative changes at critical nodal points can result in significant qualitative changes.

For the manager who comes on board after a ship has set sail, the timelessness of her interventions may assure or frustrate program effectiveness. Redirecting the flow of services and the investment of personnel and support staff in a situation of severe time constraints poses a serious ethical dilemma. If the survival of the program is at stake, one can accept the principle as formulated by Gewirth (1978) in terms of human survival. Given his lexical ordering of choice, survival would take precedence over other imperatives, and the manager would justify her interventions on such grounds. But staff may see their own survival on the job as taking precedence over program survival. After all, if staff survives, other programs can be initiated; not so if the cost of program survival is their demise.

Return to the initial observation that directed our attention to attributes of the manager, rather than to the consequences of her actions. We have to anticipate that she may have little time to communicate to those she views as her clients, the bases for their trusting her motives as well as her competence.

We are then compelled to consider the morality of the organization and its trustworthiness, as a critical influence in promoting or depleting one's trust in the manager. If we assume that institutions shape the behavior and values of those who work within them, one can argue that those individuals (in this case the managers) have a responsibility to reflect upon their organizations and to change them. To insist that these are immoral institutions in which managers have no moral responsibility, is impossible (Michel, 1981). Thus, in focusing on the manager's attributes one anticipates that her behavior will exemplify that ethical stance one seeks to have supported by the organizational environment in which she works. Hopefully, her behavior in time will generate the trust in her motives. Until such trust is earned, she will be judged by the clientele she relates to in light of the reputation of the institution that hires her and sanctions her practice. It is important, therefore, that the institution be viewed as operating on principles, in addition to the manager evidencing virtues in her behavior. As Rosemarie Tong (1986) argues, "character and conduct go hand in hand." This is as true for the organization as for the individual.

DO ETHICAL CONSIDERATIONS STRENGTHEN OR WEAKEN OTHER FUNCTIONS?

Every manager encounters dilemmas in practice, not all of which are ethical dilemmas. As a rule of thumb, where increments in information dissipate the contradictions that generated the dilemma, a practice issue, not an ethical issue, is involved. Where, on the other hand, increased information heightens rather than dissipates the dilemma, an ethical issue is probably involved. Typically, certain dilemmas affecting management behavior are as likely to surface in the practice of a manager in social welfare programs as in any other management assignment. According to Aram (1978) these dilemmas most often stem from the following contradictory requirements of the manager's job:

1. self-interest versus collective responsibility;
2. organizational control versus individual development and initiative;
3. organizational and personal criteria in administrative decision-making;
4. individual preferences and group norms;
5. leadership requirements for adhering to and changing group norms.

Having rational procedures that could assure the resolution of instances where these contradictory requirements generate dilemmas, is desirable. However, the reasonable expectation is that the rationale will often not provide guidance in situations in which a decision must be made of what is good or bad. As we noted earlier, for this reason one is pressed to consider the virtues of the person making the choice. But given the replaceability of persons in managerial positions and the relative constancy of the organization, it is also necessary that the organization follow certain principles, lest it be judged solely by the attributes of transient individuals. We need ethical principles that will guide an organization's choices when faced with ethical dilemmas. Prescribing such principles is not easy, but a more difficult challenge is to decide whether adherence to such principles is likely to strengthen or weaken the organization's managerial effort toward achieving program effectiveness.

One major contribution to program effectiveness that an ethical practice can make is to communicate by word and deed that the end sought by the organization is consistently supported by the means employed to achieve it. To warrant this reputation the manager and the organization must do more than evidence strong motivation to behave in an ethical manner; they must also demonstrate in concrete ways the actual impact of such behavior on program procedures and policies. The need is to do more than advocate for the principles; it also is necessary to actively oppose departures from such ethical principles in organizational as well as personal performance.

A second contribution that ethics can make is to clarify the relevance of criteria used to monitor and evaluate programs. Defining the conditions under which paternalism, equal access, privacy, the right to know, etc., are to be judged as just and fair, require criteria which guard against the error that assumes that what works is necessarily good.

Ethical principles, such as those incorporated into codes of ethics by professions, also provide guidelines for personal relationships between colleagues, between staff and service recipients, and between management and other client constituencies.

These possible positive contributions of ethics to program effectiveness are sufficiently self-evident not to warrant spending more time on them. Of equal interest is the possibility that adherence to ethical principles may prove detrimental to program effectiveness.

In the normal course of events ethical dilemmas will surface where two competing goods, two competing rights, or a right and a good are in conflict. When faced with such conflicts, the manager cannot help but be aware of the impact of her choices on those who benefit and those whose goods, or rights, have been sacrificed. Examples of such conflicts might help sharpen our understanding of problems such choices generate. Two goods are in conflict when the manager decides to limit workloads in order to lessen the burden on the staff, and in so doing reduces the number of recipients who can be served. The ethical justification for such action is the obligation of the manager to promote the well-being and efficiency of the staff. She judges this to take precedence over the obligation owed potential clients. Two rights may be in conflict when the manager chooses to give preferential treatment to one worker over another, not on the basis of merit, but on the basis of the needs of the organization. Here the rights of the worker to fair and equal consideration based on competence, may be in conflict with the right of the organization to consider political, financial or other factors in its allocations of resources. As is true when choosing among goods, so in choosing among rights, the manager must be guided by a higher ordering principle if such choices are expected to meet an ethical standard.

Finally, in choosing between a right and a good, the choice of the latter generally develops into a paternalism that must be justified, lest the right that is sacrificed be more costly to the recipient than the good that such choice promotes. When the manager neutralizes the role of a troublesome board member because she believes the member's emotional instability is disrupting the functioning of the board and subjecting the board member to unnecessary ridicule, we have an instance of limiting the rights of the board member for his or her own good.

Note that in all three examples, adhering to an ethical imperative in attempting to resolve a dilemma will pose the possibility of a loss of some rights, goods, or both, by some party even as a gain is registered by another. In addition, it is entirely possible that a manager who acts in an ethically commendable fashion may contribute to a less effective service for some and a more effective service for others. In approaching such choices in a consequential framework, it is hoped that the net gains for the sum total of managers' clients will exceed the net loss.

Having briefly addressed three of the four issues, we come to the most difficult and most significant for managerial practice. Are there practice principles that managers should follow in order to avoid unprincipled behavior and to concurrently improved on program effectiveness? First, let us consider some "thou shalt not" principles which most managers would find reasonable:

1. Managers should not advocate against the interests of the organization that employs them. The difficulty in implementing this principle stems from acts of omission and commission, which may or may not be categorized as adversarial. To adhere to this principle, there should be prior agreement on what constitutes the organization's interests. Such agreement, at critical times, may be impossible to achieve.
2. Managers should not assume or accept responsibilities which they are not competent to fulfill. This principle hinges on making judgments of competencies which must rely on incomplete information or information that becomes available in the process generated by these judgments.
3. Managers should not allocate resources in a manner that promotes distrust of their motives among the various clientele they must serve. The problems associated with priority determination, conflicting interest, and insufficient resource all make adherence to this principle problematic.

These illustrative "thou shalt nots," and others that can be formulated, all call for ethical judgments in uncertain situations, pointing to the choices that are to be preferred. They call on managers to act in a virtuous mode, but are sufficiently constrained by unclear definitions as to be almost irrelevant as guides for actions in particular cases. They have one positive attribute in common that warrants their formulation. All share a lack of constraint upon a manager. They limit their guidance to what managers should not do, thus leaving room for creativity and innovation.

More precise, and probably more controlling guidance, is provided by "thou shalt" principles. Toulmin (1981) cautions against such principles, just as Feyerabend (1978) cautions against method, and Salanick, (1981) against effectiveness criteria. All share in common the theoritician's abhorrence of rules that dictate premature discarding of doubts which cuts off the pursuit of truth. Such cautions, unfortunately, are anathema to the practitioner. Where the intent is to do, rather than to know, certainties are essential. For this reason, at the risk of seeming anti-theoretical, I will venture some principles stated in the affirmative. Hopefully, they will engage us in an exploration of the issues addressed earlier in the paper and move the discussion beyond the effort to merely identify them.

Having argued for the possibility of ethical management, and the possibility of the manager acting as a moral agent, I was led to conclude that no manager can reasonably lay claim to neutrality when confronted with ethical choices in her practice.

— *Principle*: Managers must evidence adherence to the values that justify their organizational goals. Such adherence should be demonstrated by ethical imperatives that justify practice principles. When these imperatives are not identified and subscribed to in both word and deed, the manager may justifiably be judged an unprincipled practitioner.

— *Principle*: The possibility that the manager may experience success in meeting the interests of some clients, while concurrently failing to meet the interests of others, should be anticipated in the choice of criterion variables used to evaluate her performance.

— *Principle*: The effects of a manager's interventions should be evaluated before attempting to evaluate the contribution of management to overall program effectiveness.

— *Principle*: Where a consequentialist ethical assessment of manager's behavior is not possible, the trustworthiness of the manager's and the organization's intentions may substitute for consequences. This assumes that a principled person (manager) will be more likely to act in a principled way, than one whose past behavior has failed to generate trust in her intentions.

— *Principle:* In ethical ambiguous situations not all dilemmas will be resolved to the satisfaction of all parties concerned. Recognizing that managerial choices may detract from, as well as enhance, service effectiveness, every effort should be made to approximate a nonzero sum game resolution of the dilemma. As a minimum, the outcome sought ought to aim for a just and fair resolution.

In real-life situations, where managers enter organizations which are in process of realizing their own intentions, I have argued against the possibility of a non-involved, neutral stance, as regards ethical issues. In developing my argument, I have sought to identify the elements that must be considered in arriving at an evaluation of the influence of ethics in managerial behavior, and ultimately on the organization's service effectiveness. As the illustrative "thou shalt not" and "thou shalt" principles make evident, it is feasible to arrive at a set of guiding practice principles, grounded in an ethical framework, which can be defended on empirical as well as ethical grounds.

REFERENCES

Aram, J.D. *Dilemmas of administrative behavior.* Englewood Cliffs, NJ: Prentice-Hall, Inc., 1978.

Feyerabend, P. *Against method.* Vers: Editor-lander, 1978.

Gewirth, A. *Reason and morality.* Chicago: University of Chicago Press, 1978.

Gould, S.J. A short way to big ends. *Natural History,* 1986, *95,* 18-29.

Meyer, J.W., Scott, W.R. & Deal, T.E. Institutional and technical services of organizational structure: Explaining the structure of educational organizations. In H. Stein (Ed.), *Organization and the human services.* Philadelphia: Temple University Press, 1981.

Michel, R. Comments in conference report. National Institute of Mental Health. *Ethical issues in mental health policy and administration.* Washington, DC: U.S. Department of Health and Human Service, 1981.

New York Times, January 30, 1986, B6.

Salanick, G.R. The effectiveness of inactive social service systems. In H. Stein (Ed.), *Organization and the human services.* Philadelphia: Temple University Press, 1981.

Thompson, D.F. The possibility of administrative ethics. *Public Administration Review,* 1985, 560.

Tong, R. *Ethics in policy analysis.* Englewood Cliffs, NJ: Prentice-Hall, Inc., 1986.

Toulimin, S. The tyranny of principles. *The Hastings Center Report,* 1981, *11,* 31-39.

Index

Accountability, 235-236
  of adult protection services, 84
  of child protection services, 85
  client outcome measurement and, 33-35,
    73-88
  computer technology effects, 86
  conditions for, 77-81
  consensus, 83-86
  feedback and, 79,86-87
  implementation, 81-82
  key administrators and, 82-83
  model, 87-88
  resistance to, 74-75
  strategies, 78-79
  successful outcome definitions, 76-77
  time frame, 83
  definition, 115-116
  of drug abuse services, 84-85
  of employment and training services, 85
  of family planning services, 85
  of foster care services, 85
  management by measurement and, 91
  of manager, 7-8
  of mental health services, 84
  multiple constituencies and, 235-236
  of rehabilitation services, 85
  social program design and, 115-126
    implications, 125-126
    model, 116-125
    problem definition, 117-119
    program goal, 117,119-120,121
    program objectives, 117,121-122
    service plan, 117,122-125
    target population, 117,119-120,121
  technological complexity and, 127
Action rationality, 230
Action strategies, for multiple constituencies,
    224,227-236
  accountability control, 235-236
  action rationality, 230
  basic values, 235
  education of constituents, 232

environmental values, 229
power use, 231
record-keeping, 236
service delivery, 232
skills to implement, 228-229
symbols into action, 233
vision of purpose, 228,233-234
web of influence, 230-231
Administrator. *See* Manager
Adult protective services, accountability
  levels, 84
Advocacy, managerial, 282
Advocacy organizations
  purpose, 11
  service effectiveness criteria, 12,13
Affective change, as client outcome measure,
  27
  assessment, 29-30
Affective involvement, 125
Affective responses, to feedback, 195
Arrangement, organizational, 15-17
Assessment centers, for staff, 155
At-risk population, 120-121
Audits, of case records, 49
Autonomy
  organizational, limitations of, 207
  of staff, 148
    first line workers, 75
    social workers, 92,264
    supervisory conflict and, 94-95

Baker Act, 84
Balance Theory, 247
Behavior, organizational, congruence
  hypothesis, 149
Behavior change
  as client outcome measurement, 28,30-31
  rewards and, 245
  as service effectiveness criteria, 12,13
Behavior responses, to feedback, 196-197
Behavioral check lists, 30-31

290   MANAGING FOR SERVICE EFFECTIVENESS

Legitimacy activities, 224,225-226,227,
229-236
Legitimacy Model, of service effectiveness,
225
Legitimation skills, 229
Limited programs, 134,135,136,137,138,
139,140
Living conditions. *See* Environmental
modifications
Living skills, 28,36

Management
ethics of, 271-284
client primacy and, 272-275
criterion variables, 275
functional effects, 279-284
manager's ethics, 276-279
levels, 15-17
participative, 169-171
"Management by wandering around," 228
Management Information and Program
Evaluation System, 97-100
Management information systems, 49
design, 177-190
decision support applications, 177-178,
179-180
definition of organizational productivity,
181-182,187
definition of organizational purpose,
180-181,185
design process, 184
effectiveness measures, 182-183
feedback and, 183-184
formatting, 183-184,188
housekeeping applications, 177-178,179
measurement of purpose, 185-186
performance guidance applications,
177-178,179,182-189
productivity measures, 182-183,187-188
standard setting, 183-184,188
system comparison, 179-180
Manager. *See also* Director
accountability, 7-8
advocacy by, 282
client centeredness orientation, 24
educational preparation, 241
in measurement theory, 69,70
generic social work skills, 241-254
advantages/rewards emphasis, 245,250,
251
comprehensibility, 245,250,251
examples, 249-252

high pressure tactics and, 248,250,251
influential others, 247-248,250
persuasion, 243-252
principles, 244-249
proven results citing, 246,250,251
social administration and, 242-244
threat minimization, 248-249,250,251
trialability, 246-247,250
values compatibility, 245-246,250
interaction with supervisor, 15-16
with non-human services background, 26
research training, 70
responsibility, 282
trustworthiness, 276,279,283
Marital counseling, client outcomes, 77
Market economy, social services in, 258-267
"best defense" relationship, 261-263
as complementary system, 265-267
as contradiction, 263-265
"poor copy" relationship, 258-260
social work implications, 267-269
Maxey Boys Training School, 79-80
Measurement technology, 68-69. *See also*
Client outcome measurement
Measurement theory, 69,70
Mental health services, accountability
services, 84
Mental patients, symptom deterioration
measurement, 61-62
Methadone programs, 131-132,134,135,136
Michigan, Maxey Boys Training School,
79-80
Michigan Department of Social Services, 75,
82,83
Microcomputers, client outcome
applications, 69
Milwaukee County Department of Social
Services, 80-81
Minnesota, human service program outcome
indicators, 76-77
Minnesota Community Social Services Act,
76
Minnesota Multiphasic Personality Test, 66
Model developmental approach, 111-112
Monitoring
of client outcomes, 35-36. *See also* Client
outcome measurement
of service effectiveness, 49-50
Motivation, for worker performance, 152,
153
Movement tables, 186
Multiple constituencies

.

T - #0058 - 160425 - C0 - 212/152/12 [14] - CB - 9780866566872 - Gloss Lamination